"Those who are interested in the evolutionary aspects of the twentieth century in America should not miss Cronon's book. It makes exciting reading."

The Nation

"Author Cronon places us all in his debt with an interesting and serious portrayal of a Negro leader who was at one and the same time perhaps the most controversial, loved, mocked, and criticized personality of the turbulent twenties."

The Christian Century

"A very readable, factual and well-documented biography of Marcus Garvey."

The Crisis

Culver Pictures, Inc.

Marcus Garvey

BLACK MOSES

The Story of Marcus Garvey

and the

Universal Negro Improvement Association

E. DAVID CRONON

Foreword by
JOHN HOPE FRANKLIN

The University of Wisconsin Press

The University of Wisconsin Press
1930 Monroe Street
Madison, Wisconsin 53711

3 Henrietta Street
London WC2E 8LU, England

www.wisc.edu\wisconsinpress

16   15   14   13   12   11

Printed in the United States of America

ISBN 0-299-01211-5 cloth, 0-299-01214-X paper
LC 76-101503

FOR JEAN

★ CONTENTS

vii

★ ILLUSTRATIONS

★ Much has happened in the decade and a half since I wrote *Black Moses*. At the time the book appeared in 1955, few scholars were concerned with Negro history. In fact I felt obliged in the Preface I wrote then (coincidentally finished less than a week after the Supreme Court's landmark 1954 decision outlawing school segregation) to justify my interest in Marcus Garvey in the hope of persuading a few readers of his significance as a symbol, at least in the early 1920's, of the longings and aspirations of the black masses and as an illustration of deep-seated Negro discontent with the injustice of American life. How different is the situation today, in part because of the civil rights revolution sparked by that decision and other Court actions of the 1950's. One of the most welcome changes is the great upsurge of interest in Negro history among blacks and whites alike. Books by and about Negroes appear almost daily in response to the apparently insatiable hunger of young black Americans to learn about themselves and their past, a demand whose legitimacy may not be denied and whose considerable impact upon American education is seen in rapidly proliferating black history courses and black studies programs.

How different, too, is the reaction today to the Garvey Movement. When Garvey died in 1940 he had been largely forgotten by the millions who in the 1920's had thrilled to his ambitious dream of African redemption by the proud and unified black people of the New World. Indeed, when I began my research in the late 1940's I was struck by how nearly complete Garvey's obscurity was among younger black Americans, most of whom seemed to have scant knowledge of and little interest in his career and ideas. Renewed awareness of Garvey's significance as a black nationalist leader came increasingly thereafter, however, as new black nations emerged one by one in Africa, as West Indian blacks secured their independence and experimented with a plan of federated union as envisaged by Garvey, and as militant black power leaders of the American civil rights movement, some of them, like Malcolm X, the children of Garvey followers, began to stress the race pride and separatist aspects of Garvey's philosophy. Today there is no need to justify a book about Marcus Garvey or to speculate on whether there would be a market for it. That alone is a measure of how swiftly and sharply the world has changed.

With the advantage of today's perspective, I would no doubt have written a somewhat different book, changing or adding some details based on recent information and modifying a few of my conclusions. Such changes would be relatively few, however, for in the main my account of the Garvey Movement seems valid. Garvey's legacy of racial consciousness and pride impresses me today as more significant than it did in the mid-1950's, when I tended to underestimate the extent to which a later generation could again be swayed by black chauvinist ideas. In 1955 I expressed doubts "whether Garvey could find today, in the United States at least, the ready response that greeted his early proselytizing efforts." Today the question might well be resolved in his favor. Certainly Garvey has become an increasingly important symbol of black nationalism and power, and in the process he has been rescued from the near oblivion into which he had fallen at the time of his death.

As I noted in 1955, the renewed interest in Garvey and Garveyism is greatest in his island homeland of Jamaica, though the revival is by no means insignificant elsewhere. Once scorned by the Jamaican power structure, Garvey is regarded today as a black George Washington, the father of Jamaican independence. The capital city of Kingston has named a road after him and has placed his sculptured bust in a public park. In 1964 the Jamaican government brought Garvey's remains home from his obscure London grave and triumphantly placed them in a Marcus Garvey National Shrine. Garvey was officially designated as Jamaica's first National Hero. The following year the government announced that it was establishing a £5,000 Marcus Garvey Prize for Human Rights to be awarded for the first time in 1968, on the twentieth anniversary of the adoption of the United Nations Declaration on Human Rights, to the person who in this generation had contributed most significantly to the field of human rights. With unforeseen irony the Garvey Prize was awarded in December, 1968, to the martyred Martin Luther King, whose widow in accepting the award noted the common identity of Garvey and her late husband, their "passion for the liberation of their people" (Kingston *Daily Gleaner*, December 11, 1968). To make Garvey's symbolic conquest of his homeland complete, the government is planning to replace Queen Elizabeth's portrait on Jamaican currency with that of the once forgotten black nationalist. Garvey's triumph in Jamaica could hardly be more impressive or total.

In the United States the resurrection has been less spectacular, but interest in Garvey and his teachings has mounted as black power spokesmen invoke his name and as Negroes generally discover their past and recall the audacious black prophet whose daring ideas outran his time. One of the factors in the Garvey revival in America and elsewhere is surely the effort of his devoted widow, Amy Jacques Garvey, who for many years has kept in touch with black nationalists throughout the New World and Africa, stressing the relevance of her husband's philosophy for today. To make Garvey's ideas better known, she recently published two accounts of his life and work that add new details to the familiar story: *Garvey and Garveyism* (Kingston: A. Jacques Garvey, 1963) and *Black Power in America* (Kingston: Amy Jacques Garvey, 1968). The two volumes of *The Philosophy and Opinions of Marcus Garvey*, which she had edited in the 1920's and which had been long out of print and had become extremely rare, have lately been reprinted in both the United States and England. Unlike her husband, who never visited the motherland of Africa, Mrs. Garvey in 1960 was the honored guest of the governments of Nigeria and Ghana. There she proudly reviewed the ships and facilities of Ghana's new national steamship company, the Black Star Line. In the light of these developments who can dismiss as mere bombast Garvey's farewell message to his followers when he went to prison in 1925:

When I am dead wrap the mantle of the Red, Black and Green around me, for in the new life I shall rise with God's grace and blessing to lead the millions up the heights of triumph with the colors that you well know. Look for me in the whirlwind or the storm, look for me all around you, for, with God's grace, I shall come and bring with me countless millions of black slaves who have died in America and the West Indies and the millions in Africa to aid you in the fight for Liberty, Freedom and Life (*Philosophy and Opinions,* II, 239).

E. David Cronon

Madison, Wisconsin
September 12, 1969

★ On one Sunday afternoon in the summer of 1954, I heard two speakers in London's Hyde Park mention Marcus Garvey. These references to a man who had been rather thoroughly discredited at the time of his death more than a decade ago emphasized once more for me the considerable impact he had on the outlook of darker peoples in many parts of the world. As I stood there musing over the fantastic career of this man of many talents and many imperfections, I tried to recall my first contact with his name. I was not altogether successful, but I did remember that as a child I saw people avidly reading copies of the *Negro World*. I knew that this was Marcus Garvey's paper, although I had not the slightest idea of what Garvey or the *Negro World* stood for. I also remembered that less than two years ago one of the leading Negro newspapers suggested that the uprisings of the Mau Mau in Kenya could well have been inspired by the teachings of Garvey. I could not escape the conclusion that for more than a generation Marcus Garvey had attracted the attention of thousands of people and that he had made a distinct impression, favorable or unfavorable, on most of them.

Garvey wrote and spoke freely, beginning with his first attempts to organize a mass movement among Negroes in his native Jamaica more than forty years ago. In the course of his trial in the federal court for using the mails to defraud, his numerous activities were fully aired. Many articles and several books, including a collection of his principal writings, have been devoted to the man and the movement. We know, therefore, a good deal about him in a general and superficial way: his remarkably dynamic personality, his flamboyant oratory, his wide and successful appeal, his numerous encounters with Negro leaders who vigorously opposed his philosophy and approach, and his tragic downfall. Yet Garvey remains an enigma—stolid, almost sphinxlike in his defiance of analysis and understanding. We do not know much about the extent of his following or which aspects of his program had the greatest appeal. We know all too little about the quality of his insights, of his appreciation of the coincidence of his program with the desperate plight of the Negro in the United States. Nor do we know very much about the fundamental traits of the man's character, of his integrity and sincerity in projecting the movement which bore his name. We do not know how to assess the relative influence of the opposition and of Garvey's own mistakes, unwitting or otherwise, in bringing about his own downfall.

Now comes David Cronon's *Black Moses,* which happily answers many of the questions that arise in the mind of one who would seek to understand Marcus Garvey. Mr. Cronon's book enjoys two praiseworthy distinctions. It is the first full-length biography of this colorful and important figure; and Mr. Cronon's thorough search for all the surviving Garvey material led him to newspapers difficult to get, to the unpublished records of the trial in New York, to the relics of Garvey in the second Mrs. Garvey's possession in Jamaica, and to an interview with the first Mrs. Garvey in England. An even greater distinction, perhaps, is the manner in which Mr. Cronon courageously and intelligently faces the numerous problems inherent in the treatment of this controversial figure. There is no evasion of the difficult task of analysis and evaluation. Mr. Cronon has achieved the uncommon success of being sympathetic without becoming adulatory or patronizing, of being critical without becoming derogatory or malevolent. The result is the portrayal of a man terribly human, full of contradictions and weaknesses, at times pompous and selfish, at other times humble and generous. Artfully woven into this portrait is the story of the largest Negro movement of its kind in history which, in so many ways, was a projection of the character and personality of its founder.

I am confident that thoughtful students will find this book a worthwhile guide to an understanding of the recent past and of the role of the leader in periods of crisis and frustration, while the general reader will be grateful to Mr. Cronon for writing an absorbing account of an unforgettable character.

John Hope Franklin

[*November 1954*]

★ ACKNOWLEDGMENTS

★ A debt of appreciation is due to the many persons who have helped in the preparation of this work. Mrs. Amy Jacques Garvey has given freely of both her time and her great store of information to supply needed facts that she alone was in a position to give. Mrs. Garvey kindly prepared a biographical account of her husband's early life in Jamaica and furnished me with scarce copies of his publications. I am also greatly indebted to Mr. Hodge Kirnon of New York City for his helpful advice and the generous use of his extensive collection of Garvey material. Professor Abram L. Harris of the University of Chicago, Mr. A. Philip Randolph of the Brotherhood of Sleeping Car Porters, Mr. William Pickens of the United States Treasury Department, and Mrs. Amy Ashwood Garvey commented helpfully on various aspects of the movement. Miss Jean Blackwell, curator of the Schomburg Collection of the New York Public Library, Mrs. Dorothy B. Porter, supervisor of the Moorland Collection of the Howard University Library, Dr. Percy Powell of the Division of Manuscripts of

the Library of Congress, and Mr. Charles Nowell of the
Manchester (England) City Library all helped to shorten
my research labors considerably. Professor John Hope
Franklin of Howard University patiently read the manuscript and at all stages of its production offered friendly
encouragement and wise advice. Two of my fellow Fulbright scholars at the University of Manchester, Miss M.
Janice Murphy and Mr. William R. Chadeayne, also gave
generously of their considerable editorial and literary skills.
It is no doubt fitting that I acknowledge here my debt to
Senator J. William Fulbright, the patron of postwar international education, whose legislative vision made possible
a year of study in Great Britain during which the manuscript benefited from further research and revision. In this
connection I would be remiss if I did not also express my
thanks to Mr. Alan Pifer and the staff of the United States
Educational Commission in the United Kingdom and to
Sir Ronald Adam, director-general of the British Council,
for their yeoman efforts to introduce me to British scholarly
resources and, upon occasion, to open closed doors.

Like all scholars who have had the good fortune to ask
their aid, I am indebted to the efficient staffs of the follow-
ing institutions: the University of Wisconsin Library, the
Wisconsin State Historical Society Library, the Schomburg
Collection, the Howard University Library, the Library of
Congress, the National Archives of the United States, the
British Museum, the British Colonial Office Library, the
Royal Empire Society Library, the University of Man-
chester Library, the Manchester City Library and the
Sterling Memorial Library of Yale University.

Lastly, I owe a special debt of gratitude to the two persons who have helped most to bring this work to a conclusion. To my good friend and wise teacher, Professor
Howard K. Beale of the University of Wisconsin, I am

indebted in more ways than can possibly be listed here. I owe much to Professor Beale's careful training in the techniques of historical research, but even more to his penetrating suggestions and patient criticism. His interest in and knowledge of the subject have been a source of both encouragement and enlightenment. And without the considerable assistance of my uncomplaining wife, Jean Hotmar Cronon, this study would lack a great deal of whatever merit it now possesses. *Black Moses* is in a very real sense their book, and I hope it justifies their faith in me.

Although the preceding list of acknowledgments indicates the extent to which other persons have contributed to this study, all errors of fact and interpretation are, of course, mine alone.

E. D. C.

May 23, 1954

★BLACK MOSES

A SON IS GIVEN

God did say to Moses one day,
Say, Moses go to Egypt land,
And tell him to let my people go.
　　　　　—Traditional Negro Spiritual [1]

I know no national boundary where the Negro
is concerned. The whole world is my province
until Africa is free.
　　　　　　—Marcus Garvey [2]

★ In the years immediately following World War I there
developed among the Negroes of the world a mass movement of considerable influence and importance. Under the
leadership of a remarkable Jamaican Negro, Marcus Garvey, the Universal Negro Improvement Association attracted the attention of the colored world to a degree never
before achieved by a Negro organization. Garvey's activities were world-wide in scope, and his organization
had members scattered from Africa to California, from
Nova Scotia to South America. His most important work,
however, was done in the United States, where conditions
among the Negro population were such as to assure him
of a ready following. Within a few years after its inception
Garvey's U.N.I.A. had collected more money and claimed
a larger membership than any other Negro group either
before or since. Glittering successes and glorious promises
marked the rise of Garveyism; equally spectacular dis-
illusionments accompanied its decline. Marcus Garvey was

3

a part of the American scene for only a decade, but he influenced the life and thinking of his people during that decade as have few men in a whole lifetime.

A short, stocky, largely self-educated but supremely confident black man, Garvey came to the United States at the age of twenty-eight and proceeded to build up a mass following in an incredibly brief time. His peculiar gift of oratory, a combination of bombast and stirring heroics, awakened fires of Negro nationalism that have yet to be extinguished. Garvey attracted attention chiefly because he put into powerful ringing phrases the secret thoughts of the Negro world. He told his listeners what they most wanted to hear—that a black skin was not a badge of shame but rather a glorious symbol of national greatness. He promised a Negro nation in the African homeland that would be the marvel of the modern world. He pointed to Negro triumphs in the past and described in glowing syllables the glories of the future. When Garvey spoke of the greatness of the race, Negroes everywhere could forget for a moment the shame of discrimination and the horrors of lynching. Garvey's program was strongly emotional, fiercely chauvinistic, and bitterly protestant in character. This latter-day Moses achieved little in the way of permanent improvement for his people, but he did help to point out the fires that smolder in the Negro world. Indeed, Garvey's success in catching the ear of his people indicates, as Gunnar Myrdal has observed, the existence of "a dissatisfaction so deep that it mounts to hopelessness of ever gaining a full life in America." [3]

☆

Marcus Garvey was born in the quiet little town of St. Ann's Bay, on the northern coast of Jamaica, on August 17, 1887, nearly four hundred years after Christopher Columbus had first taken note of that garden-like harbor by marking it on his charts as "Santa Gloria." The boy was named Marcus after his father, and legend has it that his mother, Sarah, sought to give him the middle name of Moses, explaining prophetically, "I hope he will be like Moses, and lead his people." [4] Not a religious man, the father compromised with the less prominent Biblical middle name of Moziah.° Marcus and Sarah Garvey were of unmixed Negro stock, and the father was said to be descended from the Maroons, those escaped African slaves whose heroic exploits in defense of their freedom form an important part of Jamaican history and folklore. The Maroons have always had a greater prestige than ordinary Jamaican Negroes as a result of their successful struggle against slavery, a fight that was rewarded with a treaty of independence from the British in 1739.[5] Garvey was later to glory in the fact that he was a full-blooded black man without any taint of white blood in his veins, a feeling of superiority that may have stemmed in part from his Maroon heritage.

In Jamaican households there is a strong sense of family life, with the father emphatically the head authority. Marcus Garvey, Sr., was no exception to this rule, and he directed the life of his family with a stern formality. A resident of the town who knew him well later described him as a man aloof from the rest of the people:

Mr. Garvey was a master mason. He did both stone and brick work beautifully, but he always acted as if he did not belong among the villagers. He was well-read and acted as a local lawyer. . . . He was silent, stern, seem[ing] to have the strength

° There are differences of opinion as to Garvey's middle name, though there seems to be no evidence at all that he ever used one. Roi Ottley uses "Manasseh," Claude McKay and others prefer "Aurelius," and Burgit Aron stands alone with "Moses." Garvey's widow is perhaps the best authority, and she asserts that although his mother wanted the name "Moses" Garvey's father insisted upon "Moziah."

of an ox. His complexion was not very black, but his features were broad and nose flat. He was "Mr. Garvey" to everyone, even to Sarah, his wife, and children.

Where her husband was cold and formal, Sarah Garvey was gentle and openhearted. "She was the direct opposite of my father," Garvey later recalled.[6] A white neighbor remembered her as "the most beautiful black woman" she had ever seen, with "features that of a European, her skin black and soft as velvet, her eyes jet black, large, liquid, and so sad." Mrs. Garvey attended church faithfully in spite of the fact that her husband showed little interest in religion other than putting in an appearance at an occasional funeral. She often found it necessary to sell cakes and pastries to augment the family income, for her husband worked only when he felt like it and often would rather lock himself in his room and read. This moodiness on the part of his father caused young Marcus, known variously as "Mose" or "Ugly Mug" at this time, to become strongly attached to his mother.

The Garvey family was a large one, for this strange union brought forth eleven children, of whom Marcus was the youngest. Most of the children died young, however, and only Marcus and his sister, Indiana, lived to maturity. Apparently the family was fairly well provided for in Marcus' early years when his father was earning enough for a comfortable livelihood.[7] Later Garvey said of his father, "He once had a fortune; he died poor." [8] The older Garvey's unreasonable stubbornness caused him to lose most of his property. For twenty years he received a newspaper under the assumption that it was a gift from the publisher, only to be billed for the sum of thirty pounds by the executors of the estate when the publisher died. Feeling that the claim was unjust, Mr. Garvey ignored the debt, was sued by his creditors, lost the case, and still refused to pay, with the result that one of his properties was attached by court order and sold at a loss to cover the claim and court costs. Adversity only increased his stubborn irritability and led to further quarrels with his neighbors over boundary and property rights. A series of ruinous court actions eventuated in the loss of all his lands except the small plot of land upon which the Garvey home stood. These developments only increased the persecution complex of the elder Garvey and he increasingly tended to lose himself for days at a time in his books and brooding meditations.

While neither parent had much formal education, Garvey's father was locally respected for his wide reading and his private library, and from this paternal trait young Marcus may have developed his similar fondness for books and learning. As a boy, Garvey attended the local elementary school and may have spent some time in the Anglican grammar school at St. Ann's Bay. It is possible that he also received additional education through the Jamaican teacher-pupil course of training.[9] If we are to believe Garvey himself, he had more than a perfunctory education. "I attended the schools of the town and was graduated from the Church of England High School," he once declared. "In addition I was tutored by the Rev. W. H. Sloely and the Rev. P. A. Conahan, and eventually I went to England and for eighteen months was a student in Bir[k]beck College." [10] The records of Birkbeck College, now a part of London University, were partly destroyed in the London blitz of 1940 and unfortunately do not indicate definitely whether Garvey was ever a student or what courses he attended. The registrar of the college believes, however, that Garvey may have attended law classes as an occasional student in 1912 and 1913.[11] "I got my education from many sources," Garvey boasted on another occasion, "through private tutors, two public schools, two grammar or high schools, and two colleges. Between school and work, at fourteen, I had under my control several men. I was strong and manly, and I made them respect me." [12] Throughout his life Garvey yearned to be considered a learned man, the intellectual equal of a Negro scholar such as his bitter enemy, Dr. W. E. Burghardt DuBois. Garvey's florid style of writing and speaking, his fondness of appearing in a richly colored academic cap and gown, and his use of the initials "D.C.L." after his name were but crude attempts to compensate for some of the educational advantages that had been denied him by reason of class and color.

Life in St. Ann's Bay completed another, more important aspect of Garvey's education. In his younger days he was unaware of any racial differences and played freely with all of the neighbor children, regardless of their color. Indeed, he had more than the usual number of white playmates, for the Garvey home adjoined the properties of two white families. One of his best friends was a little white girl, the daughter of the neighboring Methodist minister. When Garvey was fourteen, she was sent away to school in Scotland and in saying goodbye she told him that she must no longer see or write to him because he was a "nigger." This was the first time he had ever heard the term used, and he later wrote of the disturbing incident, "It was then that I found for the first time that there was some difference in humanity, and that there were different races, each having its own separate and distinct social life." After this first lesson in race distinction young Garvey "never thought of playing with white girls any more, even if they might be next-door neighbors," though he continued for some time his friendships with white boys. [13]

☆

There has been a significant race problem in Jamaica ever since the first Spanish conquistadores met and mastered the native Indian population. The question of race tended to loom ever larger on the Jamaican scene, moreover, as first the Spanish and after 1665 the British turned to Africa for Negro slaves to labor on the island's rich sugar plantations. Throughout the West Indies in general the white group has always been a small minority of the total population. At the time of Garvey's birth the population of Jamaica numbered just over 600,000, double what it had been in 1800.[14] Anglo-Saxons amounted to roughly 2 per cent of the total; Negroes, 78 per cent; and mixed bloods, or colored, about 18 per cent. Over the years the colored or mulatto group has increased steadily both in numbers and proportion, while the white population has declined drastically. Quite obviously this has been the result of intermarriage and miscegenation.

In contrast with the United States, one of the outstanding features of the Jamaican racial situation is the separate status of this mulatto group. As in the case of many colonial areas where the white minority lives as a managerial or non-laboring class, the mixed bloods approximate a middle-class status. As a middle class, the mulatto group occupies a useful role in the eyes of the whites: it is useful for economic purposes and it acts as a buffer between the two unmixed races. And since accommodation rather than protest is the dominant motive of the mixed blood, he assumes the role of a conformist anxious to defend his superior status.[15] Among some members of the mulatto group there may even be an underlying assumption that continued intermarriage will eventually wipe out the remaining color barriers between the two upper classes.[16] The colored population acts as a safety valve for any explosive racial discontent and tends eagerly to assimilate and imitate English culture. This is aided by a general lack of pride in the Negro heritage and by the stigma attached to Negro blood. There is a tendency for personal behavior to follow conformist patterns, since ambition is directed toward individual social and economic success. Any natural leaders are therefore drawn away from attempts to modify the system.

English class traditions, modified by racial considerations, are the determining forces in Jamaican society. There is no legal discrimination between the three racial groups, and while ultimate political control remains in London there is little possibility for one racial group seriously to exploit the others. Generally speaking, the white element forms the social aristocracy of the island, the mulattoes make up the middle class, and the blacks are the laborers. There is no fixed color line in the sense that a black may not rise to middle class status, but the question of color looms large in island thinking. This is particularly the case within the colored element of the population and between it and the darker Negro group. The lightest of the mixed bloods, often called "Jamaican whites" because they consider themselves white, generally possess the most racial prejudice. The mulattoes act to protect their status as "almost white" and look down upon their more Negroid brothers.

The overwhelming black majority is, however, a group apart. The Negroes far outnumber the other two classes combined, but despite their numerical superiority they are relegated to an inferior economic and social position. The blacks have tended to be helpless for want of organization and leadership. Natural black leaders are drawn into the colored class through marriage or through economic and social advancement. Neither whites nor mixed bloods are anxious for a change in the *status quo,* and they act together to prevent any enlightenment of the black majority.

It was into this environment that Marcus Garvey was

born, and from it he was to draw much of his antipathy and distrust for any but the darkest-skinned Negroes. Growing up as a black himself, Garvey understood the feelings of hopelessness and frustration among the more backward Jamaican Negroes and saw the need of expanding their outlook through greater educational and economic opportunities. Above all he desired to rebuild their racial self-respect through a new feeling of pride in the Negro heritage.

☆

When he was fourteen, family financial difficulties forced Garvey to leave school and go to work. He had hoped to go on with his secondary education in Kingston, the capital city of Jamaica, but instead he was apprenticed to learn the printing trade with his godfather, a Mr. Burrowes. This was not a complete waste of time, however, for his employer had a substantial library that was open to the youthful apprentice. Here, too, Garvey began to absorb some of the journalistic techniques that were later to play such an important part in the development of his movement. After two years at the trade, young Marcus had picked up enough skill to warrant his branching out on his own. And since prospects for the future in a small village printery did not appear particularly bright, at the age of seventeen the ambitious young man left St. Ann's Bay for Kingston in order to work at his new trade.

In Kingston, working for a maternal uncle, Garvey was able to save enough money to bring his mother to live with him. A hurricane had swept Jamaica in 1903, destroying the crops on which Mrs. Garvey's income depended and forcing her to leave the home village as a matter of financial necessity. Urban life did not agree with her, however, as her previous leisurely life in the peaceful parish had not prepared her for the hurried bustle and crowded confusion of the larger town. Mrs. Garvey made no secret of her dislike of the confining nature of city life, complaining about her financial losses and fretting over her forced existence away from the old home at St. Ann's Bay until her death shortly thereafter.

Garvey shared some of his mother's fondness for the old and the familiar, but he also found city living a new and exciting experience. Kingston offered much to interest a lad from a quiet country parish. The thronging streets and hurried atmosphere, the big ships unloading their cargoes from faraway lands were in sharp contrast with the peaceful home village. Noisy harangues and lively street debates fascinated the serious black boy; and since his country education had not prepared him for any such quick exchange of ideas, he resolved to learn the art of effective self-expression. His first attempts at public speaking met with rude rebuffs and he was bluntly told, "Country boy, shut your mouth!" He persisted, however, spending his Sundays visiting various churches to observe the techniques of delivery used by the most effective Kingston preachers and practicing reading aloud passages from the school reader while trying out various gestures before the mirror in his room. Gradually Garvey became more proficient as a platform orator, gaining confidence as he was listened to with increasing respect by his associates. Eventually he was to establish the yearly Elocution Contest, which proved so successful that it became an important annual event in Jamaica.[17] This, too, was sound training for a man who would one day sway thousands with his magnetic oratory.

Working as a printer in Kingston, Garvey made rapid advancements, until by the time he was twenty he had become a master printer and a foreman at one of the largest Jamaican firms, the P. A. Benjamin Company.[18] On the afternoon of January 14, 1907, an earthquake and fire destroyed much of Kingston.[19] Wages were low and the scarcity of commodities caused a price rise that materially decreased the purchasing power of the workers. The Printers' Union, one of the oldest and most powerful labor organizations on the island, thereupon struck for higher wages. Garvey had not been informed of the impending strike, and the walkout of his men took him by surprise. He joined them, nevertheless, and was elected to lead the strike.

As head of the striking printers, Garvey worked energetically at organizing public meetings in favor of the workers, in spite of the promise by his employers of a personal salary increase if he would abandon the struggle. The strike was finally broken, however, when the union treasurer absconded with the funds and when the employers began to introduce linotype machines with imported printers to operate them. Most of the striking printers were able to return to their jobs; but Garvey, as the only foreman who had joined the strike, found himself blacklisted.[20] This made him at twenty something of a local labor martyr but left him contemptuous of labor organizations and their ability to solve the problems of the worker, particularly the Negro worker. Throughout his life Garvey remained skeptical of the value of the labor movement and refused to bring about any understanding between labor forces and his Negro improvement movement.

Unable to find private employment as a printer because of his activity as a strike leader, Garvey went to work at the government printing office. His experience in the strike had emphasized the need of organized action to improve the lot of the black worker, however, and about 1910 he began editing a periodical known as *Garvey's Watchman*.[21] This venture proved unsuccessful, and he next helped to establish a political organization, the National Club, with a fortnightly publication called *Our Own*. A well-educated Negro, a Dr. Love, publisher of the *Advocate*, gave Garvey much inspirational encouragement at this time. Dr. Love had studied in England and had returned to devote much of his time and money to the enlightenment of the Jamaican Negro peasants. His example and helpful support meant much to the young reformer after the initial rebuffs as labor leader and editor.

Garvey soon realized that any effective program would demand his full-time attention and more money than he had any immediate prospects of obtaining in Jamaica. He therefore left his job at the printing office and traveled to Costa Rica, where he hoped to be able to earn enough money to enable him to return and continue his organizational work. The United Fruit Company was currently expanding its operations in Costa Rica, and Garvey's uncle secured a job for the Jamaican as timekeeper on one of the company's banana plantations. The plight of the Negro field workers, many of them his countrymen, only increased Garvey's determination to improve the lot of Negroes everywhere. He soon gave up his plantation job to go to Limon, where he protested to the British consul over the treatment of Jamaican Negroes working on the banana plantations. This official's nonchalant indifference convinced Garvey that no white person would ever "regard the life of a black man equal to that of a white man." And in Limon he tried to establish another newspaper called *La Nacionale*, but again his journalistic efforts failed to break through the apathy of the indifferent Negro peasants.[22]

Disconcerted at his young nephew's idealistic efforts at radical journalism and reform, Garvey's uncle gave him enough money to go to Bocas-del-Toro, Panama. Here Garvey found a job, but after a few months he drifted on to Colon, where he started another newspaper, *La Prensa.* In Panama Garvey observed with great indignation the inferior status of Negro workers on the Panama Canal, which was nearing completion at this time. From Colon Garvey moved to Ecuador, where he observed Negro laborers being exploited in the mines and tobacco fields, and then went on to compare conditions in Nicaragua, Honduras, Colombia, and Venezuela. His widow records that "sickened with fever and sick at heart over appeals from his people for help on their behalf" he returned to Jamaica.

In 1912, Garvey journeyed to London to learn what he could about the condition of Negroes in other parts of the British Empire. Here he became associated with the half-Negro, half-Egyptian author, Duse Mohammed Ali. Duse Mohammed was greatly interested in Africa and published a monthly magazine, the *Africa Times and Orient Review.* One of his chief interests was the campaign for home rule in Egypt; but his part-Negro ancestry made him quick to notice the presence of an insidious color bar in England, and his writing often reflected his bitterness at this insult to colored people.[23] Garvey's contacts with this African scholar stimulated a keen interest in Africa, its culture, and its administration under colonial rule. The young Jamaican learned a great deal about his ancestral homeland, absorbing much of the African nationalism so characteristic of his later activities. In London Garvey met other young Negroes—students from Africa and the West Indies, African nationalists, sailors, and dock workers—and from them he picked up information about Negro conditions throughout the world. He read avidly on the subject of Africa in the rich libaries of the city and may even have spent a few months in an English college.[24]

Garvey also became interested in the position of Negroes in the United States, and it was in London that he came across a copy of Booker T. Washington's autobiography, *Up from Slavery*. This book had a profound effect upon him as he later testified: "I read *Up from Slavery* by Booker T. Washington, and then my doom—if I may so call it—of being a race leader dawned upon me. . . . I asked: 'Where is the black man's Government? Where is his King and his kingdom? Where is his President, his country, and his ambassador, his army, his navy, his men of big affairs?' I could not find them, and then I declared, 'I will help to make them.' " [25] The seeds of Garveyism had unwittingly been sown by the great compromiser and advocate of accommodation, the venerable Sage of Tuskegee!

In the summer of 1914 Garvey hastened home to Jamaica, his head spinning with big plans for a program of race redemption. "My brain was afire," he recalled as he considered the possibility of "uniting all the Negro peoples of the world into one great body to establish a country and Government absolutely their own." Garvey was "determined that the black man would not continue to be kicked about by all the other races and nations of the world," and he had a glorious vision of "a new world of black men, not peons, serfs, dogs and slaves, but a nation of sturdy men making their impress upon civilization and causing a new light to dawn upon the human race." [26]

Back in Jamaica Garvey contacted some of his old friends, and on August 1, 1914, he established the organization which was henceforth to occupy all his time and energy until his death. The imposing title of the new organization, the Universal Negro Improvement and Conservation Association and African Communities League, implied its stated interest in "drawing the peoples of the race together." Its manifesto, drawn with great care, warned of "the universal disunity existing among the people of the Negro or African race" and called upon "all people of Negro or African parentage" to join in a great crusade to rehabilitate the race. Garvey itemized the ambitious general objects of the association:

To establish a Universal Confraternity among the race; to promote the spirit of race pride and love; to reclaim the fallen of the race; to administer to and assist the needy; to assist in civilizing the backward tribes of Africa; to strengthen the imperialism of independent African States; to establish Commissionaries or Agencies in the principal countries of the world for the protection of all Negroes, irrespective of nationality; to promote a conscientious Christian worship among the native tribes of Africa; to establish Universities, Colleges and Secondary Schools for the further education and culture of the boys and girls of the race; to conduct a world-wide commercial and industrial intercourse.[27]

It is interesting to note that these general objects were modified slightly in later published versions of the U.N.I.A. manifesto. The word "race" was dropped from the second and third objects; instead of promoting "Christian" worship among African tribes, the later version spoke only of "spiritual" worship; and the word "imperialism" was abandoned with reference to the independence of African states. In addition, a new object spoke of the need "to establish a central nation for the race." [28]

The preamble to the constitution of the new organization contained a strong plea for universal brotherhood, but it indicated that the achievement of this goal must come through the concerted action of the Negro people of the world. The Universal Negro Improvement Association was described as "a social, friendly, humanitarian, charitable, educational, institutional, constructive, and expansive society," whatever that might mean, and its organizers pledged themselves "to work for the general uplift of the Negro peoples of the world" and "to do all in their power to conserve the rights of their noble race and to respect the rights of all mankind." The motto of the association was both stirring and succinct: "One God! One Aim! One Destiny!" "Let justice be done to all mankind," thundered Garvey in the preamble, "realizing that if the strong oppresses the weak, confusion and discontent will ever mark the path of man, but with love, faith, and charity toward all, the reign of peace and plenty will be heralded into the world and generations of men shall be called Blessed." [29] Garvey was designated as President and Traveling Commissioner of the new organization and was to be assisted by Thomas Smikle as Vice President, Eva Aldred as President of the Ladies' Division, and T. A. McCormack as General Secretary. Garvey's future wife, Amy Ashwood, held the post of Associate Secretary. The headquarters of the association were located in Kingston at 30 Charles Street. [30]

In addition to its general program of race redemption, the U.N.I.A., as it soon came to be called, had a definite plan of action for Negro betterment in Jamaica. The keystone of the local program was the establishment of educational and industrial colleges for Jamaican Negroes, and in this Garvey was borrowing from Booker T. Washington, whose Tuskegee Institute in Alabama had been the inspiration for so many similar ventures in Negro education. The U.N.I.A. campaign for a Jamaican Tuskegee received favorable publicity and gained the support of such eminent white citizens as the mayor of Kingston, a Roman Catholic bishop, and the governor of the island. The blacks, the chief beneficiaries of the scheme, were indifferent, however, and the association was actively opposed by the mulatto group. "I was openly hated and persecuted," Garvey explained later, "by some of these colored men of the island who did not want to be classified as Negroes but as white." They could not understand why any man with talent would concern himself with improving the lot of the lower-class blacks. To them Garvey was "simply an impossible man to use openly the term 'Negro'; yet everyone beneath his breath was calling the black man a nigger." [31] Obstructed by hostile mulattoes and ignored by unimpressed blacks, Garvey soon came to the ironic conclusion that the chief support for Negro betterment in Jamaica must depend upon public-spirited members of the white group.

In the spring of 1915, Garvey decided that it would be necessary to call upon the Negroes of the United States for support of his program in Jamaica. Previously he had written to the founder of Tuskegee Institute and had received an invitation from Washington to visit the school. Accordingly, on April 12, 1915, Garvey wrote again informing Washington that he was now planning a visit to the United States "to lecture in the interest of my Association" and would do "most of my public speaking in the South among the people of our race." He asked for Washington's assistance as he would "be coming there a stranger to the people." [32] The Sage of Tuskegee, who undoubtedly received countless such requests from unknown hopefuls representing obscure organizations, responded politely, but he refrained from committing himself to any definite promise of support other than the courteous offer to make Garvey's stay "as pleasant and as profitable as we can." [33]

It seems clear that at this time Garvey had given no thought to moving his base of operations permanently to the United States, but doubtless he had heard of the generous financial support given the Tuskegee Institute and felt that Booker T. Washington was the only American who might be able to help him to secure funds for the U.N.I.A.'s educational program in Jamaica. The plans for industrial and agricultural education would be bound to appeal to

the man who had done so much to channel American Negro
education along those lines. It might even be possible to
organize branches of the Universal Negro Improvement
Association under the leadership of American Negroes before returning to Jamaica to establish the trade school. But
before Garvey could complete his travel plans late in 1915,
Booker T. Washington was dead, and with him died Garvey's strongest hope for a sympathetic reception in America. In spite of this unfortunate development, Garvey went
ahead with his plans for an American visit; and on March
23, 1916, the stocky Jamaican arrived in Harlem to see how
American Negroes would receive his program of race improvement.[34]

★ T W O

HOW LONG, O LORD,

HOW LONG?

Slabery an' freedom
Dey's mos' de same
No difference hahdly
Cep' in de name.
— Negro Folk Song [1]

A race without authority and power is
a race without respect.
— Marcus Garvey [2]

★ When Marcus Garvey, as yet an obscure foreigner, stepped ashore in New York on that bleak March day early in 1916, the American Negro world was undergoing a series of profound social changes that would play no small part in the acceptance of Garvey's leadership by large numbers of American Negroes. There were many reasons why colored Americans would be receptive to Garveyism at this time, some stemming directly from the effect of World War I on Negro life and others having their origin in factors that had been shaping Negro thought for years prior to the war. The profound disillusionment felt by Negroes at the end of the war had much to do with their widespread acceptance of a new and alien leader with an extreme program of racial nationalism. Americans in general experienced a postwar disillusionment as it became apparent that the war had not been fought entirely for the noble democratic ideals given so much publicity during the struggle by the Wilson administration. But American Negroes, expecting much and obtaining little in the way of improved status, were deeply discouraged over the results of the war here at home. It did not take Garvey long to realize that the growing mood of frustration and despair on the part of many Negro Americans was a favorable climate in which to promote his ideas of race redemption.

☆

The Negro population of the United States has traditionally been located in the southeast section of the country, the area known as the American South. Here among the cotton and tobacco fields to which the original African slaves had been brought the large bulk of American Negroes continued to dwell, working the red clay of Georgia or the rich soil of the Black Belt in much the same fashion as their forefathers. With the abolition of slavery, southern Negroes began to experience forces acting from within and without the South that tended to increase their mobility. Sometimes a long period of poor crops or a brutal lynching acted to drive Negroes from the area. At other times reports of high wages and more favorable conditions in other parts of the country tended to pull them away from their traditional homes.

During World War I, large numbers of southern Negroes migrated to fill the empty workbenches of the war-stimulated industry in the North and the West. This movement from the South was not new in character, but its magnitude far exceeded any of the earlier significant Negro migrations out of the South. Like the remarkable trek into Kansas in 1879, led by Henry Adams of Louisiana and Moses Singleton of Tennessee,[3] and the more spontaneous movement into Arkansas and Texas in 1888–89, the exodus of 1916–18 was caused partly by economic conditions and partly by the discriminatory treatment accorded Negroes in the South.[4] Even before the United States entered the war in April, 1917, thousands of southern blacks were moving northward in search of a better life.

While it is difficult to determine exactly the number of Negroes who left the South in this period, probably a half million Negroes moved to the North in the years 1916–18.[5] The movement coincided with the greatest industrial demand for unskilled labor, tapering off in 1919 during the period of postwar industrial reconversion and depression and reviving somewhat from 1921 to 1924.[6] Some northern cities experienced a phenomenal increase in Negro population in the space of a few months. The number of Negroes living in Gary, Indiana, to take one extreme example, increased by more than 1200 per cent in the decade between 1910 and 1920. Chicago's Negro population increased from 44,103 to 109,594 during the same decade, a rise of nearly 150 per cent at a time when the white population was increasing only 21 per cent.[7] Other northern industrial cities showed similar rapid growth in the number of colored citizens arriving in search of work and housing.

The general depression of southern agriculture prior to the entry of the United States into the war made southern Negroes especially receptive to inducements to move north.[8] The low price of cotton and the general labor depression in the South after 1914 undoubtedly had a considerable influence on the exodus. The appearance of the boll weevil in much of the cotton belt during the summers of 1915 and 1916, moreover, was another cause of the demoralization of Negro agricultural workers.[9] This cotton pest had first entered the United States in the southern part of Texas in 1892. It traveled slowly but inexorably, reaching Louisiana in 1903, but by 1908 the boll weevil had

covered most of the cotton belt west of the Mississippi
River. It spread through most of Georgia in 1916 and had
conquered South Carolina by 1919.[10] Thus in the years
when northern industry was sending its agents southward
in search of new sources of unskilled labor, farmers in
many parts of the South were experiencing severe hard-
ships as a result of the depredations of the boll weevil. "De
merchant got half de cotton," sang southern Negroes in a
mournful ballad, "de boll weevil got de res'. Didn't leave
de farmer's wife but one old cotton dress, an' it's full of
holes, it's full of holes." [11] Added to crop losses caused by
weevil attacks was the distress in some areas resulting from
a series of disastrous floods during the summer of 1915.[12]

Northern industry embarked on a great campaign to secure Negro labor after the demands of the European war
had overtaxed the northern industrial labor market and the
war itself had shut off the traditional supply of European
immigrant labor. This demand for unskilled labor could
best be met in the South, where the agricultural conditions
outlined above had led to a large labor surplus. Wages were
low in the South and, in spite of the rising cost of living,
southern wages tended to remain depressed because of the
large labor surplus. In the North, however, wages and
working conditions were much more attractive. A detailed
study of the Negro migrants to the Pittsburgh area showed
that the wage differential between the two sections was an
important factor in persuading many Negroes to make the
move.[13]

Northern industrialists used various methods to attract
Negro workers. The Negro press was utilized to spread the
word of the golden economic opportunities to be found in
the North; colored editors devoted a large amount of editorial and advertising space to descriptions of the great
possibilities for lucrative employment north of the Mason

and Dixon Line. Coupled with this newspaper campaign was the energetic activity of the labor agents sent to make direct contact with southern Negroes. These agents operated at one time or another in every section from which Negroes emigrated.[14] The labor agents worked mainly in the cities where their activities would not be so easily observed by anxious southern whites. After the effects of the migration on the southern labor market began to alarm the local authorities, it became necessary to conduct much of the promotional work through the mails. In some cases, free railroad passes were used to encourage Negroes to leave the South.[15]

The migration was greatly stimulated by enthusiastic letters home from friends and relatives who had made the move and by the editorial encouragement of northern Negro newspapers, many of which had a large circulation in the South. The heavy traffic of Negroes moving northward influenced others living along the main routes to follow suit. One migrant from Decatur, Alabama, estimated that a third of the Negro population was persuaded to leave the city, largely because of encouragement from other migrants on the trains passing through the town. "And when the moving fever hit them," he declared, "there was no changing their minds." [16] Towns not located on main rail lines were much less affected by the migration.

The weekly Chicago *Defender* was a particularly effective stimulus in the development of the migration. The newspaper's militant approach to racial equality, its violent criticism of the South, and its strident advocacy of retaliation in kind for the barbarities of southern whites found a wide audience among southern Negroes. Indeed, the circulation of the *Defender* jumped from 50,000 to 125,000 during the migration.[17] In the *Defender* Negroes could read fierce protests against the injustices of southern life, protests expressed in an unrestrained fashion no southern paper would dare to imitate. The paper acted as a clearing house for inquiries about the North and received many letters from southern Negroes seeking encouragement for the move.[18] When southern whites began to spread word that the migrants would freeze to death in the North, the *Defender* scornfully declared that "to die from the bite of frost is far more glorious than at the hands of a mob," and it begged southern Negroes "to leave the benighted land." Noting numerous instances where Negroes had frozen to death during southern winters, the *Defender* asked pointedly: "If you can freeze to death in the North and be free, why freeze to death in the South and be a slave, where your mother, sister, and daughter are raped and burned at the stake; where your father, brother, and sons are treated with contempt and hung to a pole, riddled with bullets at the least mention that he [*sic*] does not like the way he is treated. . . . The *Defender* says come." [19]

In spite of repressive measures instituted by worried southern officials and employers to halt the flood of cheap labor out of the South, large numbers of southern Negroes left their homes because they were dissatisfied with economic conditions and believed that the move north would better their status. Poor housing, low wages, a lack of police protection, the difficulty of securing justice in southern courts, limited educational opportunities, and the general position of inferiority accorded them in the South caused many Negroes to seek new homes where they could hope for a better life.[20] The fantastic rumors about the unlimited opportunities to be found in the North did little to prepare the southern migrants for wretched housing conditions, a higher cost of living, and a war boom in industrial employment that would prove only temporary in nature.

By the end of the war, then, there were in the North large

numbers of nearly illiterate southern Negroes who had left their homes in search of better conditions. Unused to the climatic rigors of northern life, and for the most part unskilled in the trades, this group of native migrants presented a problem of assimilation much more difficult than that raised by the presence of old-world immigrants. The general slackening of employment during the period of reconversion and recession after the war disheartened many of these new arrivals. Their initial feeling of delight at the comparative equality of treatment in the North rapidly gave way to a wave of discouragement as it became apparent that even in the fabled North Negroes were still only second-class citizens, herded into black ghettos, the last to be hired and the first to be fired. To this group of poorly educated, superstitious, disillusioned Negroes Marcus Garvey would make his strongest appeal, and from this element of the colored world Garveyism would draw some of its staunchest support.

☆

In addition to the disorganization of southern agriculture prior to the war and the wave of migration northward during the struggle, the war itself acted to stimulate unrest among American Negroes. Wartime propaganda emphasized the democratic way of life as one of the important ideals for which America was fighting. The war speeches of President Wilson on the rights of subject minorities clearly raised issues that had domestic implications. This war-stimulated discussion of the democratic ideal brought to white Americans a vague realization of certain embarrassing inconsistencies in the operation of American democracy. There was even an appreciation by many of the need to improve the status of minority groups in order to demonstrate the sincerity of American war aims. These developments tended not only to raise the hopes of American Negroes but also to emphasize to them their role of inferiority in a nation that prided itself on its democratic heritage.

On the whole, American Negroes responded loyally to the call to arms. A few radical periodicals, notably the *Messenger*, published by A. Philip Randolph and Chandler Owen, cynically questioned the advisability of dying for a country that denied all of its citizens equal treatment; but this group was only a very tiny, though vociferous, minority. The overwhelming majority of the Negro people wanted to prove their patriotic loyalty and supported the war effort in every way possible. Nearly 400,000 Negroes served in the armed forces during the struggle, while on the home front Negro civilians enthusiastically purchased more than $250,000,000 worth of bonds and stamps in the five major Liberty Loan drives.[21]

With but few exceptions, the Negro press gave strong support to the war effort. Negro newspapers carried glowing, if often exaggerated, accounts of the heroic exploits of colored soldiers in France and boasted proudly of the industrial achievements of Negro workers at home. The war effort received unexpected support, moreover, when in July, 1918, W. E. B. DuBois, the respected editor of *Crisis*, published an editorial entitled "Close Ranks!" in which he urged that Negroes forget their special grievances and stand shoulder to shoulder with their white fellow citizens in the fight for democracy. Colored editors were not willing to forget completely the injustices of American life, but they concentrated on winning the war in the hope that a record of loyal service in the world struggle for democracy would help materially to extend some of that democracy at home.

American Negroes were proud of the record of their troops during the war. True, opportunities for Negro advancement were limited, it was exceedingly difficult for a Negro to obtain an officer's commission, Negro enlistments were curtailed, service was prohibited in the Marine Corps and severely restricted to menial positions in the Navy, and the War Department hesitated to form Negro combat units. In spite of these handicaps, however, Negro soldiers acquitted themselves creditably. Negro combat troops were among the first American soldiers to be sent overseas, and such regiments as the Fifteenth New York and the Eighth Illinois Infantry gave distinguished service with the French Army. The all-Negro Ninety-Second Division was handicapped by the fact that it was the only American division to receive its first training as a unit after its arrival overseas, and its organization as an effective fighting unit was therefore somewhat delayed. The Ninety-Second went into action in August, 1918, however, and shared in the heavy fighting of the last two months of the war. An entire battalion of the division was cited for bravery and awarded the Croix de Guerre by the French high command. Forty-three enlisted men and fourteen Negro officers were awarded the Distinguished Service Cross for bravery in action.[22]

An important aspect of Negro military service overseas was the treatment accorded colored soldiers in England and France. For the most part Negro soldiers moved about freely in France and enjoyed friendly relations with the French population, often to the great chagrin of their white comrades in arms.[23] The comparative absence of racial prejudice in France was for most of the American Negro troops a new and vividly unforgettable experience. The practical demonstration that all whites were not inherently antagonistic toward their darker brothers was responsible for much of the mounting dissatisfaction with conditions in the United States. The returning Negro soldier, both emboldened and embittered, was in no mood to slip quietly back into the old prewar caste system. And in spite of the determination of some white Americans to maintain the old racial *status quo*, many Negroes were now willing to fight, if necessary, to gain what they considered their rightful place in American life.

☆

As might be expected, the increased mobility of the Negro population during the war years brought with it a marked rise in the friction between Negroes and whites. Some of this tension was traceable to the forced mingling of the two races in the armed forces, though this was kept to a minimum by the use of segregated units and cantonments. The hostility of southern whites to the presence of Negro troops caused the War Department grave concern and was one of the reasons for the appointment of Emmett J. Scott, former private secretary to Booker T. Washington for eighteen years, as Special Assistant to Secretary of War Newton D. Baker.[24]

There were several serious clashes between Negro soldiers and white civilians in the South. In September, 1917, troops from the Twenty-Fourth Infantry Regiment were involved in a riot with white civilians in Houston, and in October of the same year the Fifteenth New York Infantry barely avoided similar trouble at Spartanburg, South Carolina. The summary trial and speedy execution of thirteen of the soldiers involved in the Houston affair and the imprisonment for life of forty-one others did much to shake the confidence of the colored world in the integrity of federal justice.[25] For years afterward the Negro press was bitter in its denunciation of what colored Americans considered a serious travesty on justice, and ultimately Negroes launched a successful campaign to obtain pardons and reinstatement for the imprisoned men.

Race friction was not limited merely to the armed services. The influx of southern Negroes into the North brought
serious problems of assimilation during a period when officials of northern cities had little time to cope with them
adequately. More than a decade earlier Mr. Dooley, the
homespun Irish philosopher created by humorist Finley P.
Dunne, had observed with shrewd insight that if he were a
Negro he would "as lave be gently lynched in Mississippi
as baten to death in New York," and that he would "choose
th' cotton belt in prifrince to th' belt on th' neck fr'm th'
polisman's club." [26] The dislocation of the war years
proved that mob violence was not merely a southern phenomenon.

In 1917, the city of East St. Louis, Illinois, was the scene
of a violent race riot growing out of the employment of Negroes in a factory holding government war contracts. At
least forty Negroes lost their lives in a bloody struggle lasting several days.[27] Lynchings also took an upward turn
during the war years with thirty-eight Negro victims in
1917 and half again that many more the following year.[28]
But the riots of the war period were only a grim prelude to
the bloody months in 1919 that have been called the "Red
Summer," for from June to the end of the year there were
twenty-six race riots in American cities.[29] The conflicts
were not localized in any one section of the country but
developed wherever the two races were living in close
proximity and were competing for scarce housing and employment. Negroes now showed a new willingness to defend themselves and their rights, a fact that added to the
ferocity of some of the struggles.

In July, 1919, a race riot broke out in Longview, Texas,
over the sending of a dispatch to the Chicago *Defender*
concerning a lynching the previous month. When Negroes
showed some resistance, the infuriated white rioters

burned much of the Negro section of the town. The following week there was a more violent outbreak in the nation's capital, partly as a result of irresponsible newspaper reports of Negro assaults on white women. White servicemen played a large part in the three-day rioting, and the casualty lists on both sides were heavy owing to Negro retaliation.[30] Even more serious was the rioting in Chicago beginning on July 27, 1919, over the drowning of a Negro boy in a white section of a Lake Michigan beach. Rumors that he had been murdered fanned the flames of an intense racial hatred that had been building up over the months of heavy Negro migration into the city. For thirteen days the city was largely without law and order, despite the presence of the state militia after the fourth day of trouble. At the end of the reign of terror at least thirty-eight persons were dead and hundreds more injured. More than a thousand families, mainly Negroes, were homeless as the result of the worst outbreak of racial strife in the nation's history.[31] During the next two months other race riots occurred in such widely separated cities as Knoxville, Tennessee, Elaine, Arkansas, and Omaha, Nebraska.

The pattern of violence evidenced in the great increase of lynching and race riots demonstrated that American Negroes were now determined to adopt more militant measures in defense of their rights. It was no longer true, as Mr. Dooley had once remarked, that "th' black has manny fine qualities. He is joyous, light-hearted, an' aisily lynched." [32] One Negro, a veteran of the Chicago rioting, spoke the determination of countless others of his race when he warned: "It is the duty of every man here to provide himself with guns and ammunition. I, myself, have at least one gun and at least enough ammunition to make it useful." [33] Another Chicago Negro explained the attitude of the new Negro: "We are only defending ourselves against American prejudice." [34] This new element of forceful protest indicated not only a deep dissatisfaction with the workings of American democracy but implied as well a fierce determination to improve the status of the colored citizen.

☆

The growth of bigotry and intolerance in America was stimulated by the rebirth of the Ku Klux Klan after 1915. This tragicomic organization of white-sheeted knights advocated a broad program of white supremacy and the preservation of American institutions—as interpreted by the Klan. From beneath their burning crosses the hooded leaders of the Klan exhorted all true Americans (native born, white, Protestant) to unite against Negroes, Roman Catholics, Jews, Orientals, and all foreigners. The reaction against wartime internationalism soon enabled the Klan to thrive in areas where there had been little previous manifestation of racial bigotry. The K.K.K. was particularly strong in the South, where its energies were directed largely against Negroes. The South was not the only part of the country susceptible to the spread of K.K.K. "Americanism," however, and within ten months after the end of the war the Klan had made appearances in twenty-seven states, including parts of New England, New York, Indiana, Michigan, and Illinois.[35]

The Ku Klux Klan acted in such a way as to leave little doubt in Negro minds as to its determination to make the United States a white man's country. "We would not rob the colored population of their right," announced a klansman at one konklave, "but we demand that they respect the rights of the white race in whose country they are permitted to reside." [36] In Portland, Oregon, the Knights of the White Light, an adjunct of the K.K.K., mailed circulars to prominent whites demanding that all Negroes be deported to Africa. The Knights proposed that agents be sent among the colored population to emphasize the desirability of returning to the ancestral homeland, observing with quaint insight, "Some Negroes will be found quite willing, for they can be made to feel dissatisfied with conditions as they are." [37]

Just as the race riots after the war helped to shake the faith of Negroes in their future as American citizens, so also the nocturnal activities of the Ku Klux Klan and its associated organizations caused many colored citizens to doubt whether the Negro could ever hope to achieve equality of opportunity and treatment in the United States. The great hopes of the war years dissolved into bitter cynicism in the face of the brutal realities of the postwar situation. It is not surprising that many Negroes sought escape in radicalism or looked for a new leader to point the way to relief from the injustices of American life.

☆

The death of Booker T. Washington late in 1915 removed from the American scene the one Negro who had commanded national respect from both races. Washington had always counseled patience and moderation. In his teaching he had repeatedly emphasized the necessity of gaining white respect through the cheerful and efficient performance of lowly tasks. His program of industrial education at Tuskegee Institute in Alabama had won him nationwide respect as an educator. After his widely publicized address at the Atlanta Exposition in 1895, white Americans everywhere had come to look upon him as the national spokesman for the Negro people.

Washington's essentially conservative program of race relations had been under attack almost from the start, however, by a more militant group of younger Negroes. These critics resented Washington's narrow philosophy of industrial and agricultural education and denounced his apparent submission to the increasing curbs on Negro civil and political rights in the South. The beginnings of a revolt against the Washington technique of racial accommodation, as evidenced by the strong protests framed by the Niagara Movement of 1905, were further strengthened by the formation in 1910 of the interracial National Association for the Advancement of Colored People. Dr. W. E. B. DuBois, a brilliant Negro scholar whose militant views pointed the direction of the new organization, was appointed director of publicity and research with the primary function of editing the monthly magazine of the association, *Crisis*. The N.A.A.C.P. embarked at once upon a publicity campaign to point out the injustices and abuses of American race relations, but its successes were won largely through tedious legal proceedings. For many Negroes this recourse to the courts was still too slow to be really effective.

These impatient champions of what came to be called the New Negro, as contrasted with what was scornfully termed the "Uncle Tom" Negro of the Washington school of moderation, included such men as Chandler Owen, A. Philip Randolph, Hubert H. Harrison, Cyril V. Briggs, William H. Ferris, and William Bridges. Under their able direction a new radical press sprang up in Harlem after the war. Such periodicals as the *Messenger*, the *Voice*, the *Crusader*, the *Challenge*, the *Emancipator*, and the *Negro World* were thought sufficiently dangerous to be cited in a 1919 Department of Justice report on Negro radicalism and sedition.[38] The following year the Lusk Committee, created to investigate seditious activities in the State of New York, devoted forty-four pages to this New Negro press in a report entitled *Revolutionary Radicalism*.[39]

The new militancy of the Negro press was shown in the

call issued by the *People's Pilot* of Richmond, Virginia, during the bloody summer of 1919 to "wisely use the greatest opportunity that has ever come to our race." Warning that the white man, victorious over his European enemy in the war, was now turning "to devour the darker peoples who helped him to conquer his foe," the Negro paper declared, "we must do as he did and overcome him or let him treat us as he has treated his enemy." [40] Cartoon and editorial comment in the Negro press cited Japan as an example of how the colored races could successfully stand up to white nations. [41] Much of the poetry appearing in Negro publications at this time was concerned with the ironic negation of the Negro's wartime contribution and often urged violent measures to secure Negro rights. [42] Even the relatively mild-mannered *Challenge* published in every issue an oath swearing "never to love any flag simply for its color, nor any country for its name," and asserting that "the flag of my affections must rest over me as a banner of protection, not as a sable shroud." Though the New Negroes and their radical press did not attract a large following and were never united on any specific program, their strident voices helped to arouse and prepare the black world for a movement that would gain mass support and confidence.

☆

By 1919 American Negroes were ready for any program that would tend to restore even a measure of their lost dignity and self-respect. Discontent with existing conditions was widespread, and the old Uncle Tom race leader was being replaced by more vigorous spokesmen, who spoke of equality in general rather than limited terms. The Negro population of the North had greatly increased during the war and was concentrated in urban centers where mass organization could be more easily accomplished than in the predominantly rural South. Bad living conditions and poor job opportunities tended to discourage even the most optimistic Negro, while the outbreak of mass intolerance as evidenced in the violence of the race riots and the resurgence of the Ku Klux Klan seemed to prove the need of a new approach to the race problem. More and more Negroes were beginning to agree with Cassy, who over half a century earlier had declared bitterly in *Uncle Tom's Cabin,* "There's no use calling on the Lord—He never hears." Rather, they were coming to believe that more drastic steps would have to be taken before Negroes could achieve their full rights.

Up to this time no Negro organization had either seriously attempted or succeeded in the organization of the Negro masses. None of the racial improvement groups, such as the National Urban League or the National Association for the Advancement of Colored People, had directed much attention to lower-class Negroes, but had instead depended upon the upper classes, both white and Negro, for intellectual and financial support. This was a basic weakness that tended to separate the bulk of the colored population from its leadership, and the unfortunate result was that Negroes were denied any very effective racial organization. A really comprehensive alignment within the Negro world would need to gear its program to the suspicions, prejudices, aspirations, and limited intellectual attainments of the black masses. And in the process of attracting the mass of Negroes it might conceivably alienate white public opinion.

Fresh from the easy-going lethargy of tropical Jamaica, Garvey would find the quicker tempo of American life more in accord with his own restless ambition and unbounded energy. American conditions were, however, sufficiently unlike the Jamaican environment that had shaped Garvey's thinking to warrant speculation as to his ability to interpret correctly the problem of race relations in the United States. The war years had greatly accelerated the drift of Negroes to the cities; and while this development would simplify any large-scale organization of American Negroes, it also meant that Negro problems were increasingly of an urban character, for which Garvey's West Indian background had given him little preparation. As a Jamaican black, Garvey had developed strong feelings of distrust and even hatred toward the light-skinned mulatto group, whose superior caste status was tacitly recognized by all shades of island society. In the United States there existed no such clear-cut color distinction, especially on the part of the dominant white group, and any move to unite blacks against mulattoes or to repudiate mulatto leadership could only serve to divide and weaken the Negro world. Moreover, American Negroes would need much more than a fund-raising campaign for a new agricultural and industrial school in Jamaica to rouse them from their angry mood of postwar frustration and disillusionment. The increasing militancy of the New Negroes and the determined resistance of the Negro victims of the race riots of 1917–19 seemed to indicate that Garvey would have to come up with something considerably more exciting than a West Indian extension of Booker T. Washington's prosaic educational philosophy if he were to win the attention of more than a few Negro Americans. The new belligerency did not necessarily mean, however, that Negroes could be persuaded to abandon their stake in American society. Nevertheless, the Negro people were ready for a black Moses, and equally ready to lead them into the promised land was Marcus Garvey.

THREE

UP,

YOU MIGHTY RACE!

> *One God, our firm endeavor,*
> *One Aim, most glorious bent,*
> *One Destiny forever,*
> *God Bless our President.*
> —U.N.I.A. Hymn [1]

> *Now we have started to speak, and I am only*
> *the forerunner of an awakened Africa that*
> *shall never go back to sleep.*
> —Marcus Garvey [2]

★ Harlem in 1916 was the logical place to begin any organization of American Negroes. Within the crowded confines of the Negro section of New York City a would-be leader could find support for almost any type of movement. A compact black ghetto, Harlem boasted more publications than any other Negro community and could rightfully claim to be the seat of Negro urban society. Here were to be found representatives of all elements in the colored world, a sable mélange of sensitive artists, successful businessmen, self-anointed preachers, poorly paid day laborers, and ignorant sidewalk loafers. Although its teeming tenements were already jammed to groaning capacity, the next few years would see the arrival of many thousands more immigrants from the West Indies and the American

South as northern industry expanded to meet the demands of World War I. These new arrivals would be for the most part poorly educated agricultural workers, Negro peasants who would find urban life new and strange and who could therefore be reached by an emotional appeal that might be ignored by more sophisticated Harlemites. A movement that offered gaudy uniforms, colorful parades, high-sounding titles, and grandiose dreams would make a strong appeal to this lower strata of Harlem society.

At first skeptical Harlemites paid but scant attention to the stocky black Jamaican whose big ideas on race redemption had sounded so impressive in Kingston.° The sidewalk crowds loitering on Lenox Avenue ignored his harangues and dismissed him as just another West Indian carpet-bagger. Even the brief but favorable notice of Garvey's visit printed in the *Crisis* failed to arouse more than a casual interest in the Jamaican stranger.[3] Not daunted by this seeming indifference on the part of his future legions, Garvey made a tour of the country, visiting some thirty-eight states in order to study Negro conditions in America. He

° Much of the information in Chapters 3, 4, and 5 concerning Garvey's activities in the United States is taken from the record of the Black Star mail fraud trial in 1923. Nearly three thousand printed pages of testimony and exhibits are included in Garvey's appeal of his conviction to the U.S. Circuit Court of Appeals, Second Circuit, and other unpublished documents pertaining to the Black Star Line are filed with the U.S. District Court for the Southern District of New York. For facility of reference these records have been coded as Case *A* and Case *B*, although Case *B* refers to the trial and Case *A* refers to the record on appeal. Whenever practicable the citation is made in parentheses in the text. The full legal citation for the two cases is:

Case *A*. *Garvey* v. *United States,* no. 8317, Ct. App., 2d Cir., Feb. 2, 1925.
Case *B*. *United States* v. *Garvey,* no. C33–688, S.D.N.Y., June 19, 1923.

Citations of Case *A* are followed by the numbered pages from the trial record. Unless otherwise noted, citations from Case *B* pertain to an unnumbered collection of Black Star Line manuscripts included in the docket.

went to see some of what he scornfully termed the "so-called Negro leaders" and was shocked to discover "that they had no program, but were mere opportunists who were living off their so-called leadership while the poor people were groping in the dark." [4] The fact that some of these leaders were light-skinned mulattoes may well have been one of the reasons for Garvey's distrust. Another reason was the reliance of many Negro leaders upon the support of white philanthropists. Garvey feared such dependence upon white charity and contemptuously termed this type of Negro leader "the most dangerous member of our society" because of his willingness "to turn back the clock of progress when his benefactors ask him to do so." [5]

On June 12, 1917, Marcus Garvey was among the several thousand persons present at a Harlem mass meeting held in the Bethel African Methodist Episcopal Church for the purpose of organizing a group called the Liberty League. Hubert H. Harrison, a well-known Negro writer and lecturer, was chairman of the meeting and he introduced Garvey to the audience. This was the best opportunity Garvey had yet had to try his eloquent oratory and magnetic personality on an American group of any size, and he made the most of it, sweeping the audience along with him in an impassioned plea for support of the new organization. It was not in Garvey's make-up, however, to be a follower; he must be the unconditional leader of any enterprise to which he devoted his talents. Yet in this brief contact he had seen a Harlem audience come alive to his words and the experience undoubtedly dispelled any lingering doubts over the question of establishing his movement in the United States. [6]

In Harlem Garvey found not only a mass of Negroes overshadowed by the larger white world but also a large number of West Indians isolated from the native American Negro population. As a West Indian himself, Garvey quite naturally turned to this group as a focal point for the establishment of his organization.[7] Garvey had been brought up in the Roman Catholic faith and carried letters of introduction from officials of the Jamaican church. Seeking support in this direction, he arranged to hold his first American meeting in the annex of St. Mark's Roman Catholic Church in Harlem. Apparently the gathering was rather poorly attended, with the small audience composed largely of Jamaicans who were familiar with Garvey's lack of success in the island homeland. His plans for an industrial school of the Tuskegee type made a favorable impression, nonetheless, and during this phase of his talk Garvey enjoyed the respectful attention of his listeners. His vision of an international organization working for the redemption of Africa, however, was greeted with hoots of derision, and in the excitement Garvey fell off the platform, injuring himself slightly. His enemies later charged that this was a deliberate attempt to win popular sympathy.[8]

In spite of the discouraging aspects of this initial meeting, Garvey went ahead with his organizational plans and in 1917 established the New York division of the Universal Negro Improvement Association. Garvey's original plan seems to have been to start the movement in America and then return to Jamaica to perfect the parent organization; but after several hundred members had been enrolled in the Harlem branch and had elected officers, Garvey discovered that a few Negro politicians were attempting to turn the movement into a political club. In the fight to rid the organization of this unwelcome political infiltration, Garvey made his first enemies in Harlem, and they were able to smash the New York association late in 1917. One of the opposition had received a letter from Garvey's old

London employer, Duse Mohammed Ali, in which serious charges were raised against Garvey's character and his leadership was discredited. This letter was read at a meeting of the association and the ensuing controversy resulted in the breakup of the organization.[9] Garvey later employed Duse Mohammed on his newspaper, the *Negro World,* but the old Egyptian nationalist always remained somewhat jealous of the success of his former protégé and rather skeptical of the wisdom of tying African nationalism to Negro redemption.[10] Years later he was still telling anyone in London who would listen that because of Garvey's "laziness and general worthless character" he had been discharged from his messenger job in 1913.[11]

Garvey made a new start and in two months claimed to have built up a new organization of about 1,500 members.[12] Once again the politicians attempted to acquire control of the association and managed to split the group into two factions. At this juncture, thirteen of the loyal members, most of them Jamaicans, came to Garvey with the request that he take over the active leadership of the Harlem organization until it could be consolidated. Garvey was technically not an officer of the New York division at this time, working only as an organizer while retaining the presidency of the parent Jamaica association. He consented to this request and was immediately elected president general of the New York U.N.I.A. A quick reorganization was effected and the Universal Negro Improvement Association was incorporated as a membership corporation under New York law to prevent rival groups from using its name. In its New York charter the association pledged itself "to promote and practice the principles of benevolence" and described its purpose as "the protection and social intercourse of its members" (Case A, 2330). Garvey boasted that "in three weeks more than 2,000 new members had joined" the new incorporated organization. As for the rival group, "in two weeks the politicians had stolen all the people's money and smashed up their faction." [13] Garvey now saw that he must keep his movement free of entanglements with established political parties if it were to embrace all Negroes and focus their attention upon the burning issue of African redemption.

During 1919 and 1920 the Universal Negro Improvement Association enjoyed a remarkable growth. Garvey traveled extensively throughout the United States and established branches of the association in most urban centers of Negro population. The spread of the movement was not confined to the United States, moreover, as Garvey made every effort to interest Negroes in the West Indies and Central America in his ideas. He now dropped the fiction that the headquarters of the U.N.I.A. was in Jamaica and it was obvious that the headquarters of the movement was wherever its founder happened to be, that in fact Marcus Garvey was the U.N.I.A. By the middle of 1919, Garvey was making the dubious claim of more than two million members and thirty branches.[14] Whatever the exact membership of the U.N.I.A. at this or any other time, and Garvey's figures are always questionable, there is no doubt that large numbers of Negroes were listening with ever increasing interest to the serious black man whose persuasive words seemed to point the way to race deliverance.

The movement received unexpected publicity when in October, 1919, Garvey was attacked by an insane former employee. The assailant, George Tyler, dashed into Garvey's office in an old brownstone house on 135 Street in Harlem and, after an argument over an alleged twenty-five dollar debt owed him by Garvey, drew a revolver and fired at the U.N.I.A. leader. Two of his shots found their mark, one grazing Garvey's forehead and narrowly missing his right eye, and the other imbedding itself in Garvey's right leg. Tyler was captured by the police after a running chase through Harlem streets, but he leaped to his death from a prison balcony before he could be brought to trial.[15] The whole affair was made to order for Harlem scandal sheets. Garvey's attractive secretary and future wife, Amy Ashwood, had wrestled with the intruder and had courageously placed herself between her employer and the gunman. Garvey himself had rushed after the assassin with blood streaming down his face. The assault assumed heroic proportions in the Negro press and Garvey became overnight a persecuted martyr working for the salvation of his people. Harlem began to take a deeper interest in Marcus Garvey and his newly reorganized branch of the Universal Negro Improvement Association.

☆

One of the important reasons for Garvey's amazing success in the rapid organization of the Negro masses was his establishment in January, 1918, of the *Negro World*, the U.N.I.A.'s New York newspaper. This was one of the most remarkable journalistic ventures ever attempted by a Negro in the United States, and it drew from Claude McKay, a sometime Garvey critic, the grudging praise of being "the best edited colored weekly in New York." [16] Within the space of a few months the *Negro World* became one of the leading Negro weeklies, and as such it proved to be a most effective instrument for the promulgation of Garvey's program. The circulation of the paper has been variously estimated at from 60,000 to 200,000 during its most prosperous years.[17] In its issue of August 2, 1920, the paper itself more modestly claimed a guaranteed circulation of 50,000 "reaching the mass of Negroes throughout the world." Later issues claimed only to be "reaching the mass of Negroes." The *Negro World* was disseminated all over the world until it was banned by many of the colonial governments for its dangerous nationalism.[18]

The character of this newspaper merits some consideration. Separating the two words *Negro* and *World* was a sphinxlike seal bearing the motto of the organization, "One Aim, One God, One Destiny." Under this was the phrase, "A Newspaper Devoted Solely to the Interests of the Negro Race." The paper was priced within the low-income range of Garvey's followers and generally sold for five cents in New York, seven cents elsewhere in the United States, and ten cents in foreign countries. Certain sections of the *Negro World* were printed in French and Spanish for the benefit of those West Indian and Central American Negroes who could not read English. The front page of the paper always carried a lengthy editorial proudly addressed to the "Fellowmen of the Negro Race" and signed, "Your obedient servant, Marcus Garvey, President General." These editorials covered a wide variety of subjects, ranging from grand visions of the past glories of Negro history to undisguised promotional appeals on behalf of the association. "Africa must be redeemed," Garvey asserted in an early editorial, "and all of us pledge our manhood, our wealth and our blood to this sacred cause. Yes, the Negroes of the world have found a George Washington, yea more; they have found a Toussant L'Overture [*sic*], and he will be announced to the world when the time comes." [19] Garvey soon turned over most of the burden of editing the paper to the able William H. Ferris, who was assisted by men like Hubert H. Harrison, Eric D. Walrond, and Hudson C. Pryce. The *Negro World* always remained, nevertheless, the personal propaganda organ of its founder.

The pages of the *Negro World*, usually ten to sixteen in number, were filled with long articles expounding the ideas and philosophy of Garveyism. Often guest contributors

such as William Pickens, T. Thomas Fortune, Hodge Kirnon, and John E. Bruce wrote accounts of some aspect of
the movement. The paper made a great effort to remind its
readers of their glorious history, with particular emphasis
on the regal splendors of ancient Africa. Garvey proudly
recalled for his followers, though not always with complete
accuracy, the stirring heroism of such leaders of American
slave rebellions as Denmark Vesey, Gabriel Prosser, and
Nat Turner. The struggles of Zulu and Hottentot warriors
against European rule, the histories of Moorish and
Ethiopian empires, and the intrepid exploits of Toussaint
L'Ouverture against the French in Haiti were not neglected in the effort to make Negroes conscious and proud
of their racial heritage. Garvey delighted in references to
the greatness of colored civilizations at a time when white
men were only barbarians and savages. This emphasis on
racism was one of the reasons that the *Negro World* was
cited by the Department of Justice and the Lusk Committee of New York in two separate reports on Negro radicalism in 1919 and 1920.

The newspaper also carried news of the activities of the
various divisions and branches of the Universal Negro
Improvement Association, and the *Negro World's* wide
circulation helped to direct and unify the efforts of the
component parts of the organization. Readers were urged
to write and speak on behalf of race equality and unity.
The author of a strongly nationalistic pamphlet published
in Pittsburgh in 1921 declared that he was endeavoring "to
create and stimulate a spirit of racial pride and unity
among Negroes" because of "a powerful article that appeared in the *Negro World*." [20] Subscribers were encouraged to send the editor their thoughts on any subject and
these letters from all over the world were printed to show
the wide circulation of the paper and the universal charac-

ter of the movement. One of the more popular sections was a page devoted to "Poetry for the People," in which the loyal devotion of the Garvey following could be expressed poetically. A typical offering by a Mexican Negro asked, "Can We Forget Marcus Garvey?":

> Negroes, can we ever forget
> This great bold Negro man,
> The man God has resurrect,
> To lead us to our land.
>
> A braver Negro than he
> The earth hath never seen;
> He fearlessly outlines his plans,
> And bids our unity.[21]

Another popular attraction was a feature entitled "Bruce Grit's Column" contributed by John E. Bruce, a well-known New York journalist active in the association.

The *Negro World* prided itself on its refusal to accept advertising for such race-degrading items as skin-whitening and hair-straightening compounds, lucrative sources of advertising revenue for most Negro papers. These chemical beauty aids had long provided a sizable share of the advertising income of the Negro press. As far back as 1885 the *Nation* had jocularly noted this "solution" of the race problem, as advertised in a New York Negro newspaper.[22] While Garvey refused to accept any advertisements that tended to degrade the Negro race, the *Negro World* did occasionally carry commercial plugs for hair-growing compounds similar to products that claimed ability to straighten hair. The emphasis was, however, always on growing "a wonderful head of hair." The policy probably tended to relax as the need for money, from any source, became ever more pressing.[23] Scoffers referred to the *Negro World* as the "bulletin of the Imperial Blizzard" [24] or "the

Garvey addressing a crowd at Limon, Costa Rica, in 1921

Part of mammoth U.N.I.A. parade in New York, August 1, 1922

Marcus Garvey in 1922

A Black Star Line stock certificate of 1919

Garvey (second from right) reviewing a U.N.I.A. parade

Members of the Garvey Militia, New York, 1921

The ill-fated *Yarmouth*, flagship of the Black Star Line, c.1924

weakly organ of Admiral Garvey's African Navy," [25] but the paper was a potent force among Negroes in America and its influence extended far beyond American shores.

The *Negro World* was published weekly from 1918 through 1933. Late in 1922 Garvey started a New York daily newspaper called the *Negro Times*. This paper was modeled after the *Negro World,* selling for five cents per copy, but financial pressures afforded it only a brief and spasmodic existence. A pro-Garvey paper, the *African World,* was published for a time in South Africa, and the *Negro Peace Echo* appeared briefly in 1934.[26] After the *Negro World* suspended publication in 1933, the most important Garvey publication was the monthly magazine, the *Black Man,* which will be considered in Chapter 6. Since Garvey's death in 1940 there have been at least two attempts to revive his journalistic enterprises, though without his spectacular success. James R. Stewart, an ex-Garveyite in Cleveland, Ohio, published for a few months in 1942 a monthly magazine of Negro thought and opinion called the *New Negro World*. And in 1945 the remnant of Garvey followers in New York City put out with the blessing of Garvey's widow a few issues of the *Voice of Freedom,* which had as its motto the old U.N.I.A battle cry of "One God! One Aim! One Destiny!"

☆

In 1919 Garvey's organizational activities had progressed far enough for him to purchase a large auditorium located at 114 West 138 Street in Harlem. Originally the foundation of the uncompleted Metropolitan Baptist Church, the structure had been roofed over and enlarged to provide seating space for as many as 6,000 people. Rechristened Liberty Hall, this building became the American headquarters of the Universal Negro Improvement Association. At the dedication services on July 27, 1919, the

U.N.I.A. membership was reminded that the name Liberty Hall was particularly appropriate, the more so in light of the recent bloody race riots in Washington, D.C.[27] Liberty Hall in Harlem came to symbolize the movement, and soon local Liberty Halls sprang up in other areas where Garvey's ideas on race redemption took root and flourished. During the next few years the walls of the long, low, zinc-topped building off Lenox Avenue rang with countless appeals for Negro unity. At the peak of the movement nightly meetings were held in Liberty Hall and capacity audiences thronged to listen to the compelling words and audacious ideas of the little man from Jamaica.

The work of the Universal Negro Improvement Association was more than speeches and meetings, however. Sometime early in 1919 Garvey projected the idea of an all-Negro steamship company that would link the colored peoples of the world in commercial and industrial intercourse. The bold bid to enter the white-dominated maritime industry quickly caught hold of the popular imagination and for several months money was collected at U.N.I.A. meetings to purchase ships for this promised Black Star Line. News of this activity soon reached the ears of Edwin P. Kilroe, assistant district attorney of New York, and on June 16, 1919, he called Garvey in and warned him not to attempt to sell stock unless the Black Star Line was organized as a legitimate business enterprise (Case A, 64–68, 120–23). In compliance, ten days later Garvey formally launched the Black Star Line by securing a broad charter of incorporation from the State of Delaware, whose friendly laws had long attracted businessmen and industrial entrepreneurs. Under its charter the Black Star Line was explicitly authorized to own, charter, operate, and navigate ships of various types in any part of the world and to carry passengers, freight, and mails. And in case any provision had been inadvertently omitted from the detailed permissive articles of the charter, a general article granted the company authority "to do any and all things and to exercise any and all powers necessary or advisable to accomplish one or more purposes of the corporation or which shall at any time appear to be conducive to, or for the benefit of, said corporation in connection therewith." The B.S.L. was capitalized at $500,000, composed of 100,000 shares of stock with a par value of five dollars each. Garvey and four of his associates were each listed as holding forty shares of capital stock, so that the company commenced business with a stated capital of one thousand dollars (Case A, 2434–39).

Drawn from Booker T. Washington's philosophy that Negroes must become independent of white capital and operate their own business activities, the Black Star Line was a supremely audacious move that aroused the greatest excitement in the colored world. Here was an enterprise belonging to Negroes, operated by and for them, that gave even the poorest black the chance to become a stockholder in a big business enterprise. Not only could the investor feel that he was working for the betterment of his race, he was also offered the speculative opportunity of making money in exactly the same way as such a famous financial wizard as J. Pierpont Morgan. Negroes could be pardoned for emulating their white fellow citizens in the desire to make a quick killing in true Wall Street fashion, while at the same time B.S.L. investors could take pride in the fact that they were helping to make race history. Garvey's stock circulars boldly declared: "Now is the time for the Negro to invest in the Black Star Line so that in the near future he may exert the same influence upon the world as the white man does today" (Case A, 2489–90, 2499–2507). To the hesitant Garvey promised:

The Black Star Line Corporation presents to every Black Man, Woman, and Child the opportunity to climb the great ladder of industrial and commercial progress. If you have ten dollars, one hundred dollars, or one or five thousand dollars to invest for profit, then take out shares in the Black Star Line, Inc. This corporation is chartered to trade on every sea and all waters. The Black Star Line will turn over large profits and dividends to stockholders, and operate to their interest even whilst they will be asleep.[28]

Sale of Black Star stock was limited to members of the Negro race, and no individual could purchase more than two hundred shares.[29] Garvey's *Negro World* carried full-page advertisements exhorting its readers to take a hand in guiding their destiny through "a direct line of steam-ships, owned, controlled, and manned by Negroes to reach the Negro peoples of the world."[30] Ostensibly the Black Star Line was established as a strictly commercial venture, and Garvey did not intend, as his critics sometimes claimed, that the line would merely be the vehicle for the transportation of all Negroes back to their African home-land.[31] The publicity value of the venture, however, far exceeded anything that it was likely to accomplish com-mercially; and Garvey, always the master propagandist, skillfully exploited this aspect of the undertaking to the fullest extent.

At first the scheme was laughed off by many Negroes as just another attempt to extort money from the ignorant black masses. Garvey's vision of a fleet of ships manned by Negro crews and flying the Black Star Line flag made little impression on Harlem business circles. Skeptics pointed out the great difficulty of raising sufficient capital to float one ship, let alone a whole fleet of merchant vessels plying the African trade routes in competition with established white firms. Garvey was advised not to attempt the impos-sible. The critics were struck into amazed silence, therefore, when in mid-September a B.S.L. circular proudly announced that the first ship of the new line could be viewed at her berth at West 135 Street and the North River. "The Ship will fly the Black Star Line Flag," Garvey promised (Case A, 2451).

Two days after this announcement, Garvey was once again called to the office of Assistant District Attorney Kilroe, who had discovered that the Black Star Line was as yet only negotiating for the ship Garvey had indicated could be seen flying the company's flag. Kilroe warned Garvey that if any B.S.L. stock had been sold as a direct result of this misleading circular he and the corporation could be prosecuted for commercial fraud. As before, Kilroe's admonition brought swift results. The next day, on September 17, 1919, Garvey and the other directors of the Black Star Line closed the deal on the purchase of the company's first ship, a small freighter named the *S.S. Yarmouth*. The purchase price was a stiff $165,000, of which the company paid $16,500 down, with another $83,500 due when the B.S.L. took possession. The balance was to be spread over ten equal monthly installments of $6,500 each at 6 per cent interest (Case A, 2454–59).

The *Yarmouth* was a small ship of only 1,452 gross tons that had been built in 1887, the year of Garvey's birth. It was owned by the North American Steamship Corporation, Ltd., a Canadian subsidiary of the New York firm of Harriss, Magill and Company. During the war the *Yarmouth* had been used to transport cotton, but most recently it had carried a cargo of coal (Case A, 295). The squat, grimy ship, its rakish funnel ridiculously tall, was scarcely the sort to inspire undue confidence in the future success of the Black Star Line or the business sagacity of its leaders.[32] Garvey and the rest of his landlubber board of directors had accepted without question the word of his Negro maritime adviser, Captain Joshua Cockbourne, as to the suitability and seaworthiness of the vessel.[33] Later it developed that adviser Cockbourne had been working both sides of the street and had received a commission of $1,600 from a ship brokerage firm for his help in arranging the sale (Case A, 252, 371, 2218). There is no doubt that the owner of the *Yarmouth*, a New York cotton broker named W. L. Harriss, was out to take the Black Star Line and its inexperienced officers for as large a sum as possible. Harriss informed his lawyer during the negotiations that Garvey had about $6,000,000 and through the U.N.I.A. was planning to collect a dollar apiece from all the Negroes of the world. "If this fellow has got so much money," Harriss shrewdly reasoned, "we are going to sell him this ship and make as much out of it as we can" (Case A, 231). Queried later on the ethics involved in the sale, Harriss' attorney, Leo H. Healy, could only explain lamely that when the Black Star Line "offered us such a lucrative price, the business acumen for which Mr. Harris[s] is well known in business naturally asserted itself and he made a bargain" (Case A, 255).

The Black Star Line lacked the necessary funds, however, to carry out this first purchase agreement, and on October 31, 1919, Harriss obligingly agreed to a schedule of easier time payments for the *Yarmouth*, on condition that the total purchase price be jacked up to $168,500. At the same time a charter agreement was signed whereby the Black Star Line could operate the ship until the bill of sale had been registered and the vessel legally transferred to the Negro corporation. Under this agreement the North American Steamship Corporation retained ownership of the *Yarmouth* but for a cash consideration turned it over to the B.S.L. for operation under a Negro crew (Case A, 203–7). Garvey immediately appointed the double-handed

Captain Cockbourne as master of the ship and scheduled an early sailing for the West Indies. The ship would, he announced, be renamed the *S.S. Frederick Douglass,* after the great nineteenth-century American Negro leader in the fight against slavery. Even now, however, the difficulties of the Black Star Line were not at an end, for the new steamship company had trouble securing adequate insurance for the *Yarmouth* and Harriss refused to allow the vessel to sail until it was fully protected.

Late in November, 1919, the *Yarmouth* was ready for its first voyage under the red, black, and green flag of the Black Star Line. To the line's 135th Street pier came fully five thousand Negroes to cheer this great moment in the race's commercial history. Hundreds paid a dollar to go aboard and watch the proud Negro crew make ready to cast off, while at pierside the smart U.N.I.A. band added to the holiday atmosphere with a gay martial serenade. Captain Cockbourne was about to give the order to sail when anxious Leo Healy, representing the interests of the *Yarmouth's* real owner, W. L. Harriss, arrived with an order forbidding the departure until the Black Star Line had furnished adequate insurance coverage. Rather than face the riot that might develop should it appear that a white man was trying to cheat the Negro crowd of its triumph, Healy reluctantly agreed to allow the *Yarmouth* to depart on schedule, provided that he and the white port captain of the North American Steamship Corporation went along as apprehensive chaperones. With its two uninvited and unwelcome passengers the *Yarmouth* finally got under way, but its first voyage was unexpectedly short. When the *Yarmouth* had arrived in the Hudson River opposite 23d Street, Healy halted the ship, and declaring it would go no further until properly insured, clambered into a boat and rowed grimly ashore. Several days later, after the Black Star Line had taken out insurance on the *Yar-mouth,* the interrupted voyage was resumed (Case A, 208–9).

Meantime Harlem knew nothing of these difficulties and the magic name Garvey was on everyone's lips. Faced with the actuality of a steamship managed by a Negro company and manned by a black crew, even onetime Garvey critics were forced grudgingly to admit that the little Jamaican had accomplished something unique in race history. During the winter of 1919/20 thousands of shares of Black Star Line stock were sold at five dollars a share to Negroes all over the country. Students at one college in Louisiana alone raised $7,000 for the great racial undertaking.[34] Throughout the colored world the word spread of the line of Negro-owned ships that would soon ply the trade routes between America and Africa. One of the large recording companies even issued a phonograph record of a popular song entitled "Black Star Line." [35] As word of the enterprise spread to Negroes abroad, money and requests for stock poured into the New York headquarters of the U.N.I.A. From Panama one eager shareholder wrote: "I have sent twice to buy shares amounting to $125. . . . Now I am sending $35 for seven more shares. You might think I have money, but the truth, as I stated before, is that I have no money now. But if I'm to die of hunger it will be all right because I'm determined to do all that's in my power to better the conditions of my race." [36]

In February, 1920, while the *Yarmouth* was on its second voyage to the West Indies, the Black Star Line was recapitalized at $10,000,000. Garvey announced to an admiring black world, "They told us when we incorporated this corporation that we could not make it, but we are now gone from a [$500,000] corporation to one of $10,000,-000." [37] As critics like W. E. B. DuBois vainly tried to point out, this statement meant absolutely nothing, since under lax Delaware laws the larger capitalization merely involved the payment of an additional fee and had nothing to do with the actual solvency of the company. It did make excellent sales propaganda, however, and Garvey and the *Negro World* exploited it to the utmost. Garvey also ordered Captain Cockbourne to change his homeward course on the *Yarmouth's* second voyage in order to boom Black Star Line stocks in Philadelphia and Boston before discharging his cargo of cocoanuts in New York (Case A, 310–15, 1137). Business and promotion were inextricably mixed in the affairs of this steamship company.

In line with the increased capitalization of the Black Star Line, in the spring of 1920 Garvey began looking around for additions to the B.S.L. merchant fleet. Through a white ship broker, Captain Leon R. Swift, he found an excursion boat, the *S.S. Shadyside*, which he informed the B.S.L. board of directors "would be a wonderful asset as it could be used here in the summer and taken to the West Indies in the winter" (Case A, 1137, 2221–22). The *Shadyside* was an old Hudson River excursion boat of 444 gross tons that had been built in 1873 and was therefore nearly a half century old. Nevertheless, a marine survey report of April 7, 1920, declared that the vessel had been thoroughly renovated, "her engines and boilers overhauled and put in good order, and passed by U.S. local inspectors," and was thus "a fair risk for annual hull insurance when confined to inland waters" (Case B). Garvey agreed to pay $35,000 for the *Shadyside*, $10,000 down and the balance in monthly payments of $2,000 (Case A, 2657–58). The small ferry boat was intended for use on summer excursions and for B.S.L. promotional purposes. Negro organizations had for many years chartered boats for river excursions to relieve the monotony of Harlem life during the hot summer months. But never before had such a pleasure boat been owned by a Negro line. Now the U.N.I.A. and other Harlem groups would be assured of sympathetic attention when they planned their summer outings. Lacking a qualified Negro captain, Garvey finally hired a white master, Captain Jacob Wise, to operate the *Shadyside* during the summer of 1920 (Case A, 423–25).

In addition to the *Shadyside*, the persuasive Leon Swift also sold Garvey on the merits of another dubious vessel, the steam yacht *Kanawha*, formerly the expensive toy of Standard Oil magnate Henry H. Rogers, and most recently on government patrol duty during the war. "This vessel would be very desirable for your company to use in the inter-colonial trade in conjunction with your steam[er] 'Yarmouth,' " Swift declared. "If this boat intercepted your Steamer 'Yarmouth' at Jamaica port, 'Yarmouth' would make two trips to New York while she now makes one." [38] Swift failed to point out that the *Kanawha's* small size (length, 227 feet; beam, 25 feet; and depth, 15 feet) automatically precluded her successful operation as a cargo ship. Only a millionaire oil man or the United States Treasury could afford to run such a costly plaything. When Swift reported that the owner of the *Kanawha* had indicated "that if an offer of $60,000 was made for this boat in all probabilities he would accept it," Garvey and his inexperienced fellow directors rose to the bait.[39] The Black Star Line agreed to pay the asking price of $60,000 and to expend another $25,000 refitting the *Kanawha* for passenger and cargo service. Garvey informed the colored world that this ship would be rechristened the S.S. *Antonio Maceo*, after the Negro patriot of the Cuban struggle for independence from Spain, and as soon as refitting had been completed would depart on the first of a series of scheduled trips to the West Indies. "You will perhaps think the

'Kanawha' is nothing compared to the Yarmouth," wrote a B.S.L. official to the line's agent at Havana, Cuba. "In my opinion she is a better and more attractive boat than the Yarmouth, and you both must have the Cuban people inspect the boat . . . and also boost the sale of stock which is very important." [40]

On July 20, 1920, Marcus Garvey presided over the first annual meeting of the stockholders of the Black Star Line in Liberty Hall, which was packed to capacity. "We entered as a people with but little experience in the running of steamships," Garvey declared, and for that reason, "we were satisfied to purchase small boats so as to show that we can run them. We have much to be thankful for, in that no unfortunate accident has befallen us." The Black Star Line might not be the biggest in the world, but the work of the past year had been of great benefit to the Negro people, "for it has brought recognition to us as a race—it has elevated our men." Loud cheers greeted Garvey's declaration that through skillful and determined management the Black Star Line had closed its first year "as solvent and as intact as any corporation can be." George Tobias, a former railroad clerk now treasurer of the line, next presented a financial report covering the B.S.L.'s operations during the previous year. Tobias' balance sheet was impressive both for what it revealed and for what it left obscure. In one year the Black Star Line had garnered a capital through stock sales and subscriptions of $610,860. Invested assets, including real estate, equipment, and the line's three steamers, the *Yarmouth*, the *Kanawha*, and the *Shadyside*, totaled $328,190.38. Unexplained, however, was an item listed cryptically as "organization expense" amounting to $289,-066.27. Nor did Tobias or other B.S.L. officials raise the question of whether the corporation had chosen wisely in its ship acquisitions, whether in fact its invested assets were worth the large sums expended for them (Case A, 2653–56). Such questions were overlooked in the general rejoicing, however, and few Negroes had any doubt that Marcus Garvey was leading his people along the road to economic independence and social self-respect.

In addition to the Black Star Line, in 1919 Garvey also established another business enterprise, the Negro Factories Corporation. Capitalized at $1,000,000 under a charter from the State of Delaware, the corporation offered "200,000 shares of common stock to the Negro race at par value of $5.00 per share." [41] The purpose of the company, according to Garvey's *Negro World*, was to "build and operate factories in the big industrial centers of the United States, Central America, the West Indies, and Africa to manufacture every marketable commodity." [42] Negroes were called upon to support this business enterprise in order to insure steady and profitable employment for their sons and daughters.[43] This effort to develop Negro business opportunities was viewed with favor by many who questioned the wisdom of some of Garvey's other ideas on race redemption and the Negro Factories Corporation had the cautious support of some erstwhile skeptics.[44]

Among the businesses developed by the corporation were a chain of co-operative grocery stores, a restaurant, a steam laundry, a tailor and dressmaking shop, a millinery store, and a publishing house.[45] An effort was made to seek out good business opportunities and to interest Negroes in developing them. If necessary, the corporation promised to supply executive and technical guidance and would in theory be able to offer a loan of initial capital from a co-operative fund established through the sale of stock. In practice such loans were rarely possible. Strong emphasis was placed on the need of greatly expanded Negro business activity. "No race in the world," Garvey warned, "is so just as to give others, for the asking, a square deal in things economic, political and social." [46] By 1920 the Universal Millinery Store was offering "a variety of styles in chic summer hats manufactured by expert Negro designers," while the Universal Steam Laundry promised to help harassed housewives "keep cool" by doing the "rubbing and scrubbing in a modern sanitary laundry, managed and operated by Negroes." [47]

The Universal Negro Improvement Association was itself organized on a business basis. Its membership was required to pay monthly dues of thirty-five cents, of which ten cents went to the parent organization headed by Garvey and twenty-five cents remained with the local division.[48] In spite of a U.N.I.A. directive that prompt payment of dues was necessary for retention of membership in the organization, Garvey's constant appeals for the share belonging to the parent body indicate that collection of dues was never an easy task. The U.N.I.A. was modeled after other American fraternal orders in that its active membership was entitled to draw sickness and death benefits from the organization. Actually the association's central treasury rarely had enough money to meet current operating expenses, let alone any charges for benefits to ailing and deceased members. This fraternal aspect of the movement stemmed from Garvey's belief that the easiest and best approach to the black masses was through their universal search for security. "He had to start as a fraternal organization, giving sick and death benefits," writes Garvey's widow. "This was the easiest means of reaching the common man, who wanted security in his distress; hand him this first, then tell him of the spiritual, racial benefits that would come in time." [49]

☆

From his headquarters in Harlem early in 1920 Garvey issued a call for a mammoth international convention of delegates representing the entire Negro race to be held in New York during the month of August, 1920. In banner headlines the *Negro World* proclaimed that the gathering would be the largest of its kind in the history of the race. The convention would seek to consolidate the constructive work of the U.N.I.A. throughout the colored world and would furnish a spotlighted forum where delegates could report on Negro conditions in their local areas. Garvey announced that one of the important projects to be undertaken by the assembly would be the drawing up of a Negro Declaration of Rights which would then be presented to the governments of the world. As August approached and word spread of the preparations being made for the convention in Harlem, the colored world was roused to a fever pitch of excitement. While whites had their attention fixed on Geneva, Switzerland, and the newly born League of Nations, the eyes of Negroes focused on Liberty Hall in New York City, where thousands of black delegates from each of the United States, the West Indies, Central and South America, and even Africa began to arrive for the meetings.

Judged by any standards, the 1920 convention of the Universal Negro Improvement Association was a magnificent affair. Even Harlem, long used to the spectacular, found it an extravaganza not soon to be forgotten, and for the first time white America began to take notice of Marcus Garvey. Harlem streets rang with stirring martial airs and the measured tramp of smartly uniformed marching bands. The hoarse cries of little black newsboys hawking special editions of the *Negro World* added to the babel produced by cheering delegates from twenty-five countries. Garvey became literally the man of the hour. Enterprising Harlem tobacco shops offered special "Marcus Garvey" cigars, complete with a photograph of the Jamaican race leader imprinted on the band.[50] The magic of Garvey's spell and the power of his organizational ability were never better demonstrated than at this first great international convention. Throughout the black world Negroes were stirred to a new sense of their power and destiny by the fierce nationalism that pervaded every activity of the gathering.

The convention opened on Sunday, August 1, with three religious services and a silent march of all members and delegates through the streets of Harlem. "God of the right our battles fight," delegates pleaded in the U.N.I.A. special prayer, "be with us as of yore; break down the barriers of might, we rev'rently implore." [51] The next afternoon business activity in Harlem came to a standstill as thousands of cheering onlookers lined the curbs of Lenox Avenue to view the massed units of the Universal Negro Improvement Association. All the splendor and pageantry of a medieval coronation were present at this greatest of Negro shows. In a parade that was the talk of Harlem for months to come, the component parts of the U.N.I.A. were for the first time revealed to an astonished black world. First came the African Legion, smartly dressed in dark blue uniforms with narrow red trouser stripes, its members proudly conscious of the effect of their colorful garb and marching precision on the enthusiastic sidewalk crowds. Although the African Legion was unarmed except for the dress swords of its officers, its existence hinted that the redemption of the Negro people might come through force. Another group, the Black Cross Nurses, two hundred strong and neatly attired in white, indicated the readiness of the U.N.I.A. to come to the aid of stricken peoples all over the world. Here enthusiasm counted more than training, for with but few exceptions the Black Cross Nurses were medically or otherwise untrained. Amidst the marching delegates U.N.I.A. choristers sang enchantingly of the motherland. Even children had a place in the great movement for racial salvation and marched beside their elders in a special juvenile auxiliary.

On the night of August 2 the delegates gathered in Madison Square Garden to hear Garvey address an estimated 25,000 Negroes, one of the largest gatherings in the history of the hall.[52] Prominent among the delegates, and the objects of intense interest on the part of the assembled black host, were an African prince and several tribal chiefs and descendants of chiefs. Three massed bands accompanied the audience as it solemnly sang the new U.N.I.A. anthem, "Ethiopia, Thou Land of Our Fathers." The black, green, and crimson banners of the delegates were waved enthusiastically while for two hours the crowd applauded the preliminary entertainment of a quartet, several vocal soloists, and the bands. When Garvey finally stepped forward to speak, clad in a richly colored academic cap and gown of purple, green, and gold, he received a tumultuous ovation that lasted for fully five minutes.[53]

Garvey's opening words set the tone of the convention with the announcement of a telegram sent to the Irish Republican leader, Eamon De Valera. "Twenty-five thousand Negro delegates assembled in Madison Square Garden in mass meeting, representing 400,000,000 Negroes of the world," the telegram ran, "send you greetings as President of the Irish Republic." Conveying the sympathy of all Negroes for the justness of the Irish cause, Garvey's wire concluded, "We believe Ireland should be free even as Africa shall be free for the Negroes of the world. Keep up the fight for a free Ireland." [54] If British ministers in Whitehall had never before heard of this particular one of His Majesty's Jamaican subjects, there was good reason to listen to him now.

"We are the descendants of a suffering people," Garvey told his attentive listeners; "we are the descendants of a people determined to suffer no longer." Gazing out over the colorful sea of waving U.N.I.A. banners, the new Negro Moses promised, "We shall now organize the 400,000,000 Negroes of the world into a vast organization to plant the banner of freedom on the great continent of Africa."

We do not desire what has belonged to others, though others have always sought to deprive us of that which belonged to us. . . . If Europe is for the Europeans, then Africa shall be for the black peoples of the world. We say it; we mean it. . . . The other races have countries of their own and it is time for the 400,000,000 Negroes to claim Africa for themselves.[55]

This emphasis on African nationalism was to be repeated in every speech of this and future U.N.I.A. conventions. The gospel of Garveyism was now written for all to see and take warning.

Other speakers raised their voices in approval of Garvey's words. "We shall ask, demand, and expect of the world a free Africa," warned an American delegate. "We have decided, because of our numerical strength and religious nature, that we are now able to teach the world the truth of the doctrine of do unto others as you would they should do unto you." [56] Another delegate declared at a Liberty Hall meeting, "We're mighty grateful for all the white man has done for us, but we want to go home now." "You brought us over," he told the white world; "be manly and let us go back." [57]

Later in the month in a speech delivered before the convention in Carnegie Hall Garvey spelled out his warning to the white man in more explicit terms:

The Negroes of the world say, "We are striking homewards towards Africa to make her the big black republic." And in the making of Africa a big black republic, what is the barrier? The barrier is the white man; and we say to the white man who now dominates Africa that it is to his interest to clear out of Africa now, because we are coming not as in the time of Father Abraham, 200,000 strong, but we are coming 400,000,000 strong, and we mean to retake every square inch of the 12,000,000 square miles of African territory belonging to us by right Divine. . . . We are out to get what has belonged to us politically, socially, economically, and in every way. And what 15,000,000 of us cannot get we will call in 400,000,000 to help us get.

From now on, according to this belligerent Jamaican, the white man need expect no more Negro blood shed on his behalf. "The first dying that is to be done by the black man in the future," Garvey warned, "will be done to make himself free." And when this was accomplished, he continued, "if we have any charity to bestow, we may die for the white man." "But as for me," and the words had an ominous portent for every colonial government, "I think I have stopped dying for him." This speech was sufficiently frightening to white legislators in New York that it was cited in the Lusk report on radicalism and sedition in that State.[58]

Getting seriously to work, the delegates next drafted the long-awaited "Declaration of the Rights of the Negro Peoples of the World," which was adopted by the convention on August 13, 1920.[59] As background for the declaration, the convention had listened to each delegate's recital of the grievances existing among Negro residents of his community.[60] These were then compiled into a powerful "protest against the wrongs and injustices" that Negroes were suffering "at the hands of their white brethren." The declaration went on to "demand and insist" upon certain basic rights "in order to encourage our race all over the world and to stimulate it to a higher and grander destiny." The enumerated Negro rights were embodied in a series of fifty-four articles covering such topics as political and judicial equality, complete racial self-determination, and a free Africa under a Negro government. Article 45 went so far as to declare the League of Nations "null and void as far as the Negro is concerned, in that it seeks to deprive Negroes of their liberty." This was a reference to the former German colonies in Africa that had been given to France and Great Britain under a mandate from the League. There was also a demand that the word "Negro" be spelled with a capital "N," in keeping with the dignity and self-respect of the New Negro.[61] Over the next decade this campaign to capitalize "Negro" was generally successful, at least in the United States. In 1929 the New York State Board of Education ordered that all New York schools must teach the spelling of "Negro" with a capital "N," [62] and the next year the *New York Times* followed suit, "in recognition," as a *Times* editorial explained, "of racial self-respect for those who have been for generations in 'the lower case.' " [63]

The convention also put its stamp of approval on the official colors of the movement: red for the blood of the race, nobly shed in the past and dedicated to the future; black to symbolize pride in the color of its skin; and green for the promise of a new and better life in Africa. Garvey, the driving force and inspiration for this Negro reformation, was designated by the convention Provisional President of the African Republic, a sort of government in exile. He was to be aided in the work of African redemption by such executive assistants as a Supreme Potentate, a Supreme Deputy Potentate, and a whole cabinet of other officials bearing equally impressive titles. Rumor had it that the Leader of American Negroes, a Philadelphia minister named James W. H. Eason, planned to reside in Washington in a symbolic Black House. Annual salaries voted by the convention to this leadership ran as high as $12,000, though there seemed to be little or no thought given to the problem of their payment. This heavy financial commitment was in fact eventually to place a severe strain on the resources of the movement.[64] The emphasis on African nationalism was further reflected in the official anthem of the movement, sung to the tune of a militant old Jamaican missionary hymn:

> Ethiopia, thou land of our fathers,
> Thou land where the gods loved to be,
> As storm cloud at night suddenly gathers
> Our armies come rushing to thee.
> We must in the fight be victorious
> When swords are thrust outward to gleam;
> For us will the vict'ry be glorious
> When led by the red, black, and green.
>
> Advance, advance to victory,
> Let Africa be free;
> Advance to meet the foe
> With the might
> Of the red, the black, and the green.[65]

Stock of the various business enterprises of the U.N.I.A. was sold in large amounts during the convention. The *Negro World* stressed the importance of support for the Black Star Line and delegates were urged to patronize the shops of the Negro Factories Corporation. Garvey ordered African Redemption medals struck: a bronze cross for subscribers of $50–$100, silver for those giving $100–$500, and a special gold cross for those subscribing more than $500.[66] Everywhere buttons and cockades of red, black, and green began to appear on Negro lapels, signifying a fervent belief in the miracles the race could accomplish now that it was at last being united under an aggressive leader.

The convention also created a nobility and freely bestowed impressive titles upon the favored elite of the organization. Membership in such honorary orders as the Knights of the Nile or the Distinguished Service Order of Ethiopia was a reward for past services to the race and brought with it immeasurably enhanced prestige. Along with the prestige went added responsibility, and this nobility was generally a serious ruling caste with special duties to perform as district or sectional leaders of the U.N.I.A. Even the lowliest follower was not forgotten, moreover, and every black man could square his shoulders with pride when Garvey addressed him as a "Fellowman of the Negro Race." No ego need remain unbolstered in this crusade.

Although much of Garvey's support came from the unsophisticated and unlettered masses, a number of prominent Negroes were associated with the movement in the early days of its sweeping success. Gabriel Johnson, mayor of Monrovia, Liberia, was named by the 1920 convention to the $12,000 a year post of Potentate of the association and Secretary of State in the cabinet of the Provisional President of Africa. Apparently Johnson attempted to use his new position to demand precedence over the President of Liberia upon his return to Africa and for his upstart airs was very nearly lynched by the irate Liberian aristocracy.[67] In addition to the Reverend James W. H. Eason, named American Organizer, a prominent Episcopal clergyman, George Alexander McGuire, was elected Chaplain General of the U.N.I.A. Henrietta Vinton Davis, one of the finest Negro elocutionists and a sensitive interpreter of Shakespearean roles, was given the job of International Organizer and dubbed a Lady Commander of the Sublime Order of the Nile. John E. Bruce, a popular Harlem columnist, was similarly knighted for his services to the association.

Perhaps the most prominent American Negro to become

interested in Garveyism was the registrar of Howard University, Dr. Emmett J. Scott. Scott had been Booker T. Washington's private secretary for many years and during the war had served as Secretary of War Newton D. Baker's special assistant in matters relating to Negro troops. His services to the Negro people were honored at a later convention when he was made a Knight Commander of the Sublime Order of the Nile.[68] William Pickens, an educator active in the National Association for the Advancement of Colored People, for several years showed considerable interest in the Garvey movement.[69] In 1922, however, Pickens repudiated the offer of a title similar to the one given Scott on the ground that "Americans would be foolish to give up their citizenship here for a one thousand year improbability in Africa or anywhere else." [70]

☆

When the U.N.I.A. convention adjourned at the end of August and the last delegate had turned toward his distant home, Harlem and the Negro world were aware of a potent new force in the field of race relations. Cutting across national lines and banishing national allegiances, the racial doctrines of Marcus Garvey were infusing in Negroes everywhere a strong sense of pride in being black. For the first time in the long bitter centuries since their ancestors had left Africa in chains, masses of Negroes in the United States and elsewhere in the New World were glorying in their color. Garveyism had suddenly emerged as a movement of world significance, with a spiritual power that reached deep down into the colored peoples of the world and swept them along on the currents of a potent racism. "Up, you mighty race," Garvey thundered, "you can accomplish what you will," and the Negro people responded with an enthusiastic determination born of centuries of frustration and despair.[71]

The striking triumph of the 1920 convention and the successful launching of the Black Star Line and the Negro Factories Corporation marked the peak of Marcus Garvey's influence and prestige in America. The initial successes of Garveyism might well be attributed to the daring magnitude of the plans and dreams of its founder. Even Negroes not active in the movement gloried vicariously in the achievements of the dedicated Garvey followers. To many the Universal Negro Improvement Association seemed the answer to the hopes and prayers of countless generations of oppressed and downtrodden blacks. Its inspiration was providing the basis for a regeneration of Negro life. Few could dispute Garvey's proud boast that "the nations of the world are aware that the Negro of yesterday has disappeared from the scene of human activities and his place taken by a new Negro who stands erect, conscious of his manhood rights and fully determined to preserve them at all costs." [72] The shaping of the New Negro was due in no small measure to the dreams and schemes of the stocky little black man from Jamaica.

No wonder the colored world, confronted with the seemingly limitless possibilities of a truly mass organization of the Negroes of the world, waited breathlessly for new developments in the Garvey plan for race redemption. Marcus Garvey's rapid rise to a position of great prominence as a world leader indicated, however, that his movement was built upon the unstable foundations of personal rather than organizational power. Consequently there was grave danger that the Universal Negro Improvement Association would collapse should its leadership ever falter. The white trade journal, the *Nautical Gazette,* pointed its editorial pen at one of Garvey's major problems when it took flattering note of the organization of his Black Star Line. "There is nothing in the record of the black race," the

Gazette observed, "to justify doubts as to their being capable navigators. But the success of the Black Star Line as a trading venture and as an instrumentality of disposing of goods made by Americans to African Negroes will depend on the business acumen displayed by its backers." [73] As much could be said of Garvey's other projects. His dreams would need to be implemented by successful action if the initial impetus of his movement was to be maintained. Having launched a great program with bombast and grandiloquence, Garvey would have to continue to hold his followers with constantly expanding promises and ever more dazzling actions. And if his enterprises should fail or his leadership be discredited in any way, in all likelihood the daring dreams of 1920 would dissolve into a deep disillusionment that would mark the end of this promising chapter in the history of Negro aspirations.

BLACK STARS

AND EMPTY DREAMS

> *Garvey, Garvey is a big man*
> *To take his folks to monkey-land.*
> *If he does, I'm sure I can*
> *Stay right here with Uncle Sam.*
> —Harlem Jingle [1]

> *You will see that from the start we tried to dignify our*
> *race. If I am to be condemned for that I am satisfied.*
> —Marcus Garvey [2]

★ In spite of the colorful triumphs of the 1920 convention, Garvey's Universal Negro Improvement Association soon began to draw criticism, and this opposition grew in volume and strength as the weaknesses of Garveyism became more apparent. Part of the difficulty of organizing American Negroes stemmed from the traditional distrust of the upper classes for any mass movement. All too frequently in the past impressive Negro organizations had been created chiefly for the personal enrichment of their founders, and the black bourgoisie had learned to distrust the popular race leaders. The strong class distinctions within the Negro caste also acted to defeat large-scale organization. Upper-class Negroes, conscious of their status in colored society and anxious to improve their position in the eyes of the white world, hesitated to take part in any movement embracing the ignorant black masses. Their hostility to Garvey increased as he adapted his program to the superstitions and resentment of the lower-class blacks. Some of the opposition to Garvey may be explained as pure jealousy over the striking successes of an upstart foreigner. Much of it, however, was based on a legitimate fear that Garvey was leading the Negro people down a blind alley, the end of which would reveal only further disillusionment and unhappiness for the race.

At first the skeptics were inclined to dismiss Marcus Garvey as just another of the many Negro messiahs claiming a special knowledge of the road to the promised land. Harlem had been mother to many strange cults; in fact, the multitude of bizarre movements and eccentric prophets in the black metropolis was one of its most interesting features. It was only when the Garvey movement began to assume large-scale proportions that many of the Negro intellectuals began to take notice of the movement and question some of its aims and aspects. The role of spokesman for the interests of millions of American Negroes was shifting to an immigrant Jamaican, and some thoughtful Americans now began to question the ability of a foreigner to interpret correctly the race problem of the United States. The unprecedented sums of money pouring into the Garvey coffers brought more reason for alarm, since the colored world could ill afford to spend its meager resources on improvement ventures unless their worth and practicability had been amply demonstrated. Thus while Garvey was increasing his power and influence by stirring appeals to the black masses, a growing number of critics, drawn largely from the ranks of the influential intelligentsia, began to raise their voices in opposition. Weak and scattered at first, this opposition assumed shape and power as Garveyism faltered and displayed its weaknesses.

Throughout his life Garvey was plagued with legal difficulties and he had barely established his organization in
the United States before he was in trouble with the law.
During the summer of 1919, as we have seen, Garvey was
warned several times by Assistant District Attorney Edwin
P. Kilroe of New York not to attempt the sale of stock for
the Black Star Line unless the company was regularly organized as a legitimate business enterprise. Through the
Negro World Garvey lashed back at Kilroe with the charge
that "certain sinister forces" were for political reasons using
the district attorney "to hound and persecute" Garvey and
the U.N.I.A. It was clearly the intention of the white man,
who feared the awakening of the Negro, Garvey declared,
to scatter the sheep by striking the shepherd.[3] Taken to
court for his libelous indiscretion, Garvey was forced to
publish a full retraction of his remarks.[4] A similar dispute
between the U.N.I.A. leader and Cyril V. Briggs, editor of
the anti-Garvey *Crusader* magazine, also resulted in court
action. Briggs was a light-skinned mulatto whom Garvey
had contemptuously referred to as a white man "passing
for Negro." The insulted Briggs replied with a legal suit
against the *Negro World* and its rash editor.[5] Again Garvey
was forced to apologize publicly for his unwise outburst
of journalistic temper.

Chicago was the scene of another Garvey setback late in
1919. The city's large Negro population, swollen by the
migration of the war years, had provided the basis for a
flourishing branch of the Universal Negro Improvement
Association. Garvey's movement was opposed from the
start, however, by Robert S. Abbott, wealthy publisher of
the powerful Negro weekly, the Chicago *Defender*. When
Garvey triumphantly announced the purchase of the S.S.
Yarmouth for the Black Star Line, the *Defender* recalled
with heavy sarcasm the maritime plans of an earlier Moses,

"Chief Sam" of Kansas. "Chief Sam" had also laid big plans for the establishment of a Negro state in Africa, and the *Defender* intimated in uncomplimentary terms that Garvey's Republic of Africa would meet the same obscure fate as its predecessor. Outraged, Garvey brought a libel suit against Abbott, claiming that this unflattering editorial had damaged his character to the tune of a million dollars. After lengthy litigation he was awarded a token sum, but it represented only a tiny fraction of what the proceedings had cost the U.N.I.A.

In the meantime Garvey and his organizers invaded Chicago to promote the sale of Black Star stock. Speaking from the platform of the Eighth Regimental Armory, the U.N.I.A. chief denounced Abbott in typically trenchant terms as an unprincipled traitor to the Negro race. At the close of the meeting Garvey was arrested for selling stock illegally, a development no doubt inspired by Abbott. After posting bond, Garvey unceremoniously left the city in what amounted to a personal triumph for the Chicago publisher.[6] Abbott brought his victory to a climax with a successful libel suit against Garvey for his Chicago address and for articles appearing in the *Negro World*.[7]

From the first a good part of Garvey's legal difficulties stemmed from his failure to choose his associates with care. Often he seemed more interested in surrounding himself with fawning sycophants than with competent advisers who might at times disagree with certain aspects of the Garvey master plan for race redemption. The Black Star Line had yet to float its first ship when Garvey angrily fired two of its executive officers, charging them with misappropriation of company funds. He denounced the two "scoundrels," Edgar M. Gray and Richard E. Warner, in the *Negro World* and went so far as to begin criminal proceedings against Gray.[8] The time sequence is unclear, but it was at this time that Gray and Warner went to District Attorney Kilroe, and, whether from feelings of revenge or newly roused civic duty, first directed that official's attention to the affairs of the new steamship line. Apparently nothing ever came of Garvey's criminal charges against Gray, but both Gray and Warner brought libel suits against Garvey and the *Negro World* for their ex-employer's unwise attacks and Gray managed to collect $200 in an out-of-court settlement.[9] Unfortunately for the movement, Garvey's court battles of 1919 were only a mild harbinger of later developments; for as the pugnacious Jamaican increased the number of his American enemies and the financial health of his enterprises became more dubious, law suits poured in like water into one of the foundering ships of his Black Star Line.

☆

In spite of these annoying legal disturbances, Garvey's work of organization went on apace. By mid-1920 the Black Star Line claimed ownership of three ships and was offering passenger and freight space on scheduled sailings to the West Indies and on excursion runs up the Hudson River. "Have you bought your shares in the Black Star Line?" asked a Garvey circular. "Three ships are now afloat and we must float one every three months until we build up a great Merchant Marine second to none." [10] "Invest your money today," a B.S.L. stock flyer urged, "so that at the end of the financial year you may be numbered among those who will have earned their dividends." [11] Garvey now began to talk of several new ships for the Black Star fleet, a *Booker T. Washington* for trade with South America and a still larger *Phyllis Wheatley* for service on the long-heralded African run. "Through the Black Star Line we will come into trade relations with our brethren on the West Coast of Africa," Garvey told the faithful, "and transport to Liberia and other African countries, those Negroes who desire to possess and enjoy the fruits of the richest country on God's green earth." [12] An all-out appeal was launched late in 1920 to raise the needed funds for these new ships and the *Negro World* intimated that the *Phyllis Wheatley* would fly the Black Star flag by the end of the year.

The outward appearance of success and stability was not enough, however, to dispel the growing cloud of rumors that all was not well with the Black Star Line. Throughout 1920 reports trickled back to Harlem of alleged mismanagement of the Black Star fleet, of unbusinesslike methods of running the company, and even of sabotage and dishonesty on the part of B.S.L. personnel. The skeptics were in fact justified in their fears. At no time in its existence was the Black Star Line in anything like a healthy financial condition, and throughout most of its life the corporation was only one step ahead of the receivers. In the first place, the wisdom of the venture was itself open to question. Although Garvey managed to collect a surprisingly large sum of money for the line, the purchase of ships at grossly inflated prices and the attempt to enter an industry plagued by ruinous competition would have spelled disaster for even a more soundly managed corporation. And though three quarters of a million dollars was big money in Harlem and would have been ample for most business ventures, it was scarcely enough to launch a steamship line.

Furthermore, neither Garvey nor his associates had the sort of business experience needed for this bold excursion into the realm of high finance. The treasurer of the Black Star Line, George Tobias, was a former railroad clerk who made no bones about his ignorance of bookkeeping practices (Case A, 2150–51). Jeremiah Certain, vice president of the line from 1919 to 1920, had been a cigar maker before joining the company (Case *A*, 1310). Elie Garcia, secretary of the line from 1920 on, was a B.S.L. stock salesman and U.N.I.A. leader in Philadelphia before moving up to his high position, and he later was convicted on a charge of petty larceny brought by Garvey (Case *A*, 2118–19). Only Orlando M. Thompson, who succeeded Certain as vice president, had any knowledge of accounting, and events were to indicate that he was not completely trustworthy. In the selection of his associates Garvey was more interested in unquestioning personal loyalty than in business competence, and the high rate of turnover in the upper echelons of his organization indicated that he was not an easy man to work with. In less than three years the Black Star Line had two vice presidents, four secretaries, and three assistant secretaries. All but two Garvey charged with dishonesty (Case *A*, 2368–69). The general lack of qualified Negro personnel for the operation of the line plus Garvey's ignorance or disregard of proper business methods soon combined to put the Black Star Line in an extremely precarious financial position.

A master propagandist, Garvey never bothered to draw a very sharp line between the promotional and the business aspects of his enterprises. Ships of the Black Star Line were diverted from scheduled runs in order to furnish graphic support to what Garvey called "the business of selling stock" (Case *A*, 2347). In at least one instance the delay resulting from such a stock-selling side excursion caused extensive damage to a perishable cargo (Case *A*, 309–15). With messianic fervor Garvey apparently believed that funds raised for any aspect of his redemption program could be used wherever he decided they were most needed. The result could only be financial chaos in the books of the U.N.I.A. and the B.S.L. U.N.I.A. funds were loaned to the Black Star Line on the dubious security of a third mortgage and were also used to purchase B.S.L. stock (Case *A*, 2160–72). Black Star money was deposited to cover outstanding checks that had previously been issued to pay bills of the U.N.I.A. restaurant and the *Negro World*.[13] Amy Ashwood, Garvey's private secretary and later his first wife, made a down payment on a house with a Black Star check and there was no evidence that this money was ever repaid to the company (Case *A*, 2274–79, 2352–53). Sometimes Garvey kept no record of money received from stock sales, merely ordering the issuance of stock certificates on the strength of his memory (Case *A*, 985). Blank B.S.L. stock certificates by the thousands were signed in advance and frequently Garvey would leave signed blank checks for the use of his staff while he was out of town (Case *A*, 1158, 1270). Once a stock stub book listing past stock purchases was lost, but Garvey declined to advertise in the *Negro World* for its return because "people might lose confidence in us" (Case *A*, 71–72).

In Garvey's mind stock selling was the most important aspect of this business enterprise, for without an ever-expanding capital base the Black Star Line could not hope to build up its fleet. Agents were appointed for most large Negro urban centers and were encouraged to work hard by a commission of 3 per cent on their sales of B.S.L. stock. Garvey and other officials traveled extensively in the United States and the West Indies to promote the sale of stock and push the organization of the U.N.I.A. Often such promotional groups were elaborate expeditions complete with a vocal quartet and a twenty-piece military band. Garvey's chief stock salesman later asserted that expenses on these trips sometimes ate up as much as 60 per cent of the proceeds, though more frequently the local U.N.I.A. group took care of part of the costs (Case *A*, 791). Supervision of B.S.L. stock salesmen and agents was never very rigorous. While Elie Garcia was a B.S.L. agent and secretary of the local U.N.I.A. division in Philadelphia, he kept Black Star and U.N.I.A. funds mixed indiscriminately in his personal checking account on the ground that it was the only way he could "keep the money in a place where it was safe" (Case A, 2108–15).

Even if the business practices of the Black Star Line's officers had been above reproach, however, the corporation still would have had great difficulty keeping its flag above water. Its unwise purchases of dubious ships at exorbitant prices were a handicap from which even a more soundly managed company would have been hard put to survive. Worse still, the muddled operation of the rusty old ships of the Black Star fleet brought only a heart-breaking series of disasters marked by bungling incompetence, individual dishonesty, and ever-increasing corporate indebtedness. The *Yarmouth*, the B.S.L.'s tiny flagship, made a total of three limping voyages to the West Indies for the line. On the first two trips the *Yarmouth* was commanded by Captain Joshua Cockbourne, the Negro master whose venal advice had originally led Garvey to purchase the vessel. After Garvey fired Cockbourne for mismanagement, the B.S.L. had trouble finding another licensed Negro officer, and on its third and final voyage the *Yarmouth* was commanded by a Captain Dickenson, a white Canadian.

The *Yarmouth*'s maiden voyage for the Black Star Line late in 1919 set a pattern of ineptitude that unfortunately was the rule on its later voyages as well. This first trip opened auspiciously enough, as we have seen, with a tremendous send-off by thousands of cheering well-wishers at the 135th Street pier, but the ship got only as far as 23d Street before it was forced to anchor while the line's directors scurried around seeking insurance. This obstacle finally met, several days later the *Yarmouth* ignominiously sneaked out of the harbor at night to prevent any further delays. The rest of the voyage was, as Captain Cockbourne cheerfully informed Garvey, "quite an adventurous trip." [14] The firemen were unable to raise more than sixty-five pounds of pressure in the *Yarmouth's* tired boilers and as a result the ship never made more than seven knots an hour. Going through the Straits of Florida, the *Yarmouth* could barely make headway against the current because steam pressure was so low. With Cockbourne asleep early one morning the ship ran aground on the Cay Sal Bank off the Bahamas and the panic-stricken crew sent out an SOS and prepared to abandon ship. Fortunately the *Yarmouth* was only stuck in soft sand and worked itself loose with no apparent damage.

"People here are just crazy about the organization and had all kinds of entertainments ready," Cockbourne reported happily from Cuba. "The people at Havana are mustering in thousands to see the ship and I have no doubt that it would be the means of collecting a Hundred Thousand of Dollars in quick time . . . so by all means the vessel ought to touch Havana before returning to New York." [15] No doubt Black Star stock sales were boosted by the long-awaited presence of the *Yarmouth* in West Indian ports, but otherwise this first voyage could hardly be called a success. Cockbourne carried a few passengers back and forth between various islands, but the *Yarmouth* was in ballast on its runs to Kingston, Jamaica, and Colon, Panama (Case A, 300). Coming back early in January, 1920, however, the ship had a full roster of passengers and a capacity cargo of 400 tons of log wood (Case A, 302).

In spite of an obvious need for extensive repairs on the *Yarmouth's* boilers, Cockbourne had barely tied up the ship in New York when he was ordered to take her out again, this time on an emergency voyage to Cuba. The new

Volstead Act prohibiting the sale of alcoholic beverages in the United States was about to go into effect and the Black Star Line had accepted a hastily awarded contract with the Pan Union Company to transport a cargo of whiskey to a safer haven in Cuba. After an agonizing delay while various attachments for B.S.L. debts were removed from the ship, the *Yarmouth's* convivial crew managed to load all but a few cases of the whiskey cargo before the Volstead Act deadline, and on January 17 the ship once more headed out to sea. As before, the voyage was unexpectedly short. Eighty miles off Sandy Hook Light the *Yarmouth's* engineer opened the sea cocks and an SOS was sent out that the ship was sinking. Under Cockbourne's orders, the crew immediately began to jettison the whiskey cargo, which was at once picked up by a swarm of small boats that for some unexplained reason had been following the *Yarmouth*. Considerably lightened of whiskey, but with bilges awash with sea water, the *Yarmouth* limped ingloriously back into port (Case A, 267–74, 1345–47).

After several weeks while repairs to the damaged ship were made, Cockbourne made another attempt to take the *Yarmouth* and what remained of its whiskey cargo to Cuba. This time the frantic owner of the whiskey decided to leave nothing to chance and, unknown to Garvey, slipped Cockbourne and Edward D. Smith-Green, secretary of the line, a commission of about $2,000 for expediting the voyage (Case A, 269–70, 385–91). Perhaps because of this extra inducement, this time Cockbourne managed to make port in Cuba, but during the jolly voyage the *Yarmouth's* undisciplined crew made considerable inroads on the unguarded cargo of whiskey and only a fraction of the original shipment was ever unloaded. In the summer of 1922 a judgment of $6,000 was awarded the Pan Union Company to cover its losses from this ill-starred voyage. The attorneys of the

Pan Union Company were unable, however, to discover any Black Star assets to satisfy this judgment.[16]

The subsequent nautical career of the ill-fated *Yarmouth*, if somewhat less exciting, was equally disappointing. Bringing the *Yarmouth* home from the unlucky whiskey voyage, Captain Cockbourne managed to run the ship aground off Boston (Case A, 1737). Relieved of his command for this and other fiascos, he was still kept on the Black Star payroll as a stock promoter.[17] Later under the command of a white master the *Yarmouth* made a final trip to the West Indies, but this less eventful voyage was no more of a success financially than the others. Late in 1921 Judge Edwin L. Garvin of the federal district court in Brooklyn penned a humiliating obituary for the B.S.L.'s once proud flagship. To satisfy a judgment against the line of only $2,320.90, Judge Garvin approved the sale by public auction of the *Yarmouth* for a piddling $1,625, less than a hundredth of its original purchase price.[18] Thus disappeared the luckless *Frederick Douglass*, alias *Yarmouth*, the rusty little ship that in a brief two years had swallowed up $194,803.08 of Black Star money (Case A, 2650).

The Black Star Line had no better luck in the operation of its other two ships, the *Kanawha* and the *Shadyside*. The excursion boat *Shadyside* made a number of trips up the Hudson during the summer of 1920, with runs as often as three times weekly during the exciting days of the 1920 U.N.I.A. convention. Garvey and his associates had expected great things promotion-wise from this first Negro-owned excursion steamer, but unfortunately Harlemites did not come flocking to the *Shadyside* in anything like overwhelming numbers. Possibly the $1.05 fare was too high, but more likely the difficulty of securing a good upstream landing for this Negro boat acted to frustrate Garvey's hopes. In any event, the *Shadyside*'s white cap-

tain, Jacob Wise, soon warned Garvey that the Black Star
Line was losing money on the old side-wheeler, that there
were not enough passengers even to pay for coal to feed
the vessel's ravenous boilers (Case A, 424–29). By the end
of August the harassed Black Star directors had voted to
take the costly *Shadyside* out of service.[19] Put up for the
season at Fort Lee on the Jersey side of the river, the
Shadyside sprang a seam during a bad ice storm the following winter and sank quietly to the bottom of the Hudson
(Case A, 1712–13). The embarrassed Black Star Line was
in no position to attempt a salvage operation even if the
battered old steamer had warranted a rescue effort. The
B.S.L. account books told a sobering story. In less than five
months' active service the inefficient *Shadyside* had cost
the Black Star Line a staggering $11,000 in operating losses,
not to mention the larger $20,000 capital investment in the
boat itself. In the *Shadyside* fiasco another $31,000 of Black
Star money was irretrievably lost (Case A, 2650, 2657).

The nautical career of the S.S. *Kanawha*, or *Antonio
Maceo* as it was renamed by the line, was perhaps the most
colorful of all Black Star ships, and just as disappointing.
The corporation paid a whopping $60,000 for this con-
verted millionaire's yacht, the only B.S.L. vessel on which
payments were ever completed (Case A, 2657–58). At the
time the deal was closed, however, rumor had it that an
asking price of $10,000 for the *Kanawha* had just been re-
fused by another, more sophisticated buyer (Case A, 436).
To conserve his company's dwindling resources, Garvey
arranged to have the necessary repairs and alterations to
the *Kanawha* made at the B.S.L.'s 135th Street pier rather
than in a regular shipyard. More important, perhaps, the
presence of the ship at a vantage point close to Harlem
would stimulate flagging stock sales. After several weeks
of repair work early in June, 1920, Garvey announced a

gala excursion trip up the Hudson in the newest addition to the Black Star fleet. He brushed aside protests from his port captain, Adrian Richardson, that the *Kanawha* had not yet been fully tested and thus had no certificate of government inspection, a legal requirement for any voyage. Crowded with Negro passengers who had cheerfully paid $1.25 to take this exciting maiden voyage, the *Kanawha* steamed only as far as 206 Street before a boiler manhole blew out, scalding a crew member to death (Case A, 438–42).

After this tragic mishap the *Kanawha* sat in port for another month while further repairs were made to her leaky old boilers. Toward the end of July the *Kanawha* finally headed out to sea, bound for Cuba under command of Captain Leon R. Swift, the foxy white ship broker who had arranged the sale of the vessel to the unsuspecting Black Star Line. This time the unlucky craft managed to get to the Delaware River before its boilers gave out again, forcing its unhappy crew to improvise sails in order to get to port (Case A, 442–44). Captain Swift chartered a Philadelphia tug for $1,500 to tow the broken-down ship to a Norfolk, Virginia, yard. Here the *Kanawha*'s master shrewdly resolved to abandon ship. "After careful thought and thinking combined with business possibilities," Swift told Garvey in a collect telegram, "I have decided that I cannot proceed any farther with the Steamer Kanawha, so would advise you to take steps and secure somebody to relieve me." Under separate cover Swift thoughtfully submitted a bill for $315.48 to cover his salary and train fare home.[20]

To take over Smith's place at the *Kanawha*'s helm, Garvey appointed Adrian Richardson, a Boston sailor who had formerly been the B.S.L.'s New York port captain. But the seemingly jinxed *Kanawha* did no better under a black master than it had under a white. Captain Richardson

made three abortive starts southward out of Norfolk, only
to have the ship's wheezing boilers give out each time after
a few miles. After the third exasperating breakdown, Richardson headed north to Wilmington, Delaware, for a thorough engine overhaul, only to be told that the Wilmington
shipyard was not equipped to repair the *Kanawha*'s special
type of boilers. With a patch-work repair job by the ship's
own engineers, Richardson brought the *Kanawha* home to
New York, crawling the last few miles on only one boiler
plus makeshift sails (Case A, 444–47). With all three of its
ships now out of service the Black Star Line hurriedly told
the National Dry Dock and Repair Company of Staten
Island to do whatever was necessary to put the *Kanawha* in
shipshape condition. When the repair bill was submitted in
March, 1921, it totaled $44,811.02, better than two-thirds
of the *Kanawha*'s original purchase price (Case A, 2225–
29, 2701).

Although the *Kanawha* was now supposedly as good as
new, its unhappy saga under the Black Star flag was not
yet completed. On March 25, 1921, Captain Adrian Richardson once again pointed the yacht's trim prow southward
toward Havana. Six hours out of New York a safety valve
blew out and, after attempting for a day to make repairs at
sea, Richardson brought the ship back to New York for a
replacement valve. Making a fresh departure on the 28th,
Richardson put in two days later at Norfolk for supplies,
or perhaps, as Garvey later charged, to spend a night with
his wife. At Norfolk Richardson also took aboard a new
passenger, a personal friend, and in landing him further
down the coast managed to back the stern of the *Kanawha*
into a pier, doing considerable damage to both items.[21] At
Jacksonville, Florida, Richardson got another friend to repair the *Kanawha*'s fan engine, which had given out, and
ordered fresh supplies of coal and water (Case A, 449).

The short run from Jacksonville to Havana took the slug-
gish *Kanawha* five days, for the temperamental fan engine
broke down shortly after the ship left Florida. Worse still,
the yacht's incompetent and drunken chief engineer,
Charles Harris, began using salt water in his boilers in
spite of his having aboard an evaporator to make fresh
water, and by the time the *Kanawha* reached Cuba its
boilers and engine cylinders were badly corroded.[22]

Meanwhile Garvey had also gone to the West Indies on
a B.S.L. stock promotional tour. In Jamaica his inflamma-
tory speeches caused the apprehensive American consul at
Kingston to warn the State Department of Garvey's ability
to "arouse considerable racial antagonism among the negroes at the Canal Zone," [23] a report that led Secretary of
State Charles Evans Hughes to cable American consular
officials in Central America to "refuse aid in securing visa
for Marcus Garvey." [24] Garvey's tour was nevertheless a
personal as well as a financial triumph. "The news of Garvey's arrival spread like wild fire," reported a Panama
newspaper, "and people could be seen running from all
directions to see and welcome him." [25] In Costa Rica Garvey managed to obtain an audience with President Acosta
and outlined U.N.I.A. plans for the establishment of a
Negro commonwealth in Africa. The general manager of
the United Fruit Company, a large employer of Negro
labor in Costa Rica, estimated that Garvey had collected
about $30,000 during his visit in that country and asserted
that United Fruit employees in Costa Rica were sending
about $2,000 monthly to Garvey.[26] Even after the Black
Star Line had folded, Central American Negroes continued
to give the U.N.I.A. loyal financial support. The United
Fruit Company—employer, banker, and paternal overseer
to many of Garvey's Negro followers in the banana repub-
lics—reported that from November, 1921, through Febru-

ary, 1922, it had sold to the inhabitants of Puerto Barrios, Guatemala, a village of only 2,400 population, bank drafts totaling $2,941.08 payable to the Black Star Line or the Universal Negro Improvement Association. An unknown number of other such drafts were undoubtedly taken out in the names of individuals and endorsed over to the Garvey movement.[27]

Garvey had counted on having the *Kanawha* available both as a convenient and fitting agency of transportation and as a potent sales argument for his stock promotional trip. Consequently he was more than a little anxious and upset when he boarded the yacht at Santiago, Cuba, demanding from Captain Richardson a full explanation for the vessel's dilatory and costly trip. After new repairs were made on the ship's tired engines, Garvey ordered the *Kanawha* to Kingston, Jamaica, and signed himself on as ship's purser in order to avoid anticipated difficulties with immigration authorities upon his return to the United States (Case A, 452–53). The American State Department, which was of the opinion that Garvey was "an undesirable, and indeed a very dangerous, alien" who was organizing "all of the negroes in the world against the white people," [28] countered by ordering its consuls to refuse visas to the entire crew list of the *Kanawha* until Garvey's name was removed from the roster.[29]

With no more than the usual complement of boiler explosions, engine failures, and agonizing delays, the *Kanawha* reached Kingston in mid-May. Here Garvey warned the ship's officers that the Black Star Line could "not afford to continue spending money in effecting repairs in this fashion from port to port." "You are hereby advised," he reminded the chief engineer sternly, "that there will be no undue and unnecessary further repairs, and that as Chief Engineer you shall make a thorough investigation leading up to those damages that have been done since the boat left New York." [30] The possibility of sabotage had entered Garvey's mind and he began to suspect that the *Kanawha's* officers had been accepting kickbacks on the surprisingly frequent repair contracts. He received a confidential report from a worried U.N.I.A. member in Kingston that the *Kanawha's* chief engineer was "a whiteman Negro" who had boldly told the informant of his intention to wreck "this God dam Black Star Line." [31] Garvey decided to handle the repair negotiations in Kingston himself and accordingly warned the chief engineer "not to enter into any agreement with any of the Contractors without my approval." [32]

When toward the end of May the *Kanawha* again broke down on a voyage from Jamaica to Panama, Garvey charged Captain Richardson and Chief Engineer Charles Harris with "destructive mismanagement." [33] In a detailed twelve-page complaint to the American consul in Kingston, Garvey listed his suspicions of the *Kanawha's* two chief officers and asked permission to dismiss them for "incompetency, neglect, and conspiracy." [34] The irate Black Star president was supported in his misgivings by a marine survey report that the yacht's engines and boilers were badly corroded from sea water. "I would say that if [the] boilers and machinery were in good condition when the vessel left the United States in March," a Kingston ship surveyor declared, "such a condition could be brought about only through sheer neglect." [35] Unfortunately for Garvey, Charles L. Latham, the American consul at Kingston, considered the B.S.L. president to be "a clever scoundrel" who was intent upon "extracting money from the ignorant Negroes for his own pocket" and who was "appealing to and inflaming every race prejudice and animosity" of Jamaican blacks. Latham called Garvey's charges against Richardson and Harris "absurd," and insisted upon a Black Star deposit to cover the severance pay of the two discharged officers.[36] Although Garvey attempted to have Richardson's and Harris' marine licenses revoked, even seeking the intervention of Secretary of State Hughes in the matter,[37] his charges against the former officers of the *Kanawha* eventually were dismissed.[38]

Leaving the luckless *Kanawha* under the command of E. R. Connors, its former first mate, with instructions to return home as soon as practicable, Garvey headed for New York to prepare for the coming 1921 U.N.I.A. convention. On second thought, the State Department decided to allow the popular Negro leader to enter the country, though Garvey and his party were detained at New Orleans long enough for him to fire a telegram of aggrieved protest to Secretary Hughes.[39] For the rest of the summer the Black Star office in Harlem was besieged with frantic cablegrams for money to keep the *Kanawha* afloat. In late July the American consul at Kingston reported that he was receiving daily complaints from the crew of the stranded vessel. Crew members informed him they were missing meals for lack of ship's stores and claimed that they had been reduced to selling their clothing to pay for living expenses.[40]

Finally toward the end of July Garvey sent enough money to pay off the ship's debts and the *Kanawha* departed from Jamaica on its homeward voyage, managing to reach Antilla, Cuba, before its machinery broke down again. "Will spend no more money on crew or boat except it is brought to New York," Garvey cabled angrily in response to a plea for more funds. "Never ordered you to Cuban ports and will not be responsible." [41] "Kanawha disabled, cannot proceed," came the disheartening reply. "Urge you cable American consul at least four thousand dollars." [42] But by this time even the incurably optimistic

Garvey had lost interest in the costly *Kanawha*. Eventually the yacht's crew was shipped home at the expense of the United States government and the vessel was left to rust in Antilla harbor. Throughout 1922 the American consul at Antilla looked after the abandoned B.S.L. ship, periodically begging the Negro corporation to send him funds to pay for a watchman so Cuban authorities would not seize the ship as a derelict. To his superiors in Washington he reported that he had frequently emphasized to the *Kanawha*'s disinterested owners "that both the hull and the machinery were fast deteriorating under the climatic conditions of the port and that the vessel would soon be little more than a wreck." The Black Star management, however, "uniformly failed to reply" to either his warnings or his entreaties.[43] In addition to its original cost of $60,000, the *Kanawha* had devoured in less than a year and a half $134,681.11 of Black Star money. Offsetting this fantastic expense record was an operating income of but $1,207.63, mostly receipts from the first tragic excursion trip up the Hudson River (Case *A*, 2650).

☆

In November, 1919, even before the battered ships of the Black Star fleet had launched their all-out assault on the line's treasury, Garvey had promised that a new and bigger ship, to be renamed the *Phyllis Wheatley,* would "be put on the African route and sail between America, Liberia and Sierra Leone, West Africa." [44] By "linking up the Negro on this side of the Atlantic with his brother in Africa," a proud and successful *Phyllis Wheatley* would mark the fulfillment of Garvey's great maritime dream.[45] The visionary Black Star president had hoped to obtain a suitable ship for the African run by the beginning of 1920; but, as he sadly admitted to a B.S.L. creditor in January, the operation of a steamship line costs "a great deal more

money" than either he or the other directors had anticipated (Case *A*, 211). With the acquisition of the *Shadyside*
and the *Kanawha* in April, 1920, the corporation was forced
to abandon for a time its plans for an African ship. In October, however, Garvey again began talking of a *Phyllis
Wheatley* and announced that early the following year the
Black Star Line planned to "send the first trading ship
manned and owned by Negroes" to the African motherland.[46]

Heavily in debt and with a credit rating near zero, however, the Black Star Line was hardly in a financial position
to purchase another, more costly ship. In fact on October
1, 1920, Orlando M. Thompson, B.S.L. vice president,
frankly admitted to a friend that the future of the corporation was "just a little doubtful," but intimated that big
plans were afoot to save the day. "Of course this is confidential," Thompson warned, "don't let this get out." [47] Five
days later three obscure New Yorkers traveled to Jersey
City to incorporate the Black Star Steamship Company of
New Jersey with a charter virtually identical to that of the
old Black Star Line of Delaware.[48] Garvey and the re-
sourceful directors of the line had hit upon a scheme that
seemed to promise further expansion. The way was now
clear for a new ship safely to fly the Black Star flag without
danger that the vessel could be attached for any of the
mounting debts of the old Black Star Line of Delaware.
The Black Star Steamship Company of New Jersey would
no doubt stand a much better chance of getting credit than
would the foundering Black Star Line of Delaware. Garvey
ordered his lieutenants to press the search for a satisfactory
Phyllis Wheatley, the ship that might yet recoup the shattered fortunes of the Black Star fleet.

Before departing on a U.N.I.A. promotional tour in the
West Indies at the end of February, 1921, Garvey made an

impassioned appeal for more funds so that the Black Star
Line could develop the African trade. "Today we control
three-quarters of a million dollars," he told an admiring
audience in Liberty Hall, "not three-quarters of a million
on mere paper, but in property value—money that can be
realized in twenty-four hours if the stockholders desire that
their money be refunded to them." Without raising the
question of how much the line might hope to realize from
the sunken *Shadyside* and the decommissioned *Yarmouth*,
Garvey declared flatly: "By a majority vote at any meeting
we can sell out the property of the Black Star Line and
realize every nickel we have placed in it." "Africa, with her
teeming millions is extending her hands towards us," the
U.N.I.A chief cried. "It may be 6 per cent; it may be 10 per
cent; it may be 100 per cent; there is no limit to the divi-
dend to be declared at the close of the year because this
depends upon the success the corporation meets with in the
year that is past." [49]

There seemed reason for some optimism. Orlando M.
Thompson, B.S.L. vice president in charge of negotiations
for a new ship, reported that the corporation would soon
complete a purchase agreement for the S.S. *Tennyson,* a
British vessel reportedly large enough for the transatlantic
run to Africa, and on February 19 the *Negro World* published a photograph of the ship.[50] It was in fact chiefly to
facilitate this deal that Garvey decided to go to the West
Indies in order to push the sale of Black Star stock. In his
absence the other B.S.L. directors were instructed to re-
double their efforts to raise new capital. Garvey had
scarcely left New York, however, when the owners of the
Tennyson withdrew the sale offer and broke off negotiations with the Black Star Line (Case A, 2041). Desperate
for a ship, Thompson next turned to Anthony Rudolph

Silverston, the white operator of a questionable one-man ship exchange on the lower Manhattan waterfront. The affable Silverston promised the anxious Black Star directors that their ship worries were over. By operating through a white broker, he asserted, the Negro company would avoid the race prejudice that had handicapped the corporation in its other negotiations.

Silverston's first offering, early in April, was a thirty-two year old British tramp steamer, the *S.S. Hong Kheng*, currently on Chinese coastal service. Through Thompson the Black Star Steamship Company of New Jersey, fronting for the old Black Star Line, contracted to pay $300,000 for the ship, with a deposit of $3,700 and another $16,300 held in escrow pending delivery. Silverston promised to have the *Hong Kheng* in New York by May 20, 1921 (Case A, 2702–5). To raise this $20,000 down payment, the Black Star directors were forced to issue an extraordinary appeal to the major branches of the Universal Negro Improvement Association (Case A, 2044). After the delivery date had come and gone with no sign of the *Hong Kheng*, the suspicious B.S.L. secretary, Elie Garcia, did some discreet cabling and learned that the vessel was in drydock in Indochina (Case A, 2048–49). Silverston brushed off the protests of the excited Black Star directors with the assertion that the *Hong Kheng* would not have been suitable, and anyway he was now negotiating for the *S.S. Orion*, an ex-German ship currently up for sale by the United States Shipping Board. The Black Star deposit money would apply to the *Orion*, he agreed. He emphasized to the race-conscious B.S.L. directorate that a white man would have a much better chance of purchasing the *Orion* than would a colored corporation. Thompson thereupon gave Silverston a power of attorney to bid for the *Orion* (Case A,

2687), and went to Norfolk to inspect the ship, reporting to his colleagues that its acquisition "would bring much credit to the company." [51]

Actually the smooth-talking Silverston made no attempt to camouflage the fact that he was acting for the Black Star Line and asserted openly to the chairman of the Shipping Board that he represented a company controlled by "over four million colored citizens." [52] When the Board delayed accepting his offer of $225,000 for the *Orion,* Silverston protested that neither he nor his Negro clients could "afford any more 'Pussey-footing.' " "We have complied with all the requirements," he disgustedly told Chairman Alfred D. Lasker, "but it seems as if I am 'bucking up' against the 'color line' or some 'under-ground' wires." [53] To this outburst the Shipping Board merely countered with a dignified but dismaying request for "a complete financial statement" of the U.N.I.A. and the Black Star Line.[54] Apparently the board was satisfied, for in a surprise decision on August 2 it awarded the *Orion* to Silverston and the Black Star Line for $225,000, with a cash down payment of $22,500 and the balance in monthly installments of 10 per cent at 5 per cent interest.[55] Although the Negro line had already handed Silverston more than $20,000— Thompson having paid over the $16,300 escrow money without telling the other B.S.L. directors (Case A, 2059, 2146)—at this time the wily ship broker had deposited with the Shipping Board only $12,500.[56] Silverston's "expenses" seem to have amounted to more than $7,500.

Many of the delegates to the second International Convention of the Negroes of the World, which convened in Harlem during the month of August, 1921, were aroused by the evasive answers given to questions about the operation of the Black Star Line. Some suspicious U.N.I.A. members were only partly reassured by the announcement

early in the convention that the United States Shipping
Board had awarded the *Orion* to the Negro line. As the
convention wore on and Garvey failed to produce the new
ship, the long-promised *Phyllis Wheatley*, mutterings of
protest came from the U.N.I.A. ranks. One delegate in particular, Noah D. Thompson, head of the Los Angeles division of the U.N.I.A., was thoroughly disillusioned by Garvey's apparent deception. Thompson returned to the West
Coast and reported apprehensively, "None of the boasted
ships were shown to the delegates, who were daily promised that on 'tomorrow' the ships would be shown." [57] Taking alarm, the Los Angeles organization wired Garvey for
an explanation, but he only sent his Minister of Legions,
E. L. Gaines, to oust the schismatic faction. Thompson
thereupon withdrew from the U.N.I.A. with a substantial
part of its Los Angeles membership and formed the rival
Pacific Coast Improvement Association.[58]

Others were also concerned about the fate of the Black
Star fleet, particularly the much heralded *Phyllis Wheatley*. As far back as December, 1920, Dr. W. E. Burghardt
DuBois, editor of *Crisis*, had published a severe indictment
of the management of the Black Star Line, based on a
shrewd analysis of its financial reports.[59] Critics began to
ask why the Black Star Line had been advertising a schedule of *Phyllis Wheatley* sailings in the *Negro World* [60] and
why the corporation had been accepting deposits on steamship tickets to Africa (Case A, 2656). "Whatever might
have been the errors of the past," declared a B.S.L. circular
reassuringly, "the present administration of the Black Star
Line is composed of trained business men and specialty
service help, unquestionably equal to their responsible
tasks" (Case A, 2562). Skeptical Harlemites were not convinced.

To head off this mounting criticism, late in August Garvey angrily warned his vice president, Orlando Thompson, to complete the deal for the *Orion* or face prosecution for his mysterious dealings with the ship broker Silverston (Case A, 2233–36). Roused to action by this threat, on August 30 Silverston borrowed the necessary $10,000 on a two-month promissory note (at interest of $1,000), which was then endorsed by Thompson representing the Black Star Line (Case A, 2707–10). Thompson next contracted for freight for the *Orion*'s maiden voyage under the Black Star flag so that money would be available to pay off Silverston's promissory note (Case A, 1987). This was devious financing at its worst, but still the Shipping Board refused to release the *Orion*. Finally on December 13, 1921, Wilford H. Smith, B.S.L. attorney and one of the few directors Garvey still trusted, wrote to the Shipping Board for an explanation and discovered to his horror that the Black Star deposit was still only $12,500 of the required $22,500 down payment.[61] For some reason never explained the missing $10,000 did not reach the Board until December 22, when a check dated August 30 was submitted by E. H. Duff, an associate of broker Silverston.[62] Silverston later sought to claim this $10,000 as his personal property (Case A, 1888) despite the fact that the Black Star Line was repeatedly dunned for payment of the wily broker's promissory note (Case A, 2707–10). Was there any wonder that Garvey belatedly began to suspect treachery in the Black Star camp?[63]

But there was another reason for the Shipping Board's unusual delay in releasing the *Orion* to the Black Star Line. Late in August, 1921, William J. Burns, the director of the Federal Bureau of Investigation, broadly hinted to the Board that it should reconsider its decision to sell Marcus Garvey a ship.[64] Basing his allegations on highly colored F.B.I. files, the Shipping Board's own zealous security officer reported excitedly that Garvey's Universal Negro Improvement Association was "the communist party which is affiliated with the Russian Soviet Government." Garvey was declared to be "a ratical [*sic*] agitator" who "advocates and teaches the overthrow of the United States Government by force and violence," while the Jamaican's associates were also "anarchists and agitators." [65] This report was probably the reason that it took the reluctant Shipping Board six months to prepare a sale contract for the *Orion* and why it then included a demand for an extraordinary performance bond of $450,000, or twice the purchase price. The Black Star Line might possibly have been able to secure the the customary performance bond covering the $200,000 remaining to be paid, but the battered Negro corporation could not hope to find a guarantor for this large and unreasonable amount. Negotiations collapsed, leaving the Shipping Board with $22,500 of Black Star deposit money and a thorny mass of litigations for years to come.[66] In 1928 the United States Senate authorized the return of this deposit money to B.S.L. stockholders and creditors, but twice the disinterested House of Representatives failed to act upon companion measures that would permit the release of the deposit. Even the Senate bill was not adopted without some rather indifferent opposition, however, and Senator Thaddeus H. Caraway of Arkansas wondered audibly if it would not be better for all concerned to "give them the boat and let them go." [67]

☆

Meanwhile Garvey's enemies were demanding to know why the *Phyllis Wheatley*, alias *Orion*, still continued to appear only in the pages of the *Negro World*. Cyril V. Briggs, by now a full-time Garvey foe, wrote to the Department of Commerce about the Black Star fleet and received a reply from the Bureau of Navigation stating that it had been unable to find in its records any mention of the steamships *Antonio Maceo* (*Kanawha*) or *Phyllis Wheatley*. Briggs triumphantly published this exposé in his *Crusader*, asking pointedly, "Why has the Black Star Line been selling passage on a boat that does not exist?" [68] Another critic, humorist George S. Schuyler, came up with what he suspected was the answer to Briggs's question. Noting the discovery by a British physicist that ships are lighter when sailing from west to east, Schuyler suggested that in the case of the *Phyllis Wheatley* the vessel might "have gotten so light that the wind blew it away." This phenomenon might also apply to ships sailing south, Schuyler believed, for had not the *Yarmouth* also grown "lighter and lighter as the number of 'dead soldiers,' tossed in its wake by the hilarious crew, grew more numerous?" [69]

Partly through editorial agitation and partly because of complaints by a few Black Star stockholders, early in January, 1922, Garvey was arrested on a charge of using the mails to defraud. Postal authorities charged that Garvey and the Black Star Line had knowingly used "fraudulent representations" and "deceptive artifices" in the sale of stock through the mails and had advertised and sold space on a mythical vessel.[70] Garvey claimed that he had been betrayed by a few of his subordinates, and the great bulk of the U.N.I.A. immediately rallied to his support.[71] "Enemies of the Negro race and enemies of my movement within the race," Garvey told the faithful, "have been plotting for some time to besmirch my character in order to hold me up to public ridicule and to cause me to lose favor among my people." The pugnacious little Jamaican likened these enemies to the evil men who "fought and crucified Jesus Christ," and he warned, "let them crucify me and the Universal Negro Improvement Association shall succeed the more." [72]

Late in February, 1922, Garvey and three of his Black Star associates, Elie Garcia, George Tobias, and Orlando M. Thompson, were indicted on twelve counts charging fraudulent use of the mails.[73] Trial was postponed and the defendants were released on bail pending a complete federal investigation of the case. Garvey's opponents were jubilant over this blow to his racial improvement movement. "Garvey's Bunk Exposed!" screamed a headline in an extra edition of Cyril Briggs's abusive *Crusader;* "Faker who defrauded Negroes with worthless stocks and fake tickets on fake steamships now poses as 'martyr.'"[74]

Lacking seaworthy ships for his bankrupt line and under heavy fire for his alleged mismanagement, Garvey announced sadly, "We have suspended the activities of the Black Star Line."[75] The excuses given for the collapse were many. Garvey took refuge in the prevailing temper of public opinion and claimed that Bolshevist agents had paid for attacks on the line.[76] At the same time he declared that a million-dollar campaign had been waged by the white shipping industry "to boycott and put out of existence the Black Star Line."[77] He charged that certain "Negro Advancement Associations" had "paid men to dismantle our machinery and otherwise damage it so as to bring about the downfall of the movement."[78] Referring to the unfaithfulness and dishonesty of some of his employees,[79] Garvey asked, "What can Marcus Garvey do if men are employed to do their work and they prove to be dishonest and dishonorable in the performance of that work?" It was a fair question, but the obvious answer only emphasized the need of competent and vigilant leadership at the head of the enterprise. "Marcus Garvey is not a navigator," the unhappy Jamaican explained; "he is not a marine engineer; he is not even a good sailor; therefore the individual who would criticize Marcus Garvey for a ship of the Black Star

Line not making a success at sea is a fool." [80] Not all of those who had invested their savings in the sunken Black Star Line were able to see the logic of this equation, however.

FIVE

WEIGHED

IN THE BALANCE

*It is not Garvey who is being weighed in the balance of
the world's judgment, but his race, and particularly his
jealous and unworthy rivals who conspired against him.*
—George Alexander McGuire [1]

Men who are in earnest are not afraid of consequences.
—Marcus Garvey [2]

★ With the arrest and indictment of the four officers of the
Black Star Line there quickly came a new high in the organized opposition to Marcus Garvey and his Negro improvement schemes. Finanical failure, coupled with un-
denied rumors of Garvey's secret negotiations with officials
of the hated Ku Klux Klan, aroused a great deal of bitter
feeling against the Universal Negro Improvement Association and its cocky leader. No doubt a man with less spirit
and determination would have been crushed by the collapse of his business enterprises and the prospect of a possible prison sentence. But Garvey, undismayed by the swift
descent of his fortunes and still firmly convinced of the
righteousness of his cause, calmly set out to salvage what
remained of his Negro movement. The task was not so
formidable as might be expected. An overwhelming majority of the fiercely devoted U.N.I.A. membership still believed implicitly in its martyred leader and accepted un-

questioningly his bitter account of the dishonesty and treachery that had caused the downfall of the Black Star Line.

This is not to say that adversity did not bring a number of important desertions from the U.N.I.A. ranks. A few disappointed Black Star stockholders and disgruntled former U.N.I.A. employees now sought to recover their investment in the sunken line or to collect back salaries. In May, 1922, for example, Garvey was sued for $105, representing the investment in Black Star stock of a former B.S.L. stockholder, Edward Orr. The trial in Bronx superior court revealed part of the sorry history of the Black Star Line. Garvey confessed that the assets of the corporation were nonexistent and that two years of operation had cost more than $600,000, but he denied having overstated the business potentialities of the line in his stock promotional campaigns. The Black Star Line had never paid any dividends and currently owed $200,000 with no assets, holding only a mortgaged interest in two ships, the sunken *Shadyside* and the abandoned *Kanawha.* "It seems to me that you have been preying upon the gullibility of your own people," Judge Jacob Panken told Garvey in summing up his judgment in favor of the plaintiff Orr, "having kept no proper accounts of the money received for investment, being an organization of high finance in which the officers received outrageously high salaries and were permitted to have exorbitant expense accounts for pleasure jaunts throughout the country." The "dupes" who had invested in the Black Star Line were advised to ask for the appointment of a receiver. "You should have taken this $600,000 and built a hospital for colored people in this city instead of purchasing a few old boats," the distressed jurist declared. "There is a form of paranoia which manifests itself in believing oneself to be a great man." [3]

Heaped upon Garvey's mounting pile of business troubles was a series of legal difficulties concerning his domestic life. In December, 1919, he had married his pretty secretary, Amy Ashwood, who had been active in the movement since its early days in Jamaica.[4] The marriage was not a success and during the following year Garvey sought a divorce, though his suit was dropped in April, 1921. In July, 1921, however, Mrs. Garvey sued for a separation on the ground that her husband had been overattentive to his private secretary, Amy Jacques, who had taken over Amy Ashwood's desk when she became Mrs. Garvey.[5] There was something of irony in the fact that Amy Jacques had first come to the United States at the invitation of her girlhood friend, Amy Ashwood, and had now taken her friend's place in Garvey's heart as well as in his office. Mrs. Garvey then left on a trip to England and while she was out of the country, on June 15, 1922, in Kansas City, Missouri, Garvey received an uncontested divorce. This was followed a month later by his marriage to his secretary, Amy Jacques. The first Mrs. Garvey, who had apparently been unaware of any pending divorce action, immediately filed a counter-suit, denying the validity of the Missouri proceedings and naming Amy Jacques as corespondent.[6] The Negro press, always predominantly hostile to Garvey, gave a sympathetic ear to Amy Ashwood's legal battle, and throughout the period of most bitter anti-Garvey agitation colored newspapers played up her lurid charges of cruelty and misconduct.[7] Efforts to nullify the second marriage were unsuccessful, however, and Amy Jacques Garvey remained a devoted wife and loyal co-worker throughout the rest of Garvey's frustrated life.

When the third annual convention of the Universal Negro Improvement Association met in Harlem during the month of August, 1922, the growing number of Garvey op-

ponents united to hold anti-Garvey meetings elsewhere in
the city under the auspices of a group called the Friends of
Negro Freedom. Sparked by Chandler Owen and A. Philip
Randolph, the Negro editors of the radical *Messenger*
magazine, the Friends of Negro Freedom adopted the ve-
hement slogan, "Garvey must go!" At open-air street meetings and Harlem social gatherings the cry was raised for
the immediate deportation of the alien race leader whose
bankrupt schemes had cost American Negroes so dearly.

Speaking to the Friends of Negro Freedom early in
August, William Pickens, field organizer for the National
Association for the Advancement of Colored People and
formerly a Garvey sympathizer, told how he had received
threats from Garveyites after refusing the offer of an honorary award by the U.N.I.A. "We feel that you have done
exemplary work in the cause of Africa," Garvey had written Pickens, "and that your services should be rewarded
and appreciated by those of us on whose shoulders it falls
to take cognizance of the things that are done in the name
of scattered Ethiopia." Pickens' rejection was direct and to
the point. "I cannot feel myself quite bad enough to accept
any honor or alliance with such an organization as the Ku
Klux Klan or the Black Hand Society," he had retorted,
recalling Garvey's rumored deal with the Klan. "You compare the aim of the Ku Klux Klan in America with your aim
in Africa—and if that be true no civilized man can endorse
either one of you." [8] Before his Harlem audience Pickens
charged Garvey with seeking "to get on the right side of the
Ku Klux Klan so he could go and collect money from Southern Negroes." [9]

Similar warnings were expressed by others. Mokete
Manoedi, himself a native of Basutoland, South Africa, informed a street meeting of Garvey foes that African Negroes were "not favorably impressed with the unmitigated

presumption of this man Garvey in electing himself Provisional President of Africa." [10] This unpalatable bit of news so enraged the Garvey supporters in the crowd that the meeting broke up in a fight. Some of the intensity of the emotions aroused by the anti-Garvey controversy may be recaptured in a bitter description of the Jamaican race leader given by Dr. Robert W. Bagnall. In a discourse entitled "The Madness of Marcus Garvey," Bagnall called Garvey "a sheer opportunist and demogogic charlatan." The verbal portrait was in fact a veritable thesaurus of uncomplimentary terms:

A Jamaican Negro of unmixed stock, squat, stocky, fat and sleek, with protruding jaws, and heavy jowls, small bright pig-like eyes and rather bulldog-like face. Boastful, egotistic, tyrannical, intolerant, cunning, shifty, smooth and suave, avaricious; ... gifted at self-advertisement, without shame in self-laudation, ... without regard for veracity, a lover of pomp and tawdry finery and garish display.[11]

Bagnall declared that he opposed Garvey's Back to Africa movement on the grounds that it was "impractical, visionary, and ridiculous," and asserted that "Garvey must go, because like Judas Iscariot, he sold himself for thirty pieces of silver" in order to curry favor with the hated Klan.[12]

Another critic of Garvey's African dream was A. Philip Randolph, who told a Harlem audience scornfully, "people now are fighting for the erection of democracies, not of empires." Randolph doubted that Garvey's black republic would be run along democratic lines, and he emphasized his conviction that Negroes would not want "to be the victims of black despotism any more than white despotism." [13] Randolph's colleague, Chandler Owen, also joined in the attack on the embattled U.N.I.A. leader. When Garvey instituted a libel suit against him for allegedly damaging utterances, Owen challenged Garvey to point out the offending words so that his reinforced speeches might cause the Jamaican to sue "for a million dollars every day next week." [14]

Stung by these damaging attacks, Garvey lashed back furiously at his enemies in the *Negro World.* "Let me tell you somebody is going to be smashed in New York between the 1st and the 31st of August," he stormed. "Any Negro individual or Negro organization ... that thinks it can fight and intimidate the Universal Negro Improvement Association—let you be the National Association for the Advancement of Colored People—let you be Negro socialists—let me tell you, you are preparing for your Waterloo." With a special warning to William Pickens and Chandler Owen, Garvey declared defiantly, "The Universal Negro Improvement Association has no fear of anybody, and when you interfere ... you will take the consequences." [15]

Although the 1922 U.N.I.A. convention was not well attended in spite of herculean efforts of the *Negro World* to recapture the sparkling excitement of the two previous gatherings, Garvey's loyal followers took his warning to heart and used force and intimidation in their attempts to break up the opposition meetings. Often police action was necessary to maintain order in Harlem during the turbulent period of the third Garvey convention. Typical of the temper of loyal Garveyites was the statement of William Sherrill, Baltimore attorney and U.N.I.A. delegate to the League of Nations in 1922. "Black folk as well as white who tamper with the Universal Negro Improvement Association are going to die," Sherrill predicted ominously. "Black men and black women will be free even though the price of freedom is blood." [16]

Shortly after the close of the U.N.I.A. convention, A. Philip Randolph received a small package containing a human hand. Apparently mailed from New Orleans, the grisly parcel also contained a note signed by the Ku Klux Klan which told Randolph bluntly, "If you are not in favor with your own race movement, you can't be with ours." The dread K.K.K. demanded "to see your name in your nigger improvement association as a member, paid up too, in about a week from now," and warned, "be careful . . . or we may have to send your hand to someone else." [17] Randolph and other U.N.I.A. opponents were inclined to believe that the threat had come from a Negro Garveyite rather than from a white Klansman,[18] but Randolph admitted the possibility that "the klan had come to the rescue of its Negro leader, Marcus Garvey." [19] Whatever the motivation, the gruesome incident provided the Garvey attackers with further ammunition.

One of the sternest and most effective critics of Garveyism was also one of its former high priests, James W. H. Eason, the Philadelphia minister who had in 1920 been named Leader of American Negroes. Garvey and Eason quarreled violently during the 1922 convention and at one point the two men almost came to blows on the platform before the delegates in Liberty Hall. Garvey accused Eason of double-crossing him, and the Philadelphian thereupon withdrew from the U.N.I.A. and formed a rival organization called the Universal Negro Alliance.[20] After the break Eason traveled extensively about the country lecturing against Garvey and the U.N.I.A., explaining that he had quit the association over the issue of sending a delegation to the League of Nations to ask for a mandate over certain parts of Africa.[21] Instead of attempting the immediate redemption of Africa, Eason believed the U.N.I.A. should seek to solve the many difficult race problems of the United States. It was rumored that the Philadelphia clergyman would be a key government witness in the forthcoming mail fraud trial of Garvey and the other Black Star officers.

While in New Orleans to address an anti-Garvey meeting, Eason was shot from ambush and murdered. Evidence indicated that two minor officials of the U.N.I.A., "Chief of Police" William Shakespeare and "Patrolman" F. W. Dyer, both Jamaicans, had arrived coincidentally with Eason, and the two were accordingly apprehended and charged with the crime. Police reported that before his death Eason had claimed that Garvey was behind the assassination, but the murdered man did not live long enough to identify the two alleged assailants.[22] Eventually Shakespeare and Dyer were acquitted of any complicity in the Eason murder and the case was dropped.[23] The incident caused a real flurry in the Negro press, however, and gave the Department of Justice an excuse to raid the New Orleans branch of the U.N.I.A. A week after the murder, F.B.I. agents arrested ten local U.N.I.A. officials and claimed to have uncovered "evidence of a nation-wide anarchistic plot."[24] In New York Garvey immediately denied that his organization either was radical or had had anything to do with the killing of Eason,[25] but the growing number of Garvey critics merely winked at each other knowingly and recalled the U.N.I.A leader's excellent reason for wishing Eason out of the way. Whether or not the U.N.I.A. was in any way connected with the murder, the episode certainly was damaging to Garvey and his movement.

☆

On January 15, 1923, less than a week after the Eason shooting, eight prominent American Negroes sent an open letter to Attorney General Harry M. Daugherty protesting against the delay of nearly a year in the trial of Marcus

Garvey and his associates. The signers, Harry H. Pace, Robert S. Abbott, John E. Nail, Dr. Julia P. Coleman, William Pickens, Chandler Owen, Robert W. Bagnall, and George W. Harris, were all respected leaders in their various fields. The "Committee of Eight" condemned Garveyism as a philosophy seeking "to arouse ill-feeling between the races," and it attacked Garvey himself as "an unscrupulous demagogue, who has ceaselessly and assiduously sought to spread among Negroes distrust and hatred of all white people." The U.N.I.A. was alleged to consist "in the main of Negro sharks and ignorant Negro fanatics," and the committee listed in great detail the more obvious defects of the association. Instances of Garvey-inspired violence were cited to show the lawless and dangerous character of the movement. The letter concluded with a plea "that the Attorney General use his full influence completely to disband and extirpate this vicious movement, and that he vigorously and speedily push the government's case against Marcus Garvey for using the mails to defraud." [26]

"Good old darkies," "Uncle Tom Negroes," "wicked maligners," Garvey raged in angry retaliation. He termed the letter to the Attorney General "the greatest bit of treachery and wickedness that any group of Negroes could be capable of," in that it sought to prejudice white America "against fellow Negroes whose only crime has been that of making an effort to improve the condition of the race." The "Committee of Eight" had not only sought to rob Garvey of his good name; its members had "written their names down everlastingly as enemies of their own race." According to the indignant U.N.I.A. president, his assailants were "nearly all Octoroons and Quadroons" or were "married to Octoroons," an indication of their solution of the race problem. One was a "race defamer" whose newspaper published "week after week the grossest scandals against the race"; another was a "real estate shark" who delighted "under the guise of race patriotism, to raise the rent of poor colored people even beyond that of white landlords"; still another was "a hair straightener and face bleacher," whose loyalty to the race was "to get the race to be dissatisfied with itself." In short, the eight critics were nothing but "a bunch of selfish grafters who have been living off the blood of the race and who feel that the Universal Negro Improvement Association has come upon the scene to so change and improve conditions as to make it impossible for them to continue to suck the last drop of blood out of our people." [27]

Whatever the effect of this letter to the Attorney General, the trial of Garvey and his three codefendants finally got under way in mid-May, 1923. The former Black Star executives were defended by separate attorneys, Garvey being represented by Cornelius W. McDougald, one of the ablest Negro lawyers in the country. Even before the selection of a jury, Garvey petitioned for the disqualification of Circuit Judge Julian W. Mack, who had been designated trial judge, on the ground that the jurist's membership in the National Association for the Advancement of Colored People precluded an impartial hearing. Garvey's plea recalled the protest to the Attorney General by the "Committee of Eight," most of whose members were active in the N.A.A.C.P., and noted the vigorous campaign that had been waged against his movement by *Crisis*, the N.A.A.C.P. organ. Garvey therefore believed that Judge Mack "would be unconsciously swayed to the side of the Government" and he respectfully requested the naming of another judge who was not a supporter of "any institution or influence which would assist the prosecution" (Case *A*, 36–53). In denying this motion Judge Mack admitted having contributed to the N.A.A.C.P., but he firmly rejected Garvey's contention that this fact implied personal bias against the defendants. Indeed, his state of mind was "one of extreme friendliness toward the colored people," and he thus would not only endeavor to protect the rights of a Negro defendant but would also "be glad to see one wronging colored people or any other people punished" (Case A, 54–59). Reading through the lengthy trial record today, one must conclude that Judge Mack's conduct was a model of judicial patience and wise impartiality.

After the trial had been in progress only one day, Garvey peremptorily dismissed his Negro attorney and announced that he would thereafter take personal charge of his case. Always fearful of plotting associates, the suspicious U.N.I.A. leader complained that McDougald had not properly cross-examined the first three government witnesses and intimated that the lawyer was part of a general conspiracy to convict his own client. Judge Mack agreed that Garvey had a perfect right to present his own case but warned that he would be allowed no special privileges because he was a layman and that the trial would nevertheless "be tried in the proper way and with the same expedition" as under normal circumstances (Case A, 184–86). As it turned out, however, the judge tolerantly gave the inexperienced Garvey wide latitude during the course of the trial and allowed him to drag out the proceedings interminably. Garvey apparently had read some law while he was in England in 1912, and, always the inveterate showman, he could not resist this golden opportunity to display his legal talents before a white jury and a courtroom crowded with admiring Negro spectators.

To bolster the government's charge that the four Black Star directors had knowingly used the mails to defraud, prosecutor Maxwell S. Mattuck called some thirty witnesses, many of them former Black Star employees and stockholders, and introduced into the record an impressive array of exhibits—B.S.L. account and minute books, damaging articles in the *Negro World,* and pertinent correspondence. A complete picture of the business activities of the ill-fated Black Star Line was at last brought to light. Much of the testimony revealed the extremely informal system of bookkeeping used in the various Garvey enterprises. It was soon apparent that the defendants had only the barest knowledge of high finance and that Garvey had naïvely assumed that funds collected for one U.N.I.A. project could be freely used for any phase of the race redemption program. Captains Joshua Cockbourne and Adrian Richardson of the steamers *Yarmouth* and *Kanawha* gave mournful accounts of the many troubles attending their unhappy voyages under the Black Star flag (Case A, 292–423, 433–570). A government accountant testified that for the first year of the Black Star Line's existence no ledger had been kept and that he therefore had to reconstruct a new financial record piecemeal in order to get a true analysis of the corporation's affairs. His picture of Black Star finances was as impressive as it was damning. During its brief history the line had sold 155,510 shares of stock to nearly 40,000 Negroes. Altogether it had taken in more than three-quarters of a million dollars. Yet in disbursing a total of $387,251.89 for dubious capital assets and incurring an operating deficit of $476,169.58, the hapless Black Star directors had managed in less than three years completely to dissipate their capital and bankrupt the company. The sad state of Black Star affairs was graphically emphasized by the B.S.L. cash balance as of January 5, 1922—$31.12 (Case A, 988–96, 1028–70, 2648–58).

But withal, the government's case rested upon the weak assumption that Garvey and his codefendants had knowingly and with criminal intent used the mails to promote the sale of Black Star stock after they were aware that the financial condition of the line was hopeless. Here the evidence was meager. There was nothing to indicate that the Black Star Line had been formed for anything other than what it purported to be, a Negro improvement venture. Prosecutor Mattuck was unable to get his government accountants to testify that Garvey and the other Black Star directors had been granted lavish salaries or exorbitant expense accounts (Case A, 1053, 1061–62). Indeed, the cost of stock promotion had amounted to less than 13 per cent, not an unreasonably high figure (Case A, 1057–58). Clearly the collapse of the corporation could be attributed chiefly to poor judgment in the purchase and maintenance of the decrepit Black Star fleet, and here the real criminals were the white culprits who had unloaded the rusty hulks on unsuspecting and inexperienced Negroes. Garvey managed to introduce enough evidence of dishonesty and questionable maneuvering on the part of some of his subordinates, moreover, to raise serious doubts as to the reliability of some of the key government witnesses. The heart of the government's case was a series of highly optimistic and exaggerated Black Star stock promotional circulars that had allegedly been mailed to prospective subscribers. The prosecution produced a B.S.L. envelope that had been mailed to a Harlem Negro on December 13, 1920; but the recipient, one Benny Dancy, was unable to recall clearly what, if anything, the envelope in question had contained. His testimony was halting, uncertain, and riddled with inconsistencies and frightened confusion (Case A, 860–65, 2626).

Although the evidence against him was admittedly weak, Garvey's bumptious activities in the courtroom were such as to prejudice him in the eyes of any jury, white or black. He arrogantly lectured and harangued hostile witnesses, invariably took exception to every ruling from the bench, and carried his examination down obscure paths far removed from the subject at hand. Unquestionably his belligerent efforts to vindicate himself and his entire race movement, even those aspects not on trial, doubled the length of the proceedings, a fact not calculated to impress favorably a jury of restless businessmen.

After Garvey had repeatedly objected to every adverse ruling, Judge Mack stated for the record that to save time he would allow the unhappy lawyer-defendant an automatic exception to all future rulings (Case A, 1505–6). Garvey's cross-examinations were frequently irrelevant to the point at issue. Once he got a reluctant Negro witness to admit he was married to a white woman, and then asked sharply: "You beat her up often, don't you?" (Case A, 795). Another time, after Orlando Thompson had testified to signing a certain B.S.L. contract, Garvey asked the former Black Star vice president if he could write. "Objection sustained," rebuked the tired judge. "Let's go on. Of course he can write" (Case A, 1867). Several times Judge Mack jokingly remarked that he was having to conduct a regular law school for Garvey's benefit,[28] but when he urged the self-assured Jamaican to seek legal advice Garvey retorted superciliously: "The defendant bows, your Honor, and feels confident of his own ability to protect his own constitutional rights" (Case A, 1421). Actually, Garvey's conceit and inexperience cost him dearly. In cross-examining Adrian Richardson, for example, he permitted the ex-captain of the *Kanawha* to testify that Garvey had been improper in his relations with his unmarried secretary while a passenger on the *Kanawha*, a damaging bit of irrelevancy that no amount of later denials by the outraged B.S.L. president could quite erase (Case A, 552–66). On another occasion Garvey called on his own behalf a character witness who could only testify that the U.N.I.A. leader's reputation for truth and veracity was "doubtful" (Case A, 2020).

Toward the close of the trial Garvey wisely began to rely on advice and counsel from an experienced white lawyer, Armin Kohn. At once there was a noticeable improvement in the quality of his defense. Indeed, Garvey's most effective moments were when he finally took the stand and under Kohn's shrewd and searching questioning told the story of his shattered hopes for a great Negro steamship line to bring badly needed self-respect and commercial opportunity to his downtrodden people. Even the bitterly hostile Chicago *Defender* was moved to admit that many of Garvey's objectives were highly praiseworthy. "At times even a degree of admiration must be felt at the nerve of the man in shattering court customs," a *Defender* reporter commented.[29] Garvey's address to the jury at the end of the trial was a moving plea to judge the Black Star Line on what it sought to do for the Negro race. "We had no monetary considerations or reward before us, but the good we could do for our race, for this and succeeding generations," he declared with quiet dignity. "You will say it was bad business. But, gentlemen, there is something spiritual beside business." "I ask no mercy," Garvey concluded. "I ask no sympathy. I ask but for justice." [30]

In spite of Garvey's early protest that Judge Mack was prejudiced against the defendants by virtue of his membership in the N.A.A.C.P., the *Negro World* asserted that his charge to the jury was "a masterpiece of fairness and impartiality." The Garvey *Negro Times* reported in banner headlines, "Judge Mack charges the jury in an able and impartial way," and announced, "Garvey, man of destiny, calmly awaits verdict." [31] The result was not, however, the vindication that the members of the Universal Negro Improvement Association so eagerly expected. After deliberating six hours and receiving further instructions from Judge Mack, the jury reported that it had found Garvey guilty as charged. Specifically, Garvey was guilty on one count of having caused promotional material to be sent through the mails to Benny Dancy, who had testified with some confusion to having received such matter before he purchased his fifty-three shares of Black Star stock. The verdict was somewhat strange in that the other three Black Star defendants were acquitted of any complicity in the crime. Garvey's devoted followers received a further blow, moreover, when several days later Judge Mack indicated his full agreement with the verdict and sentenced the U.N.I.A. leader to pay a fine of $1,000 and to serve the maximum term of five years in prison. Garvey's attorneys immediately laid plans to appeal the case and the convicted Black Star president was remanded to Tombs Prison in New York until his supporters arranged his release on September 10, 1923, on $25,000 bail.[32]

For the most part, the long-critical Negro press applauded the verdict against Garvey. Warning its readers "never to buy any stock that is being peddled," the Chicago *Defender* emphasized that the conviction demonstrated the gullibility of many Negroes when exploited by a cunning promoter.[33] The New York *Age* reviewed Garvey's *opéra bouffe* performance in court and concluded that he was "a self-convicted criminal." [34] "For the time being at least, the most promising menace the race has had in recent years is removed," rejoiced the New York *Amsterdam News*. "Marcus Garvey is a gigantic blunderer whose tactics are compelled to fail and whose wisdom is exceeded by his foolhardiness." [35] Always a ready wit, George S. Schuyler, the anti-Garvey columnist in the *Messenger* magazine, noted that the U.N.I.A.'s vaunted membership of several million was "mighty slow getting that $25,000 [bail] together," and scoffed at a report that Garvey would jump his bond. "As if you could run that guy away from this gravy-train!" chuckled Schuyler. "It is to laugh!" [36]

In his last speech at Liberty Hall before entering Tombs Prison to await the outcome of his appeal, Garvey urged his devoted U.N.I.A. followers to continue their march "forward to the redemption of a great country and the re-establishment of a greater government." The Universal Negro Improvement Association would continue the fight for African redemption and the commercial and spiritual development of the race. "We have only started; we are just on our way," Garvey told the faithful; "we have just made the first lap in the great race for existence, and for a place in the political and economic sun of men." White men were making "a tremendous and terrible mistake" if they thought they could "stamp out the souls of 400,000,000 black men," Garvey warned. "The world is crazy and foolish if they think that they can destroy the principles, the ideals of the Universal Negro Improvement Association." [37] While awaiting for his supporters to arrange his release on bail, Garvey commended the care of his wife to the loyal U.N.I.A. membership. "My work is just begun," he informed the black world, "and as I lay down my life for the cause of my people, so do I feel that succeeding generations shall be inspired by the sacrifice that I made for the rehabilitation of our race." [38]

At first disorganized and filled with dark dismay at the loss of its inspiriting leader, the Universal Negro Improvement Association soon rallied with a series of protest meetings on Garvey's behalf. Gradually the feeling began to grow among Negroes that Marcus Garvey was the hapless victim of white justice and this tended to enhance his prestige both in the United States and abroad. [39] Because of the

protracted delay in securing Garvey's release on bail, there
was no annual U.N.I.A. convention in 1923. Instead the
association concentrated on obtaining Garvey's freedom
and attempted to consolidate its loyal membership. From
his prison cell the martyred Garvey kept in close touch with
the movement, sending frequent messages of inspiration
and hope. And in spite of a series of annoying lawsuits for
back salaries brought by a few dissident ex-officials of the
movement,[40] the U.N.I.A. remained largely intact, its dedicated membership eagerly expectant for Garvey's leadership upon his return. When in September Garvey's release
was finally obtained, Liberty Hall was the scene of wild rejoicing. In a home-coming address Garvey emphasized the
anomaly of his conviction: he had been indicted for conspiracy but had been the only defendant convicted; others
had had far more to do with the actual selling of Black
Star stock, yet he alone was guilty of fraud; the imposition
of the maximum sentence, rarely resorted to in mail fraud
cases, illustrated the impossibility of a Negro's ever hoping
to get a square deal from white courts. "I was convicted,
not because any one was defrauded in the temporary failure of the Black Star Line brought about by others," Garvey asserted, "but because I represented, even as I do now,
a movement for the real emancipation of my race." Defiantly, the confident U.N.I.A. president promised to appeal his case "to the highest courts in the land, and from
there to the bar of international public opinion." "Even
though I go to jail because of prejudice," he warned, "I
will have left behind for our generations a record of injustice that will be our guide in the future rise of Ethiopia's
glory." [41]

☆

If Garvey's many opponents thought that his conviction
would mean the end of the cocky little Jamaican and his

SPECIAL EDITION | **Negro ☉ Times** | SPECIAL EDITION

VOL. 1 NO. 149   DAILY   NEW YORK, MONDAY, JUNE 18, 1923   FIVE CENTS

Garvey, Man of Destiny, Calmly Awaits Verdict

Judge Mack Charges The Jury In an Able and Impartial Way

JURY AT HALF PAST FIVE WAS STILL OUT CONSIDERING THEIR VERDICT

THE HEARING OF THE HISTORIC CASE AGAINST MARCUS GARVEY AND HIS CO-DEFENDANTS HAS COME TO AN END

THE CONCENSUS OF OPINION UP TO THE TIME OF GOING TO PRESS WAS AN ACQUITTAL OR JURY NOT AGREEING

The Indispensable Weekly
The Voice of the Awaked Negro

Negro World

Reaching the Mass of Negroes
The Best Advertising Medium

A Newspaper Devoted Solely to the Interests of the Negro Race

VOL. XI. No. 24   NEW YORK, SATURDAY, JANUARY 28, 1922   PRICE: FIVE CENTS IN GREATER NEW YORK

JUDAS ISCARIOTS WAGE COWARDLY WARFARE AGAINST LEADER OF U. N. I. A.

Like Martin Luther, George Washington and Eamon De Valera, Hon. Marcus Garvey Is a "Rebel," Willing to Die, if Need Be, for the Vindication of Ethiopia's Cause

---

The Indispensable Weekly
The Voice of the Awakened Negro—The Peerless Paper

Guaranteed Circulation 50,000
Reaching the Mass of Negroes Throughout the World

Negro World

ONE GOD! ONE AIM, ONE DESTINY

A Newspaper Devoted Solely to the Interests of the Negro Race

VOL. IX. No. 1   NEW YORK, SATURDAY, AUGUST 21, 1920   PRICE: THREE CENTS IN GREATER NEW YORK

THE DECLARATION OF RIGHTS READ IN LIBERTY HALL BEFORE THOUSANDS AMIDST TUMULTUOUS APPLAUSE

CRACKERS BEGIN WORK IN LIBERIA

NEGROES SHOULD ENFORCE THE PRINCIPLE OF AFRICA FOR AFRICANS AT HOME AND ABROAD

Voices of the Universal Negro Improvement Association

Garvey being taken by federal marshals to the Tombs Prison, New York

movement, they were sadly mistaken. While awaiting the outcome of his appeal, in 1924 Garvey organized still another maritime venture, the Black Cross Navigation and Trading Company. Patterned after the defunct Black Star Line, this corporation was chartered to engage in trade between the various Negro areas of the world, and Garvey intended that its vessels would also be used to carry American Negro colonists to Africa. On June 3, 1924, the irrepressible Garvey wired the chairman of the United States Shipping Board in Washington: "I am asking for appointment to see you in Washington on Friday 6th June re ships Presidents Arthur and Filmore and Potomac." [42] A week later the Black Cross Navigation and Trading Company submitted a firm offer for the purchase of the steamship *Susquehanna*, promising to pay the Shipping Board a total of $140,000 by August 30, 1924.[43] Privately an official of the Board admitted that this price was "an acceptable figure," but he warned: "The Company has filed firm offer with the usual deposit and doubtless could complete the payment of 10%, but would likely depend upon further stock subscriptions for the payment of the balance and if these were unsuccessful or fraudulent criticism might be directed at the Shipping Board." [44] Still holding the Black Star Line's $22,500 deposit on the S.S. *Orion*, and with the memory of its previous fruitless dealings with the earlier Negro line painfully fresh, the Shipping Board declined to do business with Garvey's new steamship corporation.

Undaunted by the governmental rebuff, Garvey turned to the Panama Railroad Company and from it purchased the *General G. W. Goethals*, a larger and more attractive vessel than the ill-fated *Yarmouth*. Obtained for a reputed $100,000 and refitted for an additional $60,000, the new ship was a much sounder purchase than any of the vessels of the old Black Star fleet.[45] Garvey had learned from dis-

aster. The U.N.I.A. leader proudly announced that the new
ship would be rechristened the *Booker T. Washington* and
said that its purchase had been made possible through the
sale of Black Cross stock to 3,600 loyal members of the association.[46] To the faithful, Garvey's surprising coup seemed
only one further proof of his wisdom and invincibility; even
his detractors were stunned by the sudden turn in his fortunes. A perennial Garvey critic could only comment bitterly: "No one objects to Mr. Garvey owning ships or going
back to Africa. American colored people do object to his
taking the name of their greatest man as a title to his com-
edy. The name of his vessel ought to be the 'Marcus A.
Garvey.' Booker T. Washington was a SUCCESS." [47]

The new Black Cross flagship was the hit of the
U.N.I.A.'s 1924 convention. The unhappy Chicago *Defender* reported that some five thousand admiring Garveyites had paid a fee of fifty cents to visit the ship on the
occasion of its presentation to the association.[48] "Marcus
Garvey thrives on adversity," admitted the amazed New
York *Amsterdam News.* "Today finds him the leading figure in a convention which is attracting more attention than
any other gathering of Negroes in modern history." [49] It
was obvious that the determined little West Indian was
still a force to be reckoned with in the colored world.

Although the *General G. W. Goethals* was both larger
and in much better condition than any of Garvey's earlier
ships, its lone voyage under the Black Cross flag followed
the old familiar pattern. Before the vessel left New York on
its first run to the West Indies late in January, 1925, Garvey
required his white captain, Jacob R. Hiorth, to promise in
writing not to "allow any expenses of any kind or bills to be
charged up against said ship without first acquainting and
getting the approval of the owners." [50] There was to be, it

seemed, no repetition of the disastrously expensive *Kana-wha* voyage. Yet Garvey expected the *General Goethals* to pay its way, and he sent along G. Emonei Carter, Secretary General of the U.N.I.A., to raise expense money through stock sales in the various ports of call.

At Havana the voyage was delayed when vigilant creditors made an unsuccessful attempt to attach the ship for old Black Star debts. The *General Goethals* reached Kingston on February 10, but Jamaicans showed little interest in the vessel and Carter could not collect enough money to cover port expenses. During the next month, according to the American consul at Kingston, the ship's passengers and crew underwent experiences that could only be described as "of a very turbulent character." Discipline, never a strong feature of life aboard a Garvey ship, soon collapsed as relations between the white officers and black passengers and crew grew more strained. The first assistant engineer jumped ship and went home, and another crew member decided to become a passenger. There were several cases of assault and violence, and once the captain had to appeal to shore authorities for protection. "Hardly a day passed," the American consul reported, "that I was not called upon to conciliate various factions and adjust their numerous wranglings and contentions."[51] On March 9, Captain Hiorth and the other white officers sought unsuccessfully to be allowed to resign their commands, declaring that the passengers and crew were "absolutely in control" of the ship.[52] Receipt of some $3,800 from New York finally enabled the *General Goethals* to weigh anchor for Colon, Panama, where it again was forced to tie up for lack of funds, its officers anxious to quit ship and its crew ready to desert. After the ship had stayed more than a month at Colon, the New York office cabled enough money to buy coal and provisions for a trip back to Kingston, but there is no record that the *General Goethals,* or *Booker T. Washington,* ever managed to return home to New York.[53]

☆

During its 1924 convention the Universal Negro Improvement Association gave final shape to its colonization program for Africa, a project that had long been under active consideration by the organization. As early as 1920 Garvey had sent a U.N.I.A. delegation to Liberia to confer with the government of the Negro republic over the possibility of transferring the headquarters of the movement to that country. Elie Garcia, head of the delegation, returned with the assurance of the Liberian government that it would "afford the association every facility legally possible in effectuating in Liberia its industrial, agricultural, and business projects." [54] Its disordered finances in recurrent crisis, Liberia was eager to accept economic aid from American Negroes. Upon his return to the United States in August, 1920, delegate Garcia submitted a report summing up his reactions to development possibilities in the African republic. Garcia was enthusiastic about the potentialities of Liberia's rich natural resources, but he denounced in vigorous terms the ruling aristocracy, which he called "the most despicable element in Liberia." He warned that the U.N.I.A. would have to play down its intention to emancipate the native tribes, at least until the movement was well established in Liberia. "As it is the Americo-Liberians are using the natives as slaves," he declared, "and human chattel slavery still exists there." [55] In this respect Garcia's reaction paralleled closely a confidential report on Liberian conditions made for the American State Department at this time.[56] In order to work with the existing Liberian government, however, Garvey decided to keep the damning Garcia report secret.

Late in 1920 Garvey launched a drive for a $2,000,000 construction loan to rehabilitate Liberia. "The purpose of this loan," he told U.N.I.A. members, "is to start construction work in Liberia, where colleges, universities, industrial plants and railroad tracks will be erected; where men will be sent to make roads, and where artisans and craftsmen will be sent to develop industries." [57] At the 1920 convention Gabriel Johnson, the mayor of Monrovia, Liberia, had been named Supreme Potentate of the U.N.I.A. In January, 1921, Johnson obtained a charter of incorporation for a local Universal Negro Improvement Association from the Liberian legislature.[58] The next month Garvey sent out a group of American Negro experts to staff what amounted to a U.N.I.A. legation in Monrovia. The party included a surveyor, a pharmacist, an agriculturalist, and a builder, and Garvey wrote Johnson that the group was to "start work immediately—putting up new buildings and starting farms, etc." [59] On March 22, Potentate Johnson and two other U.N.I.A. representatives conferred with Acting President Edwin J. Barclay and the Liberian Cabinet regarding the possibility of obtaining sites for a future U.N.I.A. colonization movement. President Barclay told the U.N.I.A. officials that the Liberian government would "be glad to have your Association occupy . . . certain settlements already laid out," but he cautioned against too much publicity for the project:

I must admit that the British and French have enquired from our representatives in America about it and have asked definite questions on the attitude of the Liberian Government towards the Universal Negro Improvement Association. . . . But it is not always advisable nor politic to openly expose our secret intentions—our secret thoughts. That is the way we do—or rather don't do—in Liberia. We don't tell them what we think; we only tell them what we like them to hear—what, in fact, they like to hear.... The Government has felt that the soft pedal should be placed on this side.[60]

By the time of its second annual convention in August, 1921, the U.N.I.A. had raised $137,458 for the construction loan; and although most of this money had unwisely been used to bail out the Black Star Line and other ailing U.N.I.A. enterprises, Garvey had purchased a $4,440 saw-mill intended for use in Liberia (Case A, 2335–40). After the convention Garvey organized the African Redemption Fund to raise money for the fight to free Africa. Apparently not much of this money reached the U.N.I.A. mission in Liberia, however, for as early as April, 1921, only a little more than a month after his arrival, Garvey's legation secretary was cabling frantically in code: "We are entirely without money. Operations compelled to stop." [61] Internal bickering, which even culminated in a murder, and a chronic shortage of funds continued to plague the U.N.I.A. representatives in Liberia until by the summer of 1921 the initial high morale had hit bottom. "I frankly could not advise our people coming out here under present conditions," one member of the party declared flatly.[62]

Nevertheless Garvey continued to make plans for the colonization program and, after his release on bond following his conviction on the mail fraud charge, the U.N.I.A. leader redoubled his activities on behalf of the Negro motherland. Another group of U.N.I.A. delegates and experts was sent to Liberia in December, 1923, to complete the final preparations for what Garvey promised would be a planned repatriation of "between twenty and thirty thousand families in the first two years, starting . . . September, 1924." [63] As before, the U.N.I.A. mission was warmly welcomed by the Liberian government and received detailed suggestions from a local advisory committee appointed by the Liberian president, Charles D. B. King. When the group returned to the United States in March, 1924, its members informed Garvey that the project had the complete approval of the Liberian government.[64] "I am glad to learn that you are busy working out our Plan and that you hope to dispatch your first colonists in September," wrote Chief Justice James J. Dossen of the Liberian Supreme Court to Garvey in May, 1924. "We shall stand ready to cooperate with you on this side, in putting over the enterprise successfully." [65]

Garvey's African colonization project aroused fully as much opposition at home and abroad, however, as did his other controversial schemes. A native of Nigeria, West Africa, told a Chicago audience that African Negroes were "prepared to fight this 'free Africa movement' to a finish." [66] One of the members of the first U.N.I.A. party of experts to Liberia complained bitterly that he was stranded in Africa without funds to return home and warned: "This movement is not doing the right thing; their speech is all right, but their business is far from what it should be." [67] The Liberian government itself seemed to be divided over the question of admitting large numbers of American Negro colonists under U.N.I.A. sponsorship. "The Marcus Garvey movement, especially in its contemplated political manifestation in Africa," declared Liberian Secretary of State Edwin Barclay to an anti-Garvey American correspondent in 1921, "does not meet with the endorsement of the Liberian government, nor is it likely that the country will be exploited by him without regard to the decision of the Liberian government." [68] Apparently Barclay was carrying out his own good advice of telling them only what they like to hear! Blaise Diagne, a Senegalese member of the French Chamber of Deputies, warned Garvey that French colonial Negroes would not support his African program. "We French natives wish to remain French, since France has given us every liberty and since she has unreservedly accepted us upon the same basis as her own European children," declared this loyal black defender of French colonialism. "None of us aspires to see French Africa delivered exclusively to the Africans as is demanded, though without any authority, by the American Negroes at the head of whom you have placed yourself." [69]

As for American Negroes, it is to be doubted whether many of them ever seriously entertained the idea of a return to the African homeland. However bad conditions might be in the United States, there was a general realization by Negro Americans that America still offered them the best hope of advancement in a world beset with racial prejudice and intolerance. Like their Jewish counterparts, most American Negroes would watch with eager interest the building of a free Negro Zionist state in Africa. They could be counted upon for generous financial support and enthusiastic moral encouragement. But only a very few would be ready to undertake the hard and thankless pioneer work needed to create a Black Israel in the African jungle. Actor Charles Gilpin no doubt spoke for many other Negro Americans when he demanded to know how he could go "back" to a place where he had never been.[70] "What has the American Negro to gain by going to Africa?" asked the Chicago *Defender* editorially. "It might be interesting to count noses and see just how many there are among us who hail from Africa . . . and yet we hear much about 'going back home,' about having a country of our own where we can salaam to a high muck-a-muck of our own." [71]

In June, 1924, Garvey dispatched a final group of U.N.I.A. technical experts to lay out and construct a series of four camps at Cape Palmas, Liberia, to house the American colonists who were scheduled to start arriving the following October. In July the U.N.I.A. shipped the first consignment of materials and machinery worth $50,000 that Garvey had ordered for the Liberian colonization project.[72] But before this shipment arrived in Liberia, it was attached on complaint of the shipping company, which alleged that the U.N.I.A. had failed to make full payment for the goods. Held in bond in the Cape Palmas customs warehouse until the matter was settled, the shipment was eventually confiscated by the Liberian customs service to cover storage charges.[73] The U.N.I.A. experts received a similarly cold welcome, for on June 30 the Liberian government had unexpectedly warned all steamship companies that "no members of the movement known as the Garvey movement" would be permitted to land in the black republic and that any shipping company that attempted to evade this prohibition against Garveyites would be "required to transport them out of the Country." [74] The now hostile Liberians were as good as their word; and when the U.N.I.A. technical experts arrived, they were ignominiously seized and held for immediate deportation.[75]

Back in the United States Ernest Lyon, the Liberian consul general in Baltimore, announced: "I am authorized to say that no person or persons leaving the United States under the auspices of the Garvey movement will be allowed to land in the Republic of Liberia." [76] Lyon anxiously persuaded the American State Department to give indirect support to the Liberian ban in an off-the-record briefing for newspaper reporters criticizing the Garvey colonization scheme.[77] The Liberian government completed the unexpected show of animosity with a diplomatic note to the United States declaring that the Negro republic was "irrevocably opposed both in principle and fact to the incendiary policy of the Universal Negro Improvement Association, headed by Marcus Garvey." [78] The *Liberian News,* believed to reflect official government views, explained that while Liberia was not opposed to immigration as such, Garveyism might tend "to throttle us if we espouse it." France and Britain were eyeing Liberia hungrily, the *News* asserted, and working with Garvey might furnish "the required pretext for the partition of our country." It developed that Liberian officials had got hold of the secret Garcia report of 1920, which "gave a clear picture of the revolutionary purposes of the U.N.I.A. in Liberia." [79] In his address on the state of the Liberian nation in January, 1925, President C. D. B. King declared that it had been necessary "to take such concrete and effective steps as would show to our friendly territorial neighbors and the world at large, that Liberia was not in any way associated or in sympathy with any movement, no matter from what sources arising, which tends to intensify racial feelings of hatred and ill will." [80]

Meeting at its fourth annual convention, the Universal Negro Improvement Association responded to this bitter blow with a lengthy appeal to the Liberian legislature and a monster petition to President Calvin Coolidge of the United States, but for all practical purposes the Back to Africa movement died with this refusal of the Liberian Republic to get behind the colonization scheme. Garvey denounced President King as a race traitor who had "terrorized and threatened the members of his own Government" in order to foil the U.N.I.A. project. He blamed his old enemy Dr. W. E. B. DuBois, who was visiting Liberia at this time as the American representative to the presidential inauguration, for the collapse of the venture, charging that DuBois had sabotaged the work of the Garvey association in order to further his own Pan African movement. [81] Later Garvey's almost pathological hatred of DuBois, whom he called "purely and simply a white man's nigger," led him to accuse the light-skinned N.A.A.C.P. leader of being the archvillain responsible for the Garvey failures in America.[82]

The bitterly disappointed Garvey also intimated that certain European powers were behind the effort to keep his movement out of Africa.[83] Certainly the British and French had good reason to fear the impact of Garvey's African nationalism upon their colonies. Secretary of State Hughes informed President Coolidge that the radical U.N.I.A. propaganda in Liberia "immediately caused protests on the part of the officials of adjoining French and British colonies." As a consequence, Hughes reported, the Liberians had a "real fear" of being absorbed "if this kind of talk is permitted." [84] When President King paid an official visit to the British colony of Sierra Leone shortly after announcing the ban on Garveyism, he received a warm demonstration of welcome. The British sent the *H.M.S. Dublin* to take the Liberian chief executive to Freetown, and at a state banquet the royal governor of the colony applauded his guest's "courage" and "statesmanship" in "slamming the door on spurious patriots from across the Atlantic, men who sought to make Liberia a focus for racial animosity in this continent." [85] Garvey charged that President King was also honored by the grateful French for his repudiation of the threat to colonialism, being named a Cavalier of the French Legion of Honor.[86]

Although it is difficult to determine the degree to which the European colonial governments were behind the Liberian rebuff to Garvey's African plans,* there is little doubt that King's action was widely and gratefully ap-

---

* While resident in England in 1950–51 I made several determined efforts to investigate the records of the British Colonial Office on the subject of

proved. A British periodical devoted to African affairs later commended President King for putting "his foot down very firmly on such misguided movements for the people of his own race, as that sponsored in the United States by Marcus Garvey and other agitators." [87] Soon after repudiating the U.N.I.A. colonization program, Liberia negotiated an agreement with the Firestone Rubber Company leasing some of the erstwhile Garvey lands to the American firm for the purpose of rubber cultivation.[88] "Again the Negro has defeated himself," Garvey noted sadly, "but his spirit is not dead." [89]

Also at the 1924 convention the irrepressible Garvey branched out with yet another U.N.I.A. venture, the Negro Political Union, designed to "consolidate the political forces of the Negro through which the race will express its political opinion." [90] This represented a rather sharp change in direction for the movement, for Garvey had heretofore tended to ignore domestic political matters in favor of the more important missions of redeeming Africa and building Negro commercial enterprises. With his customary vigor Garvey pushed the activity of the Negro Political Union in the 1924 American elections, issuing a nationwide list of approved candidates and coming out strongly in support of Calvin Coolidge, the Republican nominee for president. In New York Garvey opposed the Negro candidate for Congress from the Harlem district, Dr. Charles H. Roberts, and instead threw the support of the union to the white Tammany nominee. One shocked colored editor termed this action "silly, inane, foolish,

Garvey's influence and activities in the British African colonies. While I was generously permitted to use its excellent library on African matters, for reasons that are perhaps understandably bound up with the current African crisis, the Colonial Office declined to depart from its established policy of maintaining inviolate its archives for the period since 1902, childish, and asinine," and called Garvey "the worst menace the Negro has ever had in America." [91] In Chicago, however, the union gave its support to the Negro candidate, who later admitted that the Garveyites had "worked like Trojans" and had been "a material factor" in the campaign.[92]

☆

Regardless of these renewed efforts to perfect an organization embracing the Negroes of the world, time was fast running out for Marcus Garvey, the pudgy black Jamaican whose appealing dreams and persuasive words had caused such a tremendous stir in the Negro world. The 1924 U.N.I.A. convention had scarcely begun its meetings when a federal grand jury returned an indictment against Garvey for perjury and income tax evasion, charging that he had falsely reported an income of only $4,000 for 1921, a period when he was reputedly receiving a salary of $10,000 for his leadership of the movement. Garvey's followers quickly secured his release on $2,500 bail, but the action had a decidedly chilling effect on the convention proceedings.[93] The timing of this arrest seemed to indicate that the government was determined to harass and embarrass the little Jamaican and his Negro movement, for there was no evidence that Garvey had ever drawn the full $10,000 salary voted him as Provisional President of Africa and President General of the U.N.I.A. by the 1920 convention. Indeed, at the Black Star trial in 1923 a government accountant had testified that Garvey was paid $1,175 in 1919 and $5,168 in 1920 for his work as president of the steamship corporation, but that he had received "not a penny" of B.S.L. money in 1921 (Case A, 1053). Years later, after Garvey had been deported from the United States, the government abandoned its income tax evasion case and ordered the charges against the U.N.I.A. leader nol-prossed.[94]

On February 2, 1925, Garvey's appeal of his mail fraud conviction was rejected by the United States Circuit Court of Appeals. "It may be true that Garvey fancied himself a Moses, if not a Messiah; that he deemed himself a man with a message to deliver, and believed that he needed ships for the deliverance of his people," declared Judge Charles M. Hough, speaking for himself and Judges Henry Wade Rogers and Learned Hand; "but with this assumed, it remains true that if his gospel consisted in part of exhortations to buy worthless stock, accompanied by deceivingly false statements as to the worth thereof, he was guilty of a scheme or artifice to defraud." The court refused to accept the contention of Garvey's white attorneys, George Gordon Battle and Isaac H. Levy, that the conviction should be thrown out because the government had failed to prove that Benny Dancy had actually received Black Star promotional circulars through the mail. "It is a reasonable inference that men regularly sending out circulars in envelopes do not send out empty envelopes," said Judge Hough drily. "Judgment affirmed." [95]

Although Garvey was in Detroit on U.N.I.A. business when the Circuit Court handed down its adverse decision, he immediately returned to New York to surrender to the federal marshals, who, taking no chances, seized him when his train reached the 125th Street Station. Garvey's lawyers immediately prepared an appeal to the United States Supreme Court for a writ of certiorari, but on March 23 the high court refused to review the case.[96] Meanwhile, on February 8, the stocky black man from Jamaica who claimed to voice the secret thoughts of millions of Negroes had passed behind the grey walls of Atlanta penitentiary to begin a new life. "The Tiger," as Garvey had been called by the zealous government prosecutor during the trial, had been caged at last.

The bulk of the Negro press approved of this ignominious climax to Garvey's meteoric career, but even his most bitter foes tempered their rejoicing with an uneasy acknowledgment of the U.N.I.A. founder's place in race history. In an editorial entitled "Garvey vs. Garvey," the New York *Amsterdam News* decided that Garvey's conviction was largely the result of his own bungled handling of his defense, rather than any conspiracy by his enemies. "His tenacity, his nerve, his powers of oratory and his ability to hold his following were sufficient to defeat the purposes of all his enemies put together," declared the Harlem weekly, "but when Marcus Garvey added his strength to that of his enemies, he sealed his doom." [97] "Let no Negro take unto himself credit for this downfall," agreed the *Spokesman* magazine. "Garvey defeated Garvey." [98] Even George S. Schuyler, whose keen barbed shafts had so often drawn U.N.I.A. blood, could do no more than suggest that the annual prison show at Atlanta was certain to be a success now that "America's greatest comedian" was to be a reluctant performer.[99]

"Garvey is a Negro, but even a Negro is entitled to have the truth told about him," said the New York *Evening Bulletin,* a white daily, on February 7, 1925. "He did many strange things, it is true, but he performed many fine acts, too. . . . Had the man been given half a fair deal, his financial schemes might have been successful and he might have been able to avoid the unfortunate disasters which led him into the courts and brought punishment upon him." [100] Another white newspaper, the Buffalo *Evening Times,* also questioned whether justice had been done in Garvey's case, asserting, "There is still something that is not pleasant about this whole business." Noting regretfully that many white men who were greater offenders had received lighter sentences or no punishment whatever for crimes similar to

Garvey's, the *Times* observed: "Intent is the essence of a crime. This man's entire proceedings have a certain consistency with the possible assumption of great dreams and visions for his race." [101] Even the New York *News*, a Harlem paper long critical of Garvey and his prógram, admitted that the U.N.I.A. leader had "awakened the race consciousness and race pride of the masses of Africans everywhere as no man ever did ... save Booker T. Washington." "He made them think, he made them cooperate, he organized and marshalled their forces," said a *News* editorial. "For these things his service will be historic and epoch-making." [102] Yet perhaps the best farewell tribute to Garvey, and one with which much of the Negro world would have concurred, came from a small periodical distinguished by its efforts to remain impartial during the long controversy. "Garvey made thousands think, who had never thought before," said the *Spokesman*. "Thousands who merely dreamed dreams, now see visions." [103]

Shortly after Garvey entered prison, he sent a message of hope to his many followers throughout the world. "My work is just begun," he declared. "Be assured that I planted well the seed of Negro or black nationalism which cannot be destroyed even by the foul play that has been meted out to me." The work of the Universal Negro Improvement Association would go forward, and Marcus Garvey, in life or in death, would continue to serve the cause of the Negro people. "If I die in Atlanta my work shall then only begin," Garvey promised, "but I shall live, in the physical or spiritual to see the day of Africa's glory. When I am dead wrap the mantle of the Red, Black, and Green around me, for in the new life I shall rise with God's grace and blessing to lead the millions up the heights of triumph with the colors that you well know. Look for me in the whirlwind or the storm, look for me all around you, for, with God's grace, I shall come and bring with me countless millions of black slaves who have died in America and the West Indies and the millions in Africa to aid you in the fight for Liberty, Freedom and Life." [104] Few would question that Garvey was still a towering force in Negro life and thought, and never was his great gift of persuasive power and vivid imagery turned to more effective use than in his farewell address from Atlanta. Though the world might hold his body, the prison had yet to be built whose walls were strong enough to contain the influence of Marcus Garvey.

★ SIX

DAYS OF DECLINE

Guide him through life victorious,
Save him from accident,
Grant him his aims most glorious,
God Bless our President.

—U.N.I.A. Hymn [1]

All of us may not live to see the higher accomplishment
of an African empire—so strong and powerful, as to com-
pel the respect of mankind, but we in our life-time can so
work and act as to make the dream a possibility within
another generation.

—Marcus Garvey [2]

★ Marcus Garvey's confinement in Atlanta penitentiary did not bring about the collapse of his hardy Universal Negro Improvement Association. Amy Jacques Garvey, the loyal second wife of the imprisoned leader, directed the efforts to rally the faithful membership, and Garvey himself sent frequent messages of encouragement from his prison cell. In December, 1925, Mrs. Garvey published a lengthy compilation of her husband's speeches and writings as a source book for his racial philosophy. This work, *Philosophy and Opinions of Marcus Garvey or Africa for the Africans,* together with the shorter *Philosophy and Opinions of Marcus Garvey* that had been issued in 1923, is today the most valuable single source of information on Garveyism. Garvey was gone but he was far from forgotten. Many Negroes continued to celebrate August 17, Garvey's birthday, as an international Negro holiday.

After Garvey's imprisonment, the Universal Negro Improvement Association even made an attempt to recapture something of the palmy days of the movement's early successes with another International Convention of the Negro Peoples of the World. Four of Garvey's chief lieutenants, Sir William Ware, J. A. Craigen, S. A. Haynes, and Fred A. Toote, leaders respectively of the four largest U.N.I.A. divisions of Cincinnati, Detroit, Pittsburgh, and Philadelphia, directed the activities of the association in staging this emergency convention at Detroit in March, 1926.[3] This gathering reaffirmed allegiance to Garvey and his principles of race redemption and mapped out a U.N.I.A. holding action until the return of the movement's dynamic founder. But without Garvey's inspirational leadership the delegates were unable to generate the enthusiasm which had been so notable a characteristic of the earlier U.N.I.A. conventions. Already there was danger, moreover, that ambitious division leaders might undo the work of the association through their jealous and disruptive efforts to succeed to Garvey's mantle of authority.[4] Clearly the U.N.I.A. needed the dominating personality of its founder if it were not to break up into quarreling, schismatic factions.

One of Garvey's most active lieutenants at this time was Sir William Ware, president of the Cincinnati Division of the U.N.I.A. Ware was a heavy-set black man who had been knighted by Garvey for his U.N.I.A. work and who now demonstrated that this confidence had not been misplaced. In May, 1927, Ware organized an ambitious month-long anniversary drive at his Cincinnati Liberty Hall. The meetings were reminiscent of the larger U.N.I.A. annual conventions, with colorful parades, military demonstrations, exhilarating music, and spirited oratory. The local U.N.I.A. choir offered such old favorites as "From Green-

land's Icy Mountains" and "God Bless Our President," plus
a new piece, "When the Booker T. Washington Sails," a
musical tribute to Garvey's last ship acquisition in 1924.
Unfortunately, as we have seen, the maritime performance
of the *Booker T. Washington* did not live up to this cheery
choral promise, and ultimately this final ship of Garvey's
Negro steamship line was reported attached for debt in the
West Indies.[5] Speakers at the Cincinnati convention paid
tribute to their martyred leader with talks on such subjects
as "He Who a Dream Hath Possessed" and "Why Garvey's
Program Offers a Practical Solution of Race Problems the
World Over." Professor W. O. Brown, a sociologist at the
University of Cincinnati, spoke on "The Contribution that
Garveyism Has Made to Negro Life." The convention
urged all Negroes to petition President Coolidge to pardon
Garvey on the grounds that he was "a human being," "a
Negro," and was "sincere, honest, unselfish and consecrated" in his service as the "chosen and acknowledged
leader" of the colored world. Garvey was "the first man of
his race to propose such a big program"; he was "a pioneer,
a prophet" whose mind was "200 years ahead in its penetra-
tion of the difficulties to be encountered in the world struggle for survival by people of African blood." [6]

The U.N.I.A. was not alone in its concern for its martyred leader, for Garvey's imprisonment brought him sympathy from many who had earlier opposed the work of the
Universal Negro Improvement Association. William Pickens, who in 1923 had joined in the appeal to the Attorney
General urging the prosecution of Garvey for mail fraud,
now concluded that Garvey had been punished enough. In
August, 1927, Pickens protested against any further confinement of the Black Star president and urged his immediate pardon.[7] Even the once hostile Negro press began to
agitate for Garvey's release. "Marcus Garvey in truth was

not a criminal," proclaimed the Washington *Eagle,* "but a misinformed visionary. Garvey was right. This is certainly a white man's country." [8] A strong belief began to grow in the suspicious Negro world that Marcus Garvey had been unjustly condemned by the white man's courts. Even Negroes who had never accepted Garveyism came to believe the U.N.I.A. assertion that Garvey's treatment only vindicated his conviction that America would never be a land of justice for the black man.

Soon after Garvey's arrival at Atlanta he made application for a pardon, charging that he had been unjustly convicted in a trial marked by racial intolerance. He asserted that the government prosecutor, the trial judge, and sundry government witnesses were part of a general conspiracy to aid the National Association for the Advancement of Colored People and other rival Negro groups in their efforts to wreck the U.N.I.A. Garvey denied that he was responsible for the collapse of the Black Star Line, which he explained was only a tiny part of his larger program for the redemption of the Negro people. Indeed, the Black Star Line was not a complete failure, for it had encouraged Negroes to organize their own businesses.[9] The Department ment of Justice declined to forward Garvey's plea to the White House, however, and the petition for a presidential pardon was pigeonholed. In Atlanta Garvey was assigned to duties in the prison library and devoted his spare time to the writing of poetry. One of his poems, appropriately enough, was entitled "Keep Cool," and set to music it provided the U.N.I.A. with a pep song to encourage the languishing membership.

Although Garvey's initial effort to obtain a presidential pardon failed, the campaign for executive clemency waged by the U.N.I.A. and individual Negroes was successful in securing Garvey's release before the completion of his five-year prison term. Perhaps because Garvey's Negro Political Union had campaigned actively for the Republicans in the elections of 1924, President Calvin Coolidge commuted Garvey's sentence late in 1927 and ordered the Jamaican's immediate release. Since Garvey was not an American citizen and had been convicted of a felony, United States immigration laws required his immediate deportation as an undesirable alien. Early in December, 1927, therefore, without being permitted to visit the U.N.I.A. headquarters in New York, Garvey was taken to New Orleans and put aboard the *S.S. Saramacca*, bound for Panama and the West Indies. His farewell address to the hundreds of loyal New Orleans Negroes who came to witness his forced departure into exile moved many of his followers to tears. Garvey thanked his devoted supporters for their undiminished confidence in his leadership and promised that the best and most productive years of the movement yet lay ahead. "To the millions of members of the Universal Negro Improvement Association throughout the world," he declared firmly, "I can only say: Cheer up for the good work is just getting under way. Be firm and steadfast in holding to the principles of the organization. The greatest work is yet to be done. I shall with God's help do it." [10]

No doubt many of Garvey's critics were gratified at his swift banishment, but other Negroes were proud that a black man had aroused so much attention. "Whatever his faults or virtues," said one Harlem newspaper, "governments certainly seem afraid of him. The officers of the ship that carried Napoleon to St. Helena could not have been more careful with him than the U.S. authorities are with Garvey. This one black man has succeeded in alarming the most powerful governments of the world." [11] Kelly Miller observed that "the banishment of Garvey was epochal in its

Garvey delivers stirring farewell address, minutes before deportation,
at New Orleans, 1927

Part of large crowd of well-wishers at Garvey's deportation

Minutes before the *S.S. Saramacca* sailed, Garvey posed on deck with a group of U.N.I.A. officials, including, left to right: J. A. Craigen, executive secretary, Detroit division; S. V. Robertson, president, Cleveland division; Garvey; E. B. Knox, Garvey's personal representative; William Ware (rear, almost hidden), president, Cincinnati division; and Dr. J. J. Peters, president, New Orleans division.

significance," since it was the first time in American history
that the federal government had "paid a Negro the compli-
ment of banishment on account of his ideas or enterprise."
White Americans were afraid of Garvey, Miller said,
because the U.N.I.A. program was "calculated to give the
Negro a sense of self-respect in his own personality." [12] "A
movement that commands the fanatical devotion of two
million people—black or white, cultured or crude—must
have something in it more than red and green uniforms,"
exclaimed the New York *Amsterdam News* with something
approaching awe. "It is because Marcus Garvey made
black people proud of their race. In a world where black
is despised, he taught them that black is beautiful. He
taught them to admire and praise black things and black
people.... They rallied to him because he heard and responded to the heart beat of his race." [13]
    ☆
Garvey's return to Jamaica, although punctuated by the
painful separation from the thousands of U.N.I.A. members in the United States, was nevertheless a journey of real
triumph for the Negro Moses. When the *Saramacca* docked
at Cristobal, Panama, Garvey was refused permission to
land, but a delegation from the local U.N.I.A. division was
allowed to go aboard the ship to exchange greetings with
the exiled leader. The leader of the group told Garvey that
he spoke for two thousand active members who were steadfast in their loyalty to Garvey and the U.N.I.A. program.
"We hope that you will not be discouraged," the Pana-
manian delegation told Garvey, "but that you will be
greater energized for the stupendous task before you,
knowing that the greatest battle is fought immediately before victory." [14] Garvey accepted a small gift of money from
the welcoming committee and promised to continue the

fight for a free Africa. "To achieve success we must unite in the common cause," he agreed. "Our cause is a righteous one and it must triumph." [15]

In Jamaica great excitement prevailed over the home-coming of the martyred U.N.I.A. leader. When Garvey's ship steamed slowly into Kingston harbor, many hundreds of Jamaican Negroes were massed on the quayside, and thousands more lined the streets of the city to witness his triumphant ride from the dock area to the local Liberty Hall. The joyful reception was a far cry from Garvey's un-observed and unsung departure a decade earlier when as a serious young man of twenty-eight he had left for the United States to launch his movement among American Negroes. "As long as I live, I shall do everything for your advancement," he now promised his eager black followers, "well knowing that the organization which has been estab-lished for your uplift will always receive your fullest sup-port." [16]

Garvey immediately commenced a vigorous island-wide membership drive to rebuild the strength of the neglected Jamaica association. He told his Jamaican followers that his deportation from the United States was in fact a blessing in disguise, since it had enabled him to return to the home-land to work for race redemption among his own people. Under his driving leadership the Jamaican membership of the Universal Negro Improvement Association grew rap-idly and a number of new branches were established. Gar-vey did not neglect the movement in the United States, moreover, and each week he cabled to the *Negro World* in New York a message of inspiration and good will for the American members of the association. The serious black prophet seemed to be well on the way to a successful new stage in his fabulous career. Even *Crisis*, the magazine of the National Association for the Advancement of Colored

People that had sparked the campaign of criticism against the U.N.I.A., joined hands with Garvey supporters in wishing the Jamaican every success for his new work. "We have today, no enmity against Marcus Garvey," declared a *Crisis* editorial early in 1928. "He has a great and worthy dream. We wish him well. He is free; he has a following; he still has a chance to carry on his work in his own home and among his own people and to accomplish some of his ideals. Let him do it. We will be the first to applaud any success that he may have." [17]

In addition to his whirlwind campaign to revitalize the Jamaican U.N.I.A., in the spring of 1928 Garvey took time out to visit branches of the association elsewhere in the West Indies and Central America. "I know no national boundary where the Negro is concerned," he explained. "The whole world is my province until Africa is free." [18] Garvey realized that it was doubly important to maintain the international character of his movement now that he was barred from the chief source of his strength, the United States, and in May, 1928, he and his wife hastened to England to carry their message of Negro salvation to the European people. In London he established a European headquarters and soon after opened a branch office in Paris. This gave the U.N.I.A. an impressive international flavor, with offices in New York, Jamaica, London, and Paris, and the always imposing U.N.I.A. letterhead proudly boasted a European headquarters, a sub-European headquarters, a head office, and a foreign head office. The movement remained a Garvey-dominated affair, however, and there was never any question in his mind that the supreme headquarters was wherever he, the President General of the U.N.I.A., happened to be at any particular moment.

Garvey laid big plans for his London debut and for his first public appearance he rented the sprawling Royal

Albert Hall, a vast Victorian structure with a seating capacity of ten thousand. Fresh from his recent Jamaican triumphs and with the cheers of the Harlem multitudes still ringing in his ears, Garvey doubtless had no misgivings about his ability to draw a capacity crowd. As it turned out, he seriously misjudged both the appeal of his bombastic oratory for serious British audiences and their interest in his dramatic African program. Only a few score listeners, half of them Negroes, turned up on the night of June 6, 1928, to listen to the U.N.I.A. founder expound his racial philosophy. The only London newspaper to report the event headlined its story "9800 Empty Seats," noting with unkind sarcasm that "each member of the audience had the choice of 50 seats." [19] Even Garvey with his usual disregard of mathematics could only claim an audience of five hundred, forty of whom he said were reporters. He later explained that the British press, with its "usual blackguarding method," had ridiculed him prior to the lecture "so as to prejudice the minds of the public beforehand." [20]

The Albert Hall meeting was opened by E. B. Knox, the first assistant president general of the association, who told his scattered audience that the Universal Negro Improvement Association had "11,000,000 members with 3,000 branches in various parts of the world," an exuberant estimate that certainly erred on the side of optimism. Introducing Garvey as "the greatest Negro in the world—the most widely advertised man in the world," Knox listed some of his leader's more notable accomplishments: "He has taught us to love; he has taught us to establish a culture of our own; he has converted us to the program of Africa for the Africans." Garvey followed this flowery introduction with a long recital of his troubles in the United States, a speech that reached a sorry high for distortions and exaggerations. He intimated that one of the major American steamship companies had used its political influence to sink the Black Star Line and he accused the federal government of unfair tactics in its investigation of his affairs. He charged that the government had infiltrated his enterprises with scheming secret agents and declared that he had been sent to jail for following the advice of a U.N.I.A. attorney who had been in government pay. After Garvey's conviction, he said, this associate had been rewarded with a government post. Garvey explained that he had been rushed to prison because he could have made trouble over the Firestone rubber negotiations with Liberia. He claimed to have been honored by his association while in prison with a number of former high political figures in the United States. "Those are the morals of politics in America," he concluded impressively.

Perhaps because he was speaking to citizens of a nation with vast imperial holdings in Africa, Garvey's references to the dark continent were not as belligerent as usual. Instead of demanding a completely free Africa, he merely requested that the various colonial governments agree to relinquish certain areas under their control to Negro rule. Garvey even intimated that he would be willing to accept the less desirable parts of Africa where the white man found it difficult to live. "But we are going to have our part of Africa," he warned ominously, "whether you will it or not." [21] Whatever else might be said of this speech, it certainly indicated that prison life had failed to chasten or subdue Marcus Garvey. On the contrary, he had emerged unrepentant and entirely oblivious to his own possible failings as a leader of his people or any deficiencies in his racial philosophy.

Undaunted by the Albert Hall fiasco, Garvey moved on to Paris, where he was given a somewhat warmer reception by French intellectuals at the Club du Faubourg.[22] In September he went to Geneva, where he presented a "Petition of the Negro Race" to the League of Nations "on behalf of the hundreds of millions of black peoples who are suffering the world over." [23] The U.N.I.A. document set forth in minute detail the many grievances of the Negro people and begged for redress through the world government organization. Garvey's petition incorporated a similar appeal submitted to the League in 1922 through the Persian delegation and the U.N.I.A. president noted sadly that nothing had come of the earlier complaints except a League decision "that all nationals who had grievances should present them through their respective governments." This Garvey interpreted as a diplomatic move to destroy the effect of the U.N.I.A. appeal, though he tactfully conceded "it might not have been apparent to the League at the time." He respectfully begged the League to reconsider its ill-advised decision not to listen to direct complaints of a depressed and downtrodden people.

Garvey urged the League of Nations to pay sympathetic heed to the Negro desire for a free state in Africa. "We believe that as a people we should have a Government of our own," he declared, "in our homeland—Africa." Garvey suggested with considerably more imagination than realism that the mandates of former German colonies in Africa should be given to Negroes so that they could prove their ability to govern themselves. Failing this, he asked that parts of West Africa be brought together into a "United Commonwealth of Black Nations, and placed under the government of black men, as a solution of the Negro problem, both in Africa and the Western World." [24] In view of the later rise of African nationalist sentiment that now threatens to destroy the vestiges of white colonialism, Garvey's scheme does not seem today to have been completely impractical, only premature and unrealistic in terms of the existing political climate. Garvey was shrewd enough to recognize that the League of Nations would take no more action on this petition than it had on the earlier one, but he wanted to spell out his nationalistic program for all to read—and take warning.

Back in England after his bout with the indifferent League, Garvey rented the Century Theatre in London for another go at a British audience. This time he was received with considerably more enthusiasm, and the meeting was presided over by Dr. Charles Garnett, a controversial English clergyman, who stated his regrets that all London could not "hear the speaker and the subject." Sharing the platform with the U.N.I.A. president was his wife, Amy Jacques Garvey, who made a dignified yet moving plea for tolerance and sympathetic understanding from the white world. "Our appeal, as black people, is learn more about us as a race," she begged. "We are not asking charity of you, because we believe in self help; we believe that as a race of people struggling onward and upward we must of ourselves lift ourselves up; and all we ask you is that you treat us kindly and decently." A few minutes later Garvey joined in the entreaty for simple humanitarian justice. "Good God! What a day it will be when black, brown, yellow and white meet before that great Throne which Christian men have taught us about," he exclaimed with religious fervor. "Good God, shall we go to another Hell other than the Hell we are in now in India and in Africa?" "I stand before you this afternoon a proud black man, honoured to be a black man, who would be nothing else in God's creation but a black man," Garvey declared proudly. "Black men are not going to cringe before anyone but God." The dominant white world had better recognize that Negroes were on the march. "Now we have started to speak," he warned quietly but with ominous candor, "and

I am only the forerunner of an awakened Africa that shall never go back to sleep." [25]

But there was no inundating ground swell of enthusiasm for the Garvey program among Europeans, and the restless Jamaican decided to abandon temporarily his plans for a permanent European headquarters for his Negro movement. In the fall of 1928 he visited Canada, and, in a wistful appeal to his many supporters across the border, urged American Negroes to vote for Democrat Alfred E. Smith in the forthcoming presidential election. Al Smith was "a man from the people," a man who had "sprung from the common people" and who therefore knew "their wants and their heart beats and their pulse." The Republican candidate, Herbert Hoover, on the other hand, was "a millionaire," who had been "pampered by the monopolist class." Indeed, Hoover had been partly responsible for sending Garvey to prison, "because it was to America's interest, and, not only that, but to the interest of certain American capitalists" to put Garvey behind bars "so that Hoover could back Firestone in Liberia in connection with the rubber lands." Al Smith, a much more honorable politician, "would not tolerate such a method in politics," and American Negroes could therefore safely "put their trust in him." [26] Garvey's political agitation was noticed by the alert American consul in Montreal, who immediately complained to the Canadian authorities with the result that the controversial Jamaican was asked to leave the country.[27] Returning to Jamaica, he began to prepare his countrymen for the greatest international gathering in island history.

☆

Early in 1929 Garvey issued a call for the Sixth International Convention of the Negro Peoples of the World, which he announced would be held in Kingston during the month of August, 1929. Harlem had long since become ac-

customed to these Garvey extravaganzas, but less sophisticated Kingston was quite unprepared for the triumphant
display of U.N.I.A. power. All of Garvey's considerable organizational skill was used to recapture the pomp and
splendor of the first Harlem convention in 1920, when the
Universal Negro Improvement Association had burst like a
meteor upon a marveling black world.

On the first day of August thousands of cheering Jamaican Negroes lined the streets of Kingston to applaud
the opening parade of the convention. Many hundreds
more marched in what the Kingston *Gleaner* described enthusiastically as "a mammoth procession . . . , the like of
which has never been seen here before." [28] Jamaican Negroes, like their American cousins before them, were
visibly impressed with the various units of the association
—the smart marching bands, the elegantly uniformed
African Legion, the neat Black Cross Nurses, the Universal
Motor Corps, and the many delegates in their richly colored robes of office. The convention formally opened in the
open-air stadium at Edelweis Park, with the mayor of
Kingston present to welcome Garvey and congratulate him
on the success of the gathering. At long last Marcus Garvey
was received with honor by the Negro, colored, and white
aristocracy of his homeland. The serious black man with
the burning ideas on Negro deliverance had come a long
way from the obscurity of St. Ann's Bay.

The keynote of this convention, as of its predecessors,
was the demand for African redemption. Garvey called
upon the Negroes of the world to "dedicate their lives, souls
and bodies to a great cause of Africa's glory, the cause of
emancipation of a downtrodden race." [29] The delegates
devoted some of the sessions to the discussion of Negro
conditions in the New World, however, and representatives from various parts of the United States, the West

Indies, and Central America earnestly debated various remedies offered to end Negro grievances. After a lengthy discussion of consular systems, the convention went on record as favoring the establishment of U.N.I.A. Negro consuls in the large centers of Negro population in order to protect the rights of the race. The delegates also considered the question of proper representation at the League of Nations; but after a pessimistic report from Garvey on his recent experience at Geneva, the project was abandoned as too costly. The convention urged the U.N.I.A. to sponsor a program of school construction in order to provide social and educational centers for isolated Negro communities. To deal with the important questions of health and public instruction the convention created a new U.N.I.A. Department of Health and Public Education. The first Sunday in October was designated as National Health Day and all Negroes were urged to take extra measures to clean up their persons and property at this time. In closing the convention, Garvey announced the inauguration of a world-wide campaign to collect $600,000,000 for the new U.N.I.A. program.[30]

The convention sessions were not always devoted to hard work. On one occasion the assemblage was entertained by a debate between Garvey and Otto Huiswoud, a representative of the American Negro Labor Congress, on the subject of co-operation between white and black workers. Garvey maintained that Negroes must build up their own capital in order to become their own employers and criticized his Communist opponent for saying that capitalism should be destroyed. "The fundamental issue of life," Garvey declared, is "the appeal of race to race, the appeal of clan to clan, the appeal of tribe to tribe, of observing the rule that self-preservation was the first law of nature." Although Huiswoud made an able plea for solidarity, when

the motion was put to the house Garvey received an overwhelming victory.[31]

Toward the end of the convention, on the night of August 22, an estimated ten thousand persons packed Edelweis Park for the court reception of the Universal Negro Improvement Association, a regal ceremony that Garvey had
predicted would be "something quite unusual in Jamaica
—the resurrection of court life of ancient Africa." [32] The
eager spectators were not disappointed. The high dignitaries of the U.N.I.A., accompanied by their bejeweled
ladies, appeared resplendent in their rich robes of state,
while the officers of the African Legion fairly dazzled the
excited black multitude with their dapper uniforms, shiny
Sam Brown belts, and gleaming swords. The greatest outburst of applause was, of course, reserved for Garvey. As
the President General of the U.N.I.A. and Provisional
President of Africa passed between lines of erect legion-
naires holding aloft drawn swords, the vast assemblage
gave a mighty roar of greeting. Accompanied by his wife
and the High Potentate of the association, Garvey made his
way to a lavishly decorated stage where he informed his
audience that they were but celebrating "what had gone
before in the noble court of Ethiopia, the grandeur of past
ages." [33] The staging was right, the audience appreciative;
it was a truly magnificent show. No wonder that after this
night all shades of Jamaican society referred to Garvey
with new-found reverence and respect.

Early in the convention trouble arose over Garvey's severe castigation of certain members of the association in
the United States. He blamed his imprisonment on the dis-
loyalty of some of his associates and charged that corrupt
leaders had bankrupted the movement while he was in
prison. He stressed the fact that some U.N.I.A. officials had
demanded their full salaries regardless of the state of the

organization's treasury while he had frequently served long periods without pay or expense money. Many of the American delegates resented Garvey's accusations and soon a split appeared between Garvey and the American leaders.. The dispute centered largely over the location of the headquarters of the organization. Garvey insisted that as the U.N.I.A.'s founder and continuing leader he had a right to expect that headquarters be located wherever he happened to be. The American leaders demanded that the home office remain in New York, where the association had been incorporated and where the greatest strength and financial backing of the movement had always been found. When Garvey refused to budge from his stand, the American delegates withdrew from the convention, leaving him to establish a new organization legally known as the Parent Body of the Universal Negro Improvement Association, also called the U.N.I.A., August, 1929.[34] New charters were issued to the divisions of the organization that elected to remain loyal to Garvey, but many of the branches in the United States continued to use the old charters granted by the original U.N.I.A. under the incorporation of 1918.[35]

This 1929 split prefaced the eventual breakup of the Garvey organization. Prior to this schism there had been numerous individual dissensions within the U.N.I.A. ranks, but none had assumed dangerous proportions. Garvey's strong personal leadership had always been able to dominate or repress any of the earlier outbreaks of discontent. This time, however, the movement was seriously divided, and Garvey was not only estranged from many of his former subordinates but also cut off from much of his American support. Ultimately the 1929 schism was to deprive Garvey's organization of a $300,000 legacy.

Garvey's decision to break with the skeleton of the old New York association was encouraged by an adverse legal action that occurred during the convention. One of the former high officials of the association, George O. Mark, a native of Sierra Leone who had been a U.N.I.A. delegate to the League of Nations and later was named Supreme Deputy Potentate, had brought suit against the American organization for payment of back salary. The 1920 U.N.I.A. convention had optimistically voted to pay the Supreme Deputy Potentate an annual salary of $6,000 and Mark complained bitterly that he had never received anything like that sum. An American court had listened sympathetically and had awarded Mark a judgment against the New York U.N.I.A. Unable to collect anything from the now insolvent American association, Mark appealed to the Jamaican courts for a judgment against Garvey's revitalized association. Garvey disclaimed any present connection with the bankrupt American association and evaded queries about the assets of the Jamaican U.N.I.A., which he claimed were merely held in trust for the St. Andrew (Kingston) Division of the organization. He persisted in his refusal to turn over to the court the books of the Jamaican association and was accordingly fined twenty-five pounds for contempt, a sum cheerfully paid by the convention delegates. Unsuccessful in his efforts to extricate the U.N.I.A. from this legal dilemma, Garvey emerged from the affair convinced of the desirability of freeing himself of any restrictive ties to the old American association.[36]

Soon after the end of the Kingston convention Garvey found himself in further trouble with the law. In an intemperate campaign speech for election to the island Legislative Council, he announced that if elected he would work for a law to provide for impeachment and prison terms for judges who entered "into illicit agreement with lawyers and other prominent businessmen to deprive other subjects of the Realm of their rights." [37] This seemed to be a clear reference to the adverse decision in the Mark case, and the Jamaican court treated Garvey's attack as a threat to the integrity of Jamaican justice. Again the U.N.I.A. leader found himself before the dock on a charge of contempt of court. Although Garvey offered "to fully apolgize to this court for the words I have used," a panel of three justices of the Jamaican Supreme Court sentenced him to spend three months in jail and to pay a fine of a hundred pounds.[38] "It is impossible to ignore the fact that Garvey is not a well-meaning man guilty of an offence simply owing to his impulsiveness or folly," declared the chief justice in passing sentence. "This sentence takes much account of the fact that Garvey is a hot headed and foolish man." [39]

While Garvey was serving this sentence, his supporters elected him to a seat on the Kingston and St. Andrew Corporation, the governing body for the city of Kingston and its surrounding parish. His seat was declared vacant as a result of his failure to attend meetings during his imprisonment, but Garvey's loyal followers re-elected him once again in a special by-election after his release. This office was the highest Garvey was to reach in Jamaican politics, for his jail term had cost him much prestige among all classes of Jamaicans. This was soon demonstrated by his crushing defeat in an attempt to win a seat in the Jamaican legislature.[40] After this rebuff Garvey attempted to organize a Jamaican People's Party but gave up the project after it was effectively blocked by local politicians who were understandably not anxious to see him succeed in island politics.[41] Garvey's political aspirations were further clouded by continued legal altercations with disgruntled former officials of the movement.[42]

☆

The decade of the thirties was an era of obscurity for the pudgy black man whose bold dreams had once captured the attention of millions and whose activities had excited the anxious interest of governments. Garvey worked tirelessly to maintain and rebuild the membership in the scattered divisions of the U.N.I.A., but cut off as he was from direct contact with his greatest source of support, the American Negroes, he found his once mighty organization disintegrating into gradual impotency. In vain did he appeal to Negroes to forget the errors of the unhappy past; in vain were his assurances of a revamped U.N.I.A. program completely free of "that rascally dishonesty that swamped us in our first effort." "No old associate has any claim on me, nor on my new program of race achievement," Garvey promised. "Yes, reaching the end of association with rascals, I rise once more with the hope of finding the new company of men and women who will undertake with me to carry on the fight until victory comes." [43] Characteristically, Garvey sought to explain the failure of the Universal Negro Improvement Association in America as caused by the chicanery of certain dishonest subordinates. "If the U.N.I.A. has failed in the achievement of its high ideals," he vowed, "the fault surely will not be traceable to the masses who flock to its colors, but to selfish leaders who diverted its purposes." [44] For the Negro intelligentsia that had directed the attack on his program Garvey had nothing but unrepentant defiance and he asserted that his old opponents had gained for their pains only "the scorn and contempt of the unfortunate masses." [45]

In December, 1933, Garvey began publishing a modest magazine called the *Black Man*. This periodical succeeded the *Negro World*, which had suspended publication that year after fifteen years as the U.N.I.A. weekly newspaper in the United States. The *Black Man* appeared irregularly through the late thirties, and after November, 1934, was published from London. As far as can be ascertained from the scattered copies available, the *Black Man* appeared far less frequently than its claim of being "a monthly magazine of Negro thought and opinion" would indicate. The magazine had a definite international character and was intended to be, according to a Garvey editorial in the first issue, "the organ for reviving the great movement of the U.N.I.A. under new and honest leadership so that we may continue the battle for African redemption and for the development of the Negro race." [46]

The *Black Man* had several regular features. On its front cover was a Garvey poem, always inspirational in tone and generally dealing with some aspect of Negro salvation. The editorial section dealt with current events, particularly happenings of interest to Negroes, and often the magazine was filled with news items about prominent Negro figures taken from press accounts. More important in the make-up of the *Black Man,* however, were Garvey's regular letters to the Negro race, which tended to follow the fervent formula used so successfully in the old *Negro World.* Here Garvey aired his views on the past and future of the race and with zealous but repetitious enthusiasm outlined the ever more ambitious program of his Universal Negro Improvement Association. Here, too, Garvey found an outlet for his almost pathological hatred of such personal enemies as W. E. Burghardt DuBois and George S. Schuyler, men whom he petulantly blamed for his failures in the United States. Not only did Garvey attack certain individual Negroes; sometimes he criticized the race as a whole. One such article took the form of a dialogue between Garvey as a wise father and the younger Negro generation. In paternal tones he explained the reasons for the collapse of the U.N.I.A. program in America and then condemned elements in the Negro character that weakened the race.[47] Another article, purportedly by a white man but very likely written by Garvey himself, criticized the shortcomings of the race under the title of "Why I Hate the Negro." [48]

Garvey apparently had great difficulty in raising funds for the publication of the *Black Man*, as its irregularity and his frequent appeals for financial support indicate. "Always remember that the press is a mighty power," he declared in one such plea for assistance. "It is the object of the *Black Man* to be an educative force in the life of the race. It is to be the circulating University. Its readers will be the graduates. Help us to graduate millions. When they are graduated they will be better men and women and the race will represent a higher standard." [49] In December, 1937, Garvey appealed for help in making the *Black Man* a weekly publication because there was "so much news and so much matter to be disposed of weekly." [50] Later issues carried the names of donors and the amount of their subscription to the fund, but Garvey was never able to publish the magazine on even a regular monthly schedule. The published lists of subscribers indicated, however, that while Garvey was receiving only limited financial support, he was nonetheless still reaching a world-wide following.[51] The *Black Man*'s low price of six pence in England and ten cents in America precluded any large revenues, and its widely scattered circulation added considerably to the costs of distribution. The magazine seems to have ceased publication in late 1938 or 1939. The *Black Man* represented Garvey's final effort to regain contact with the scattered and dwindling membership of the U.N.I.A. and to rekindle the fires that had once flared so brightly in the Negro world.

In August, 1934, Garvey presided over the Kingston sessions of the Seventh International Convention of the Negro Peoples of the World. During the convention Garvey restated his belief that the Negro had no one but himself to blame for his troubles, that his plight was the result of

Negro shortcomings and was not attributable to the white man. The delegates adopted a new program of race redemption, a vague five-year plan involving the "early development of the shipping, manufacturing, mining, agricultural, and other industries which are to affect the Negroes in the United States, the West Indies, Central and South America, and Africa." [52] In order to raise the necessary fund of $300,000,000 to implement this plan, the convention authorized an individual levy of five dollars apiece on the Negroes of the world. The delegates designated August 17, Garvey's birthday, as an international Negro holiday and urged that a standard African language be adopted and used by all members of the race throughout the world. The convention went on record as condemning birth control and all religious cults (doubtless aimed at the flourishing movement of Father Divine in Harlem) and established a bureau of literary censorship to ban literature unfavorable to Negroes. Although the *Black Man* published the proceedings of the convention in its issue of November, 1934, it gave no indication of the attendance at this convention. As the resolutions were submitted by only a handful of persons, it must be surmised that the gathering was only a thin shadow of the old days of mass parades and tumultous audiences.

Important in the eclipse of Garvey's once mighty influence was the defection of many of his most important American supporters after the 1929 controversy over the location of the U.N.I.A. headquarters. Such prominent former lieutenants as Henrietta Vinton Davis, William Ware, George Alexander McGuire, and Lionel A. Francis elected to maintain a separate American organization in competition with the movement led by Garvey from the West Indies and Europe. There were now two rival Universal Negro Improvement Associations appealing for members and financial support at a time when world-wide depression had seriously impaired both the willingness and the ability of most Negroes to look beyond the pressing needs of immediate personal survival. In 1932 Lionel Francis, who had taken Garvey's place as president general of the New York U.N.I.A., issued a call for an international Negro convention sponsored by the American separatists. Except for the timely question of "means of alleviating mass unemployment," the agenda submitted for consideration by the delegates was only a warmed-over mélange of Garvey's philosophy of Negro self-help, but the master's name was conspicuously missing from the invitations and advertisements for the gathering.[53] Garveyism was fast losing its identity, even as its frustrated author was losing touch with his once devoted followers.

By 1935 Garvey had moved the headquarters of his movement to London, where he continued to agitate for a nationalistic rebirth of the Negro people. At one time he considered the possibility of campaigning for a seat in Parliament as a self-appointed representative of the colored peoples of the British Empire, and an American Negro paper went so far as to announce his candidacy as a representative of the Labour Party.[54] The report was premature, however, for Garvey's lack of any real following in England forced him to abandon his political ambitions.[55] A list of functioning divisions of Garvey's U.N.I.A. printed in the *Black Man* of October, 1935, gave little indication of the strength of the movement. Garvey's boasts of many operating branches were tempered by his constant pleas for reports and dues from the local organizations. Each issue of the *Black Man* carried earnest appeals for financial support, and frequently large advertisements urged enterprising Negroes to "start a new division" since "no well thinking community of Negroes can live without being a part of this movement." [56] During the years 1935–37 Garvey reported less than $400 collected from his various fund-raising drives, a sorry comedown from the prosperous twenties when that total could be bettered in a single frenzied evening.[57] The irregularity and ultimate cessation of the *Black Man* also provided an empty chronicle of the decline of the movement.

The unprovoked attack upon Ethiopia in the summer of 1935 aroused the Negro world to bitter denunciation of Mussolini's Italy. Garvey rushed to the defense of the beloved motherland and in characteristically defiant tones denounced the Italian dictator for his brazen attempt to despoil Africa. He joined the ragged outdoor orators in Hyde Park and appealed to the curious crowds around Marble Arch for support of the beleaguered Abyssinians.[58] He called upon Negroes everywhere to unite in defense of their ancestral homeland and he gave fair warning to Il Duce in a bit of angry verse feelingly entitled "The Smell of Mussolini":

> We'll march to crush the Italian dog
> And at the points of gleaming, shining swords,
> We'll lay quite low the violent, Roman hog.[59]

Another such poem was dedicated to "Il Duce—the Brute." [60]

After the Ethiopian Emperor Haile Selassie fled to London and discreetly let it be known that he did not desire contact with Negroes, Garvey trained his biggest guns on the snobbish Lion of Judah. "Haile Selassie is the ruler of a country where black men are chained and flogged," the *Black Man* raged. "He will go down in history as a great coward who ran away from his country." [61] Garvey called upon the Ethiopian people to forget the cowardly flight of their ruler and instead wage fierce guerilla warfare in defense of their country:

But to continue the fight there must be real patriotism. There must be a real recognition of the Negro Abyssinian. He must not be ashamed to be a member of the Negro race. If he does, he will be left alone by all the Negroes of the world, who feel proud of themselves. The new Negro doesn't give two pence about the line of Solomon. Solomon has been long dead. Solomon was a Jew. The Negro is no Jew. The Negro has a racial origin running from Sheba to the present, of which he is proud. He is proud of Sheba but he is not proud of Solomon.[62]

The following year Garvey presided at a regional conference of the U.N.I.A. at Toronto, Canada, August 20–25, 1936. The proceedings of this meeting were not published, but the *Black Man* reported that two resolutions had been passed by the delegates. One was a severe denunciation of the Harlem religious leader, the fabulous Father Divine. Previously Garvey had criticized Father Divine for permitting his followers to refer to him as God.[63] Now the conference accused Father Divine of being "blasphemist in his doctrines" and advised "all sane, intelligent, self-respecting Negroes throughout the United States and Canada not to accept and follow his blasphemous doctrine." The other resolution condemned such plays and motion pictures as *Green Pastures, Imitation of Life,* and *Emperor Jones* as part of "an international conspiracy to disparage and crush the aspirations of Negroes toward a higher culture and civilization and to impress upon them their inferiority." [64]

Another regional conference of the U.N.I.A. was held in Toronto from August 21 to 31, 1937. Immediately after this meeting Garvey opened a School of African Philosophy to train interested Negroes for world leadership in the Universal Negro Improvement Association. The *Black Man* reported that applicants were required to have at least a high school education and that Garvey had carried his students through a rigorous course of instruction covering "a range of over forty-two subjects touching vitally every phase of human life." [65] Eight of the nine students enrolled in the course were graduated and immediately appointed commissioners of the U.N.I.A. for their respective areas in the United States and Canada. Garvey announced that he would conduct a correspondence course open only to Negroes and would offer instruction leading to degrees of Bachelor, Master, and Doctor of African Philosophy.

Under Garvey's leadership, the Eighth International Convention of the Negro Peoples of the World convened in Toronto from August 1 to 17, 1938. No one was surprised when the delegates, their ranks depleted after two decades of attrition and decline, re-elected Garvey unanimously to another four-year term as president general of the U.N.I.A. The convention, only a pale reflection of its predecessors, brought forth a new five-year development plan for the association and voted to continue the School of African Philosophy inaugurated the previous year. Garvey advertised for a thousand students to obtain "an education for world-wide Negro leadership" in a "special correspondence course—$25.00." [66] The prophet was seeking younger disciples to take over command of the march into the promised land.

During the 1930's Garvey was involved in another long litigation. Back in the early days of the movement, at the 1922 convention, he had elevated a Central American Negro, Isaiah Emmanuel Morter, to knighthood in the Distinguished Service Order of Ethiopia. When Morter died in 1924, it developed that he had bequeathed to the U.N.I.A. his entire estate, consisting of a banana and cocoanut plantation of 210 square miles and twenty-one pieces of improved real estate in Belize, the seaport capital of British Honduras. [67] Since the estate was valued at more than $300,000, Morter's distressed relatives quite naturally contested the will, but eventually the local courts ruled that the property did in fact belong to the Universal Negro Improvement Association.

But by this time Garvey had split with the American association and had formed his so-called Parent Body of the Universal Negro Improvement Association. The prospect of sharing in a valuable legacy, however, quickly revived the moribund American group to the extent that its leaders greedily contested Garvey's right to the estate on the ground that he was no longer connected with the organization to which Morter had willed his property.[68] After years of bitter legal wrangling, the case was carried to the Privy Council in London, which upheld the decision of the chief justice of British Honduras in awarding the estate to the American U.N.I.A. Before this financial windfall, the New York association had been almost completely inactive, but it now revived and began operation under the leadership of Lionel Francis, a West Indian physician who had joined Garvey's movement at the 1920 convention and became successively president of the Philadelphia division and finally president general of the separatist American association. In 1940, Francis claimed for his group a membership of about seven hundred and indicated that he was far less interested in a Back to Africa movement than in providing a solution to Negro economic difficulties. "I say, if we can solve our economic problem, then to hell with the white man," he confided to an interviewer for Gunnar Myrdal's study of the Negro problem in the United States.

Sir, the Negro must learn to keep his business to himself. He must be as wise as a serpent and appear to be harmless as a dove. He must strike at the right moment. Let the European war start. Some Negroes are crying for peace. Peace, hell! Let them kill each other as long as they want to. The longer they do that, the better off the Negroes will be.[69]

Other ideological offshoots of the Garvey movement were also active at this time. The insignificant National Union for People of African Descent carried on in Garvey's extreme nationalist tradition with demands for a Negro nation with its own flag, army, and navy. The National Movement for the Establishment of a Forty-Ninth State contemplated the erection of a separate Negro state within the United States, a demand that echoed the Communist Party's agitation for self-determination in the black belt. The idea of a separate black state did not catch hold, however, and the project received but limited support from American Negroes. More in the Garvey tradition was the Peace Movement of Ethiopia, founded at a meeting in Chicago late in 1932. This group conducted a vigorous Back to Africa campaign and urged Negroes to support Senator Theodore G. Bilbo's Negro Repatriation Bill in 1939.[70] Garvey himself threw the editorial support of the *Black Man* behind Bilbo's scheme to use relief funds to resettle destitute American Negroes in Africa, and his Chicago followers launched an abortive march on Washington in support of the measure.[71] Another ideological child of Garveyism was the Pacific Movement of the Eastern World, an organization attempting to win Negro support for the Japanese in the years prior to World War II.[72] Garvey's loyal American followers occasionally were active during the thirties. A May Day parade in 1938 featured the remnants of the old African Legion marching before a limousine bearing a life-size portrait of the exiled commander-in-chief.[73]

☆

Garvey once remarked, "Leadership means everything —pain, blood, death." [74] By 1940 his own career had borne out the truth of his prophecy. The tireless efforts of the thirties had failed to recapture the exciting triumphs of

the twenties. The *Black Man's* ever lengthening column of
obituaries testified to the decline of Garvey's once powerful hold on the minds of his own generation, while younger
Negroes, preoccupied with their harsh struggle for survival
during the great depression, showed little inclination to
listen to expensive schemes for Negro salvation. A Negro
world that had been able to support Garvey's million-dollar
business ventures in the prosperous twenties found his ambitious global projects too expensive a luxury to maintain
in the hardship years of the thirties. The outbreak of the
European war in 1939 merely supplied the *coup de grâce*
to Garvey's dream of a world-wide organization of Negroes
dedicated to African liberation. The war not only restricted
Garvey's field of activity but also turned the attention of
Negroes increasingly to narrow local patriotism rather than
to Garvey's concept of a broad Negro nationalism.

Twice in the late 1930's Garvey was dangerously stricken
with pneumonia, induced by the damp chill of London
winters. His chronic asthma had given him increasing trouble in England and the two bouts with pneumonia weakened his already overtaxed heart. His Indian physician
warned him to leave the unhealthy English climate for the
mild and friendly warm air of Jamaica, but Garvey hesitated to abandon his London headquarters, the best remaining post for him to maintain contact with his broken
Negro legions. In January, 1940, he suffered a severe stroke;
and though after a lingering convalescence he recovered
sufficiently to take short rides in his beloved Hyde Park,
his right side remained badly paralyzed. The following
May a careless London news service sent out a false report
of Garvey's death and newspapers all over the world
picked up and enlarged upon the erroneous story. After
several cruel days of reading his own morbid obituary no-
tices and the many oppressive cables of condolence that

flooded in from friends around the globe, the ailing U.N.I.A. founder really collapsed and thereafter failed rapidly. The end came on June 10, 1940.[75]

Marcus Garvey was still a comparatively young man, only fifty-three; but far from his promised land of Africa and from the scene of his great triumphs in America, his death was scarcely noticed in the land where he had spent the last decade of his life. Garvey's last request was that he be buried in Jamaica and perhaps before he died he may have remembered the derisive jingle chanted by his Harlem skeptics in the early twenties:

> When a monkey-chaser dies,
> Don't need no undertaker.
> Just throw him in the Harlem River—
> He'll float back to Jamaica.[76]

But Garvey would never return to Jamaica. Neither would the Provisional President of Africa, who ironically was never able to visit the land of his dreams, witness the realization of his ideal of a powerful Negro state, respected and feared by the white world.[*]

English newspapers, feverishly intent upon the outcome of the evacuation of the British Expeditionary Force from the German trap at Dunkirk, ignored the passing of the once prominent U.N.I.A. leader. The American press, however, as yet untroubled by a personal interest in the European war news, found space to pay tribute to the memory of the cocky little black man who had once loomed so large on the American race scene. Even Garvey would have been amused to see such widely differing organs of opinion as the *New York Times* and the *Daily Worker* quarreling rather inaccurately over his significance in American life. It could scarcely be said, as the *Times* alleged, that Garvey

[* See the Preface, page xiii.—E. D. C., 1969.]

"no more represented the Negro race in this country than Mr. Capone or Mr. Hauptmann represented the white race," [77] nor was it true, as the *Daily Worker* boasted, that "the real blow to Garveyism was given by the Communist Party." [78] Perhaps the tribute Garvey would have appreciated most came from the Chicago *Defender*, the paper that had done more than any other to discredit him in the eyes of American Negroes:

Endowed with a dynamic personality, with unmatched oratorical gift, Garvey was easily the most colorful figure to have appeared in America since the historic times of Frederick Douglass and Booker T. Washington. From 1914 to 1921 he dominated the American scene from one end of the country to the other with multiple ramifications of the powerful U.N.I.A. ... Professor Albert Bushnell Hart of Harvard said of Garvey: "That is the difference between success and failure. Had Garvey succeeded in his undertakings, he would have been uncontestably the greatest figure of the twentieth century. Having failed, he is considered a fool." [79]

No matter what the final appraisal of Garvey's activities and significance as a Negro leader, black men and white, from the remotest village in Africa to the most crowded tenement in Harlem, would agree that the world had lost one of its most fascinating personalities. Marcus Garvey's like would not soon be seen again.

SEVEN

ONE AIM! ONE GOD!

ONE DESTINY!

Each race should be proud and stick to its own,
And the best of what they are should be shown;
This is no shallow song of hate to sing,
But over Blacks there should be no white king.

Every man on his own foothold should stand,
Claiming a nation and a fatherland!
White, Yellow, and Black should make their own laws,
And force no one-sided justice with flaws.
—Marcus Garvey [1]

Be as proud of your race today as our fathers were in the
days of yore. We have a beautiful history, and we shall
create another in the future that will astonish the world.
—Marcus Garvey [2]

★ Although Marcus Garvey never set foot on African soil, the basis for his race philosophy was Africa, the Negro homeland. For out of the moist green depths of the African jungle had come the endless files of hapless Negro slaves, a seemingly inexhaustible labor force to be devoured by the hungry plantations of the Americas. And in spite of the substantial but largely unrecognized contribution of these black slaves to the building of a New World civilization, their life of servitude under white masters had tended to destroy their African culture and to tear down their national and personal self-respect. To Garvey it seemed axiomatic that a redemption of the Negroes of the world must come only through a rebuilding of their shattered racial pride and a restoration of a truly Negro culture. Race pride and African nationalism were inextricably woven together in the Garvey philosophy, therefore, and the program of the Universal Negro Improvement Association centered around these two complementary objectives.

To understand Marcus Garvey and his extraordinary movement, it is necessary to consider in detail this strong emphasis on racism and African nationalism. Such a study helps not only to illumine the ideas of the man but also to show the basis for his wide appeal. Garvey's unparalleled success in capturing the imagination of masses of Negroes throughout the world can be explained only by recognizing that he put into words—and what magnificent inspiring words they were—what large numbers of his people were thinking. Garveyism as a social movement, reflecting as it did the hopes and aspirations of a substantial section of the Negro world, may best be studied by considering the ideas of its founder and leader, since these contain the key to Garvey's remarkable success.

In trying to establish a philosophy of Garveyism, however, it is important to place the movement in the context of general Negro thought in the period immediately following World War I. This was the era of the New Negro reaction to the race riots and frustrated hopes of the war years, and it was an age distinguished by the great artistic and literary activity that has been justly called the Negro Renaissance. Garveyism was for the most part decisively repudiated by the Negro intellectuals and it is thus difficult to give Garvey any credit for the flowering of the Negro Renaissance. Certainly his unceasing efforts to restore a strong sense of pride in things Negro was a march down the

same path as that trod by the New Negroes, however, and
the same forces that stimulated the Negro Renaissance
helped to create an audience for Garveyism. Garvey's bombastic efforts to whip up an intense black nationalism were
a logical counterpart to the more subtle but equally militant contemporary verse of such Negro poets as Claude
McKay, Langston Hughes, and Countee Cullen.

The significance of Garveyism lies in its appeal to the
dreams of millions of Negroes throughout the world. The
amazingly loyal support given Marcus Garvey by the Negro
masses, particularly in the United States and the West
Indies, was forthcoming because he told his followers what
they most wanted to hear, or, as E. Franklin Frazier has
said, he made them "feel like somebody among white
people who have said they were nobody." [3] Two decades
after Garvey's inglorious departure for Atlanta penitentiary
a new Harlem generation still remembered him as the man
who "brought to the Negro people for the first time a sense
of pride in being black." [4] This is the core of Marcus
Garvey's philosophy; around this ideal he centered his life.

☆

Coming at a time when Negroes generally had so little
of which to be proud, Garvey's appeal to race pride quite
naturally stirred a powerful response in the hearts of his
eager black listeners. "I am the equal of any white man,"
Garvey told his followers. "I want you to feel the same
way." [5] "We have come now to the turning point of the
Negro," he declared with calm assurance, "where we have
changed from the old cringing weakling, and transformed
into full-grown men, demanding our portion as MEN." [6]
One of the delegates to the first U.N.I.A. convention in
Harlem in 1920 served notice that "it takes 1,000 white men
to lick one Negro" and gave an illuminating preview of
the type of Negro leadership needed in the future. "The

Uncle Tom nigger has got to go, and his place must be taken by the new leader of the Negro race," he asserted. "That man will not be a white man with a black heart, nor a black man with a white heart, but a black man with a black heart." [7]

Garvey felt strongly that only through concerted action could Negroes achieve any betterment of their lowly status. "The world ought to know that it could not keep 400,000,-000 Negroes down forever," [8] he once remarked, and he constantly spoke optimistically of the Negroes of the world "standing together as one man." [9] The black man could hope to better himself, Garvey believed, only by joining his own actions with those of others of his race. "It has been said that the Negro has never yet found cause to engage himself in anything in common with his brother," the U.N.I.A. founder admitted, "but the dawn of a new day is upon us and we see things differently. We see now, not as individuals, but as a collective whole, having one common interest." [10] One of his followers put it a little more strongly:

Men and women of the Negro race, rouse ye in the name of your posterity, summon your every sense, collect your every faculty, thrust the scales from your eyes and be converted to the cause of Negro advancement and dignity; Negro power and Sovereignty; Negro freedom and integrity; thereby becoming the giants of your own destiny! Your posterity is crying out to you.[11]

This plea for racial solidarity was one in which Negroes of widely varying political persuasions could join.[12]

"It is obvious, according to the commonest principles of human action," Garvey told his followers, "that no man will do as much for you as you will do for yourself." [13] Accordingly, he counseled Negroes to work for a strong and united black nation able to demand justice instead of sympathy from the ruling powers of the world. "If we must have justice, we must be strong," he explained; "if we must be strong, we must come together; if we must come together, we can only do so through the system of organization." "Let us not waste time in breathless appeals to the strong while we are weak," he advised, "but lend our time, energy, and effort to the accumulation of strength among ourselves by which we will voluntarily attract the attention of others." [14] Create a strong Negro nation, Garvey said in essence, and never more will you fear oppression at the hands of other races.

This spirit of race confidence and solidarity pervaded all of the many activities of the Garvey movement. The Black Star Line and its successor, the Black Cross Navigation and Trading Company, the Negro Factories Corporation, and indeed the African Legion, the Black Cross Nurses, and the other components of the U.N.I.A. itself were all a part of the general plan to weld the Negro people into a racially conscious, united group for effective mass action. Outsiders might laugh or scoff at some of the antics of the various Garvey organizations, their serious members ludicrous with high-toned titles and elaborate uniforms, but the importance of this aspect of the movement in restoring the all but shattered Negro self-confidence should not be overlooked.

Garvey exalted everything black and exhorted Negroes to be proud of their distinctive features and color. Negroid characteristics were not shameful marks of inferiority to be camouflaged and altered; they were rather symbols of beauty and grace. In his poem, "The Black Woman," Garvey voiced his love of pure Negro beauty:

Black queen of beauty, thou hast given color to the world!
Among other women thou art royal and the fairest!

Like the brightest jewels in the regal diadem,
Shin'st thou, Goddess of Africa, Nature's purest emblem!

Black men worship at thy virginal shrine of purest love,
Because in thine eyes are virtue's steady and holy mark,
As we see no other, clothed in silk or fine linen,
From ancient Venus, the Goddess, to mythical Helen.[15]

These sentiments were, after all, not very different from those expressed by other, perhaps more lyric poets of the Negro Renaissance, and they reflected the growing sense of race pride developing in the Negro world.

It is perhaps significant that from this period of intensified race consciousness dates the first large-scale production of Negro dolls. Whether or not Negro children had any instinctive preference for dolls of their own color, their parents now came to believe in increasing numbers that their children should play with colored dolls.[16] In 1919 the Harlem firm of Berry and Ross started the profitable production of dolls of a dusky hue designed to satisfy the most discriminating young mistress—or parent.[17] The Universal Negro Improvement Association encouraged this revolutionary toy development, and Garvey's *Negro World* plugged the sale of black dolls. "Little Thelma Miller, eight years old, is very fond of her little colored doll," ran the caption under a U.N.I.A. photograph of a happy young mother proudly holding her very black toy baby. "She has never had the opportunity and pleasure of playing with no other doll except a colored doll. She is a real Garveyite." [18] The fact that most of these Negro dolls were advertised as "light-brown," "high-brown," or "mulatto," however, seems to indicate that Negroes continued to look upon lightness of color as a desirable characteristic.

One of the methods used by Garvey to build up a sense

of pride in the Negro heritage was his constant reference to the exploits of Negro heroes and to the land from which the race had come. He angrily accused white scholars of distorting Negro history to make it unfavorable to colored people. "Every student of history, of impartial mind," Garvey taught, "knows that the Negro once ruled the world, when white men were savages and barbarians living in caves; that thousands of Negro professors . . . taught in the universities in Alexandria."[19] The intent Negro audiences in Liberty Hall delighted in Garvey's vivid recollections of a creative black civilization at a time when white men were nothing:

When Europe was inhabited by a race of cannibals, a race of savages, naked men, heathens and pagans, Africa was peopled with a race of cultured black men, who were masters in art, science and literature; men who were cultured and refined; men, who, it was said, were like the gods. Even the great poets of old sang in beautiful sonnets of the delight it afforded the gods to be in companionship with the Ethiopians. Why, then, should we lose hope? Black men, you were once great; you shall be great again. Lose not courage, lose not faith, go forward. The thing to do is to get organized.[20]

This was in fact a subject upon which Garvey could wax angrily poetic:

Out of cold old Europe these white men came,
From caves, dens and holes, without any fame,
Eating their dead's flesh and sucking their blood,
Relics of the Mediterranean flood.[21]

Not only were white men of a low breed, far below their darker brothers, but the time had come to tell the world about the great heroes of Negro history. "Negroes, teach your children they are direct descendants of the greatest and proudest race who ever peopled the earth," Garvey preached with earnest intensity.[22] Wherever Ne-

groes had lived they had produced eminent men and accomplished notable achievements. "Sojurner Truth is
worthy of the place of sainthood alongside of Joan of Arc;
Crispus Attucks and George William Gordon are entitled
to the halo of martyrdom with no less glory than that of
the martyrs of any other race," Garvey cried. "Toussaint
L'Ouverture's brilliancy as a soldier and statesman outshone
that of a Cromwell, Napoleon, and Washington; hence he
is entitled to the highest place as a hero among men." [23]
Turn back the pages of Negro history as far as you like
and ever the result would be to the lasting glory of the
proud Negro people:

> So down the line of history we come,
> Black, courtly, courageous and handsome.
> No fear have we today of any great man
> From Napoleon back to Genghis Khan.[24]

The Garvey historical examination might not be as critical
as more objective scholars would desire, but it did act as
a massive dose of adrenalin to the nationalism now beginning to throb in Negro breasts.

☆

Along with the reborn Negro pride in the glorious past
and distinctive color of the race went a reorientation in
religion as well. Garvey believed that Negroes should end
their subserviency to the white man through the worship
of his white God. This rejection of an alien deity embodying
Caucasian features was not original with Garvey and was
in fact a logical part of any intensely race-conscious movement of this nature. Religious workers in Africa had long
noted the tendency of their converts to think of the deity
in terms of Negro pigmentation and to reject the concept
of a white God.[25] Indeed, many religious cults and sects
among American Negroes had projected the idea of a black
God long before Garvey arrived in the United States.[26]

Even some whites had suggested that Negro ministers should think in black terms, one fastidious southerner going so far as to assert that the Negro's Bible "ought to teach him that he will become a black angel and go home at death to a black God." [27] Garvey's extreme racial nationalism demanded fulfillment in a truly Negro religion, for, as his widow explains, "It is really logical that although we all know God is a spirit, yet all religions more or less visualize Him in a likeness akin to their own race. . . . Hence it was most vital that pictures of God should be in the likeness of the [Negro] Race." [28]

To implement the black religion, Garvey called upon the Reverend George Alexander McGuire, a prominent Episcopal clergyman who left his Boston pulpit in 1920 to become Chaplain General of the Universal Negro Improvement Association. On September 28, 1921, in a service conducted by dignitaries of the Greek Orthodox Church, McGuire was ordained a bishop and consecrated as head of the new African Orthodox Church.[29] Probably because Garvey had been brought up a Roman Catholic and Bishop McGuire had formerly been associated with the Episcopalian Church, the ritual of the new black religion followed much the same pattern as the liturgy of those two churches.

From the first, however, Bishop McGuire urged the Garveyites to "forget the white gods." "Erase the white gods from your hearts," he told his congregation. "We must go back to the native church, to our own true God." [30] The new Negro religion would seek to be true to the principles of Christianity without the shameful hypocrisy of the white churches.[31] Garvey himself urged Negroes to adopt their own religion, "with God as a Being, not as a Creature," a religion that would show Him "made in our own image —black." [32] When queried by a white reporter as to his reputed belief in the Negro ancestry of Christ, Garvey hedged a bit and replied that he believed "simply that Christ's ancestry included all races, so that He was Divinity incarnate in the broadest sense of the word." [33] In spite of strong opposition from the regular Negro clergy, Garvey's African Orthodox Church was able to report in its monthly magazine, the *Negro Churchman*, that "in its first year" it had "extended its missions through several states, into Canada, Cuba, and Hayti." Bishop McGuire reported that he had already recruited "10 Priests, 4 Deacons, 2 Sub-deacons and several Deaconesses, Catechists and Seminarians in training." [34]

By the time the Fourth International Convention of the Negro Peoples of the World met in 1924, moreover, the leaders of the black religion were openly demanding that Negroes worship a Negro Christ. During the opening parade through the streets of Harlem, U.N.I.A. members marched under a large portrait of a black Madonna and Child.[35] The convention session of August 5, 1924, drew the attention of the white press when Bishop McGuire advised Negroes to name the day when all members of the race would tear down and burn any pictures of the white Madonna and the white Christ found in their homes. "Then let us start our Negro painters getting busy," the Bishop declared, "and supply a black Madonna and a black Christ for the training of our children." Bishop McGuire gave added weight to his words by speaking under a large oil painting that clearly portrayed the type of Madonna and Child he had in mind.[36]

Bishop McGuire told of an aged Negro woman who had gratefully offered her African Orthodox pastor five dollars for telling her of the black Christ, because she knew that "no white man would ever die on the cross for me." Speaking emphatically so that none of his listeners might fail to catch the import of his message, the Bishop declared that

Christ had actually been a reddish brown in color, and he predicted that if the Saviour were to visit New York He would not be able to live on fashionable Riverside Drive but would have to go to Harlem, "because all the darker people live here in Harlem." Bishop McGuire complained that the western Negro was the only Negro in the world who accepted the white man's characterization of the devil as being black, and he announced that henceforth the Negro's devil would be white. Another speaker at the same meeting, the Reverend J. D. Barber of Ethiopia, prophesied that the Negro would soon have his own illustrated Bible, complete with inspiring pictures of Negro saints and angels. Reverend Barber recalled St. John's description of Christ as "a black man, with feet that shone as polished brass, hair of lamb's wool and eyes with flames of fire," a rather elastic reference to the account in the prologue of the Book of Revelation.[37]

Garvey clung to the concept of a Negro Deity until his death. To him the sufferings of Christ typified the age-old sorrows of the Negro race:

> White men the Saviour did crucify,
> For eyes not blue, but blood of Negro tie.[38]

At the Seventh U.N.I.A. Convention held at Kingston, Jamaica, in August, 1934, the delegates passed a resolution endorsing the principles of Christianity but urging Negroes to "conceive their Deity unforeign to their own creation but akin to it." Negroes were advised to worship a God whose physical form, image, and likeness would be "dramatized in the physical beauty and characteristics of the Negro himself." [39] Garvey could not conceive of a God who would differentiate between any of the children He had made to live on His earth:

> Thou art made to be so white
> That no black man has a claim:
> Could'st this, God, be ever right
> That you made us ill of fame?
> Thou art God in every way,
> Caring not for black nor white.[40]

An impartial God meant also a multiracial heaven and Garvey therefore offered for sale one of his devotional poems as a "picture motto with the design of a Negro Angel." [41]

Garvey's efforts to deny the Jewish ancestry of Christ recalled the earlier attempt of Houston Stewart Chamberlain, that pathetic Englishman turned German, to bring the Saviour into the Aryan fold. "Whoever makes the assertion that Christ was a Jew is either ignorant or insincere," the worried prophet of Nordic supremacy had written around the turn of the century. "The probability that Christ was no Jew, that He had not a drop of genuinely Jewish blood in His veins, is so great that it is almost equivalent to a certainty." [42] Like the shocked reaction to Chamberlain's ludicrous bigotry, the response to Garvey's call for an all-black religion was mostly negative. The Negro press generally shared the sentiments of George Harris, the anti-Garvey editor of the New York *News*, who indignantly declared that Garvey had installed "a black God as the deity colored folks must worship for the sake of attracting the limelight." [43] Humorist George S. Schuyler saw only the ironical aspect of Garvey's racial God and tied the black religion to the collapse of the various U.N.I.A. enterprises. "Last summer Marcus accused the Deity of being a Negro," Schuyler chuckled. "No wonder luck went against him!" [44] Kelly Miller was even more hostile in his denunciation of the new creed. "Marcus Garvey some little while ago shocked the spiritual sensibilities of the religious world by suggesting that the Negro should paint God black," he complained, adding that "the idea was revolting even to the Negro." [45]

Except for an insignificant handful of converts to the African Orthodox Church, the regular Negro clergy firmly rejected the new black religion, and it has been estimated —"guess-timated" is doubtless a more precise term—that as many as four out of five American Negro preachers were opposed to the concept of a black God.[46] William Pickens suggests that this rejection of Garvey's spiritual leadership may have amounted more to a distrust of his political aims and business methods than to any indication of convictions on the subject of color.[47] More convincing is A. Philip Randolph's explanation that Negro preachers opposed the African Orthodox Church out of fear they would lose their following, since their congregations had been conditioned in a white civilization and had thus grown up believing in a white God and in a Christian religion that had been fashioned and proselytized by white men.[48] Garvey's widow believes that the antipathy resulted largely from economic considerations, since the consolidation of Negroes into one denomination would mean the end of individual power and prestige for the preachers leading the innumerable small sects and independent churches.[49] Another consideration might be the need to retain white support in areas such as the American South where the Negro preacher has traditionally looked to white leaders for his cue in matters of politics and social action.

Unwittingly Garvey demonstrated a keen awareness of social psychology when he used a black God of Israel to stimulate racial nationalism among the Negro masses. And in spite of the loud outcries from Negro intellectuals and the horrified regular clergy when he first launched the campaign for the new religion, Garvey had the satisfaction before he died of seeing a decided shift in favor of a Negro-oriented spiritualism among certain elements of the Negro intelligentsia.[50] An eminent Negro sociologist has summed up perhaps better than anyone else Garvey's shrewd awareness of the spiritual needs of his followers. "The intellectual can laugh, if he will," wrote E. Franklin Frazier of the black God, "but let him not forget the pragmatic value of such a symbol among the type of people Garvey was dealing with."[51]

☆

Much more important in the stimulation of black nationalism was the U.N.I.A. program to lead Negroes back to their African homeland. With customary flamboyance Garvey assured his followers that a few years would see Africa as completely dominated by Negroes as Europe was by whites. "No one knows when the hour of Africa's Redemption cometh," he warned mysteriously. "It is in the wind. It is coming. One day, like a storm, it will be here."[52] To his Liberty Hall supporters Garvey exclaimed, "Let Africa be our guiding star—our star of destiny,"[53] while to the dark motherland he called, "Wake up Ethiopia! Wake up Africa! Let us work towards the one glorious end of a free, redeemed and mighty nation. Let Africa be a bright star among the constellation of nations."[54]

A great independent African nation was the essential ingredient in the Garvey recipe for race redemption and he was earnestly convinced that Negroes needed the dark continent to achieve their destiny as a great people. Like another ardent disciple of racial nationalism, Garvey demanded *Lebensraum* for his people. It fell to the U.N.I.A. to lead the struggle to regain Africa and in the fight Garvey foresaw divine intervention. "At this moment methinks I see Ethiopia stretching forth her hands unto God," he declared fervently, "and methinks I see the angel of God taking up the standard of the Red, the Black, and the Green, and saying, 'Men of the Negro race, Men of Ethiopia, follow me!' It falls to our lot to tear off the shackles that bind Mother Africa." "Climb ye the heights of liberty," Garvey exhorted the U.N.I.A. legions, "and cease not in well-doing until you have planted the banner of the Red, the Black, and the Green upon the hilltops of Africa." [55]

But what of the powerful European nations that had carved up the African continent and now controlled the homeland? Garvey frequently disclaimed any animus against the white race,[56] but at the same time he pointedly told his followers: "We shall not ask England or France or Italy or Belgium, 'Why are you here?' We shall only command them, 'Get out of here.' " [57] The barrier to a free Africa was the white man, and Garvey warned ominously: "We say to the white man who now dominates Africa that it is to his interest to clear out of Africa now, because we are coming . . . 400,000,000 strong." [58] Garvey loved to speculate on the tremendous power that would belong to the Negro people once they discovered what their numerical strength could do for them.[59] "We are going home after a long vacation," he told the U.N.I.A., "and are giving notice to the tenant to get out. If he doesn't there is such a thing as forcible ejection." [60] "You will find ten years from now, or 100 years from now," he warned a white audience, "Garvey was not an idle buffoon but was representing the new vision of the Negro who was looking forward to great accomplishments in the future." [61]

It was never Garvey's intention that all Negroes in the New World would return to Africa and in this sense it is misleading to call his scheme a Back to Africa movement. Rather he believed like many Zionists that once a strong African nation was established Negroes everywhere would automatically gain needed prestige and strength and could look to it for protection if necessary.[62] "At no time did he visualize all American Negroes returning to Africa," says his widow.[63] "We do not want all the Negroes in Africa," Garvey informed a U.N.I.A. audience in Madison Square Garden in 1924. "Some are no good here, and naturally will be no good there." [64] Those particularly needed for the work in Africa would be engineers, artisans, and willing workers of all sorts—in short, the pioneering elements upon which all civilizations are built.

Garvey's address at his inauguration as Provisional President of Africa in 1920 demonstrated his strong belief in a personal destiny as the liberator of Africa. "The signal honor of being Provisional President of Africa is mine," he exulted. "It is a political calling for me to redeem Africa. It is like asking Napoleon to take the world. . . . He failed and died at St. Helena. But may I not say that the lessons of Napoleon are but stepping stones by which we shall guide ourselves to African liberation?" [65] The possibility of going down in history as the father of his country fascinated Garvey, and after a visit to the grave of George Washington he described " a new thought, a new inspiration" that had come to him at Mount Vernon. "It was the vision of a day —near, probably—when hundreds of other men and women will be worshipping at a shrine. This time the vision leads me to the shrine of some black man, the father of African independence." [66] Garvey continued the comparison with his poem "Hail! United States of Africa!" in which he managed to mention all of the twenty-six possible African states:

> Hail! United States of Africa—free!
> Country of the brave black man's liberty;
> State of greater nationhood thou hast won,
> A new life for the race has just begun.[67]

Most American Negro editors scoffed at the Back to
Africa talk and loudly proclaimed the desire of Negroes to
remain in the United States. The Chicago *Defender,* which
generally avoided use of the word Negro in its columns,
announced proudly, "The Race considers itself African no
more than white Americans consider themselves European." The *Defender* went on to suggest pointedly that
"in the United States lunacy commissions still have legal
standing." [68] An anti-Garvey cartoon showed a strong
manly Negro holding a small nondescript "Back to Africa
fanatic" and advising, "The best thing you can do is stay
right *here* and fight out your salvation." [69] Even the white
press, when it deigned to notice Garvey, was hostile to
the idea of a redemption of Africa.[70] Negro intellectuals
generally opposed Garvey's methods if not his interest in
Africa. Booker T. Washington had preached against any
idea of a return to Africa and doubtless his philosophy
still carried great weight with many American Negroes.[71]
Sometimes, however, even Garvey's critics saw fascinating
possibilities in the awakened interest in the ancestral homeland. Writing after Garvey's confinement in Atlanta, Professor Alain Locke declared, "Garveyism may be a transient, if spectacular, phenomenon, but the possible role
of the American Negro in the future development of Africa
is one of the most constructive and universally helpful
missions that any modern people can lay claim to." [72]

It is interesting to note that the idea of setting up an
independent African state remained a part of Garvey's
program to the end of his life. One of the last issues of his
monthly magazine, the *Black Man,* contained an earnest
plea for support of U.S. Senator Theodore G. Bilbo's bill
for the repatriation of American Negroes to Africa. Garvey
admitted that the motives of this bigoted southern racist
might "not be as idealistic as Negroes may want," but he

gave the Bilbo bill his endorsement because "independent nationality is the greatest guarantee of the ability of any people to stand up in our present civilization." He therefore asked all divisions of the Universal Negro Improvement Association in the United States "to give their undivided and whole-hearted support to Senator Bilbo's Bill." [73]

☆

Garvey's passionate interest in Africa was a logical development of his firm conviction that Negroes could expect no permanent progress in a land dominated by white men.[74] No doubt he would have agreed completely with Mr. Dooley's shrewd analysis of the American race problem: "Th' throuble is that th' naygurs iv th' North have lived too long among th' white people, an' th' white people iv th' South have lived too long among th' naygurs." [75] Garvey said essentially the same thing when he told Negroes to develop "a government, a nation of our own, strong enough to lend protection to the members of our race scattered all over the world, and to compel the respect of the nations and the races of the earth." [76] When Garvey spoke of discrimination, he touched a subject painfully familiar to every Negro: "If you cannot live alongside the white man in peace, if you cannot get the same chance and opportunity alongside the white man, even though you are his fellow citizen; if he claims that you are not entitled to this chance or opportunity because the country is his by force of numbers, then find a country of your own and rise to the highest position within that country." [77] The Garvey solution for Negro ills was to make the race "so strong as to strike fear" into the hearts of the oppressor white race.[78] Only when Negroes could compel respect and justice through their connection with a strong Negro government would the position of the race be secure.

Garvey had no illusions about the white man's Christian

love and believed that it would be used only when conveniently suitable. The U.N.I.A. therefore conceded the right of whites to do as they pleased in their own lands provided that Negroes were allowed to develop a nation of their own in Africa.[79] "Political, social and industrial America," Garvey cautioned, "will never become so converted as to be willing to share up equitably between black and white." [80] Though Negroes might live as useful citizens in the United States for thousands of years, Garvey believed that as long as the white population was numerically superior to them the blacks could never hope for political justice or social equality.[81]

Garvey's plain abdication of Negro rights in America quickly brought him the open support of such white supremacy groups as the Ku Klux Klan and the Anglo-Saxon Clubs, both flourishing mightily in the postwar years. Garvey's major book, the second volume of his *Philosophy and Opinions,* carried an advertisement for Major Earnest Sevier Cox's *White America,* a polemical work strongly preaching the separation of the races. Major Cox sometimes spoke to U.N.I.A. audiences at Liberty Hall in New York, and he even dedicated a pamphlet on racial purity to Garvey, whom he called "a martyr for the independence and integrity of the Negro race." [82] Another white supporter was John Powell, the fanatical organizer of the Anglo-Saxon Clubs of America. Garvey expressed great admiration for men like Cox and Powell because of "their honesty and lack of hypocrisy" in openly working to maintain the power of the white race.[83] Speaking at Liberty Hall late in 1925, Powell congratulated the U.N.I.A. on its racial improvement program and reaffirmed the mutual desire of blacks and whites to preserve the purity of their respective races.[84] Garvey also received support from some southern whites who looked upon his movement with favor because it was likely to attract Negroes who might otherwise be resentful of their subordinate caste position in the United States.[85] After he was deported, some of Garvey's white friends were active in a campaign to permit the return of the exiled U.N.I.A. leader.[86]

"Lynchings and race riots," said Garvey with reference to the grim postwar period of racial strife and violence, "all work to our advantage by teaching the Negro that he must build a civilization of his own or forever remain the white man's victim." [87] Bishop McGuire, the religious leader of the U.N.I.A. and spiritual head of the African Orthodox Church, declared frankly that the Ku Klux Klan's campaign of intimidation and violence would benefit the movement by driving harassed Negroes into the Garvey organization.[88] In 1922 Garvey indicated his tacit support of the dread Klan, an alliance his opponents had suspected for some time. "The Ku Klux Klan is going to make this a white man's country," Garvey asserted in stating his belief that the K.K.K. was the invisible government of America. "They are perfectly honest and frank about it. Fighting them is not going to get you anywhere." [89]

Early in 1922 Garvey went to Atlanta, Georgia, for a conference with Edward Young Clarke, Imperial Giant of the Klan.[90] The purpose of the meeting was apparently to see how strong the Klan was and whether or not Garvey could hope for its support for the Back to Africa program of the U.N.I.A. Garvey's widow explains that far from approving of the Klan's violent actions against Negroes, her husband merely believed "that the prejudice exhibited by the Klan in hysteria, hate, cruelty, and mob violence was the prejudice common to most white Americans, which deep in their hearts they felt, but culture and refinement prevented many from showing any trace of it." [91] The meeting was one of expediency, then, rather than of mutual admiration, but it was nonetheless a serious tactical blunder.

Although details of the Atlanta conference were withheld, the mere thought that a responsible Negro leader would collaborate with the leading avowed enemy of his race brought down a storm of criticism upon Garvey's head. Alderman George Harris, editor of the New York *News*, denounced Garvey as "misrepresenting the attitude of 100 per cent of our native-born Americans and 75 per cent of the foreign-born group" when he surrendered to Clarke. "When Garvey agrees with the Klan's theory that this is a white man's country," Harris complained angrily, "he sadly misrepresents our people." [92] William Pickens, who had at one time very nearly accepted a high U.N.I.A. post, now spurned with contempt a Garvey title of nobility because of this rumored alliance with the Ku Klux Klan.[93] W. E. B. DuBois let go a powerful blast against the U.N.I.A. president in *Crisis*, the organ of the National Association for the Advancement of Colored People. "Marcus Garvey is, without doubt, the most dangerous enemy of the Negro race in America and the world," sputtered the indignant editor of *Crisis*. "He is either a lunatic or a traitor." [94] Unperturbed by this barrage of Negro criticism, Garvey countered with a candid appraisal of white America. "I regard the Klan, the Anglo-Saxon Clubs and White American Societies," he maintained, "as better friends of the race than all other groups of hypocritical whites put together. I like honesty and fair play. You may call me a Klansman if you will, but, potentially every white man is a Klansman, as far as the Negro in competition with whites socially, economically and politically is concerned, and there is no use lying about it." [95]

The main reason that Garvey and his organization were acceptable to the Ku Klux Klan and other white supremacy groups was that the U.N.I.A. leader preached race purity to his followers. He thundered that racial amalgamation must cease forthwith and warned that any member of the Universal Negro Improvement Association who married a white would be summarily expelled.[96] Not only did Garvey advocate race purity, but as a Jamaican black he attempted to transfer the West Indian three-way color caste system to the United States by attacking mulatto leaders. He laughed at the light-skinned mulattoes, who, he said, were always seeking "excuses to get out of the Negro Race," [97] and he scornfully accused his mulatto opponents of being "time-serving, boot-licking agencies of subserviency to the whites." [98] The average Negro leader, Garvey said, sought to establish himself as "the pet of some philanthropist of another race," thereby selling out the interests of his own people.[99]

The U.N.I.A. catered to the darker Negroes; in fact, Garvey's definition of Negro seemed to require a purity of racial origin. At first the anti-mulatto propaganda helped to inflate the egos of darker Negroes, but it was doomed to failure in the United States where neither whites nor Negroes make any appreciable distinction between Negroes of different shades of color.[100] American blacks lacked the fierce resentment toward the favored position of mulattoes that had been a part of Garvey's Jamaican conditioning. The U.N.I.A. continued to preach racial purity, however, and its founder maintained his attack on his light-skinned critics by asserting that they favored racial amalgamation. "I believe in racial purity, and in maintaining the standard of racial purity," he asserted. "I am proud I am a Negro. It is only the so-called 'colored' man who talks of social equality." [101] "We are not seeking social equality," Garvey told whites. "We do not seek intermarriage, nor do we hanker after the impossible. We want the right to have a country of our own, and there foster and re-establish a culture and civilization exclusively ours." [102] Garvey's advocacy of racial purity was noticed even in Germany, where the so-called German Emergency League against the Black Horror sought to enlist his aid in securing the removal of French Negro occupation troops from the Rhineland.[103]

In Garvey's vocabulary, as in that of most southern whites, social equality meant "the social intermingling of both races, intermarriages, and general social co-relationship." [104] Believing that such intermingling would inevitably lead to "an American race, that will neither be white nor black," [105] Garvey directed a constant stream of criticism against Dr. W. E. B. DuBois of the N.A.A.C.P. for his efforts on behalf of Negro social and political equality.[106] At least part of this animosity was doubtless due to DuBois' own dignified attacks on the U.N.I.A. and to the fact that the cultured editor of *Crisis* possessed an excellent formal education of the sort Garvey had always desired but had never been able to obtain. E. Franklin Frazier suggests that "Garvey constantly directed the animosity of his followers against the intellectuals because of his own lack of formal education." [107] Though the *Negro World* in 1922 listed DuBois as one of the "twelve greatest living Negroes" (Garvey was of course also on the list),[108] the 1924 convention of the U.N.I.A. resolved to ostracize DuBois "from the Negro race, so far as the U.N.I.A. is concerned," declaring him "an enemy of the black people of the world." [109]

Garvey denounced other Negro leaders as being bent on cultural assimilation, cravenly seeking white support, and miserably compromising between accommodation and protest.[110] The National Association for the Advancement of Colored People was the worst offender in Garvey's mind, because, he said, it "wants us all to become white by amalgamation, but they are not honest enough to come out with the truth." "To be a Negro is no disgrace, but an honor," Garvey indignantly affirmed, "and we of the U.N.I.A. do not want to become white." [111] He warned both whites and blacks that the purity of the two races was endangered by the false prophets of amalgamation. "It is the duty of the virtuous and morally pure of both the white and black races," he announced, "to thoughtfully and actively protect the future of the two peoples, by vigorously opposing the destructive propaganda and vile efforts of the miscegenationists of the white race, and their associates, the hybrids of the Negro race." [112] "I believe in a pure black race," Garvey proclaimed loudly, "just as how all self-respecting whites believe in a pure white race, as far as that can be." [113] The U.N.I.A. chief felt constrained to warn the white world of the dangers inherent in social equality. "Some Negroes believe in social equality," he cautioned. "They want to intermarry with the white women of this country, and it is going to cause trouble later on. Some Negroes want the same jobs you have. They want to be Presidents of the nation." [114]

On the other hand, white Americans need have no fears of the aims of the Universal Negro Improvement Association, which Garvey declared was stoutly opposed to "miscegenation and race suicide" and believed strongly "in the purity of the Negro race and the purity of the white race." [115] So intent was Garvey on the goal of complete racial compartmentalization that he even went so far as to warn individual whites of the danger of allowing Negroes to become elected officials, artisans, or skilled laborers while white workers were unemployed. Such ill-considered opportunities for blacks, he believed, would only lead to "bloody . . . wholesale mob violence." [116] This abandonment of Negro economic rights was too much for former sympathizer William Pickens, who exploded wrathfully, "This squat, energetic, gorilla-jawed black man is one of the worst enemies of his own Race." [117] Garvey intended, of course, that Negroes should create their own economic opportunities through such race enterprises as the Black Star Line and the Negro Factories Corporation. In this connection it is of interest to note, however, that at least five of the important operational posts in the Black Star Line were at one time or another filled by white men, including three ship captains, a first assistant engineer, and a marine superintendent. Apparently, suitably skilled Negroes were not easy to find, even for service with a Negro steamship company.

In October, 1921, President Warren G. Harding made a controversial speech on race relations while visiting Birmingham, Alabama. Quoting from Lothrop Stoddard's alarmist book, *The Rising Tide of Color against White World Supremacy,* Harding asserted his belief in the old Booker T. Washington ideal of the social separation of the two races. "There shall be recognition of the absolute divergence in things social and racial," the President declared. "Men of both races may well stand uncompromisingly against every suggestion of social equality. . . . Racial amalgamation there cannot be." [118] Though southern Negroes may have agreed with the Washington *Bee's* appraisal of the Harding speech as "a brave, courageous, fearless, heroic deed," [119] the more militant Negro leadership in the North indicated its stunned dismay at the President's apparently unfriendly attitude. Garvey, however, immediately telegraphed his congratulations to President Harding and expressed "the heartfelt thanks of four hundred million Negroes of the world for the splendid interpretation you have given the race problem." "All true Negroes are against social equality," the U.N.I.A. president asserted, "believing that all races should develop on their own social lines." [120] Harding's Birmingham address, Garvey later wrote, "was one that revealed his depth of thought for the Negro." [121] Those Negroes with an eye for the *double-entendre* could find a wry bit of humor in the assertion. Others might criticize both Harding and his predecessor, Woodrow Wilson, for their lack of sympathetic activity on behalf of colored citizens, but to Garvey they "came nearest to playing the Christ in the leadership of the American people." [122]

How well Garvey's aggressive philosophy of racial purity and social separation permeated the lowest echelons of the Universal Negro Improvement Association may be shown by a letter to the mayor of New Orleans from the women's auxiliary of the local division of the organization:

We like your "Jim Crow" laws, in that they defend the purity of races and any person married to any but a Negro cannot become a member of our organization. We are not members . . . of that class who are spending their time imitating the rich whites . . . studying Spanish so as to be able to pass for anything but a Negro, thereby getting a chance to associate with you. We are not ashamed of the Race to which we belong and we feel sure that God made black skin and kinky hair because He desired to express Himself in that type.[123]

It is not hard to see from the foregoing why Garvey was opposed so vigorously by the militant Negro rights organizations like the N.A.A.C.P., and conversely, why he received open encouragement from such white supremacy groups as the Ku Klux Klan.

☆

Garvey had a strong distaste for any alliance with white labor organizations, a skepticism that probably stemmed in part from his early failure as a strike leader in Jamaica. This distrust of the labor movement also reflected a feeling that the white worker was the Negro's greatest competitor

and most dangerous rival.[124] Rather than seek an alliance
with white workers, Garvey told Negroes that the white
employer was their best friend until such time as the race
had achieved economic independence.[125] The Negro Factories Corporation and the Black Star Line were direct
moves to set up Negro-owned business enterprises so that
Negroes would not have to beg for employment from
whites. It seemed self-evident to Garvey that "the only
convenient friend" of the American Negro worker was "the
white capitalist," who "being selfish—seeking only the largest profit out of labor—is willing and glad to 'use Negro
labor wherever possible on a scale 'reasonably' below the
standard white union wage." The white employer would
"tolerate the Negro" only if he accepted "a lower standard
of wage than the white union man." Garvey's solution for
the black worker, therefore, was to "keep his scale of wage
a little lower than the whites" and thereby "keep the good-
will of the white employer," all the time husbanding Negro
resources so that the race could ultimately become economically free.[126] Needless to say, this cheerful rejection of
trade unionism did little to endear Garvey to Negro labor
leaders, and it early won for him the bitter hostility of men
like Chandler Owen and A. Philip Randolph, who were
currently engaged in a successful campaign to establish a
union of Negro sleeping car porters.

Similarly, Garvey refused to have anything to do with
socialism and communism, despite the alarmist attempts
of the Lusk Committee and the Department of Justice to
portray him as a dangerous radical agitator. He felt that
these movements of the left, although they made a pre-
tense of helping the Negro, were inherently prejudiced
against the black race, since they were dominated by
whites. "Fundamentally what racial difference is there between a white Communist, Republican or Democrat?" Gar-

vey demanded to know. "On the appeal of race interest the Communist is as ready as either to show his racial . . . superiority over the Negro." [127] The U.N.I.A. leader suspected that for all his fine talk the Communist would just as quickly join a lynch mob as would the less radical white citizen, and consequently he believed that communism must first prove itself as a really new reform movement before the Negro could safely accept it.[128] The Communists were not initially opposed to Garvey's Universal Negro Improvement Association, though they deplored his emphasis on African Zionism. Party members inside the U.N.I.A. were ordered to push the fight for Negro equality within the United States, but they were so few in number that they were never able either to "capture" the association or to challenge successfully Garvey's leadership.[129] The Communist Party was greatly impressed with the amazing lower-class appeal of the U.N.I.A., however, and after the organization had begun to disintegrate in 1926 Robert Minor wrote disconsolately: "A breaking up of this Negro association would be a calamity to the Negro people and to the working class as a whole. . . . It is composed very largely, if not almost entirely, of Negro workers and impoverished farmers, although there is a sprinkling of small business men." [130]

In spite of Garvey's announced opposition to communism as a reform movement, he publicly mourned the death of Nikolai Lenin, the founder of the Soviet Union, in 1924. In a *Negro World* editorial he called Lenin "probably the world's greatest man between 1917 and . . . 1924," and announced that the U.N.I.A. had dispatched a cablegram to Moscow "expressing the sorrow and condolence of the 400,000,000 Negroes of the world." [131] This action need not be seen as a startling reversal of Garvey's earlier views, but merely as an example of his unexcelled flair for the dramatic and his egotistical desire to be associated with the important men of the day.

Although Garvey had once defined "radical" as "a label that is always applied to people who are endeavoring to get freedom," [132] he never hesitated to use the confusing term to discredit his opponents. In January, 1923, for example, after the "Committee of Eight" had written the Department of Justice protesting the delay in the trial of the four Black Star officials, Garvey wired the United States Attorney General to assure him of the patriotic loyalty of the U.N.I.A. In his telegram Garvey sought to smear his Negro critics. The National Association for the Advancement of Colored People was dominated by Socialists, Garvey declared, and he called the Friends of Negro Freedom "a red Socialistic organization." He accused the African Blood Brotherhood, another hostile group, of being composed of "representatives of the Bolsheviki of Russia." [133] This was a shady dodge as old as the game of politics itself: discredit your opponents by fair means or foul and perhaps they will stop asking embarrassing questions. There was just enough truth in Garvey's allegations, however, to warrant making the charges in this period of general reaction against leftist movements.

The Universal Negro Improvement Association, far from being oriented to the left, may be classified as a movement of the extreme right. Its intense nationalism and narrow racial outlook had little in common with liberal groups that were seeking to tear down these barriers between men and nations. In 1937, after Italy's legions had overrun Ethiopia, Garvey boasted that he had been the first prophet of fascism. "We were the first Fascists," he told a friend. "We had disciplined men, women, and children in training for the liberation of Africa. The black masses saw that in this extreme nationalism lay their only hope and readily sup-

ported it. Mussolini copied Fascism from me but the Negro
reactionaries sabotaged it." [134]

One may question whether Garvey was aware of all
the connotations of either fascism or communism, but certainly his U.N.I.A., with its fierce chauvinistic nationalism
and strongly centralized leadership, had fascist characteristics. Garvey talked of a democratic African republic but it
is a little hard to imagine him in such a government. Much
more likely would have been a black empire with Garvey
upon its throne. "Liberty and true Democracy means," he
once said, "that if one man can be the President, King,
Premier or Chancellor of a country then the other fellow
can be the same also." [135] There never was much doubt in
the mind of this supremely confident black man as to just
what his personal role in the "democratic" shift of power
would be.

In many respects Garveyism resembled another movement of minority group nationalism, the Jewish Zionism of
Theodor Herzl. Arnold Rose has pointed out the interesting
similarity in background and outlook shared by Herzl and
Garvey. Neither was exposed to strong anti-minority feelings in his formative years and later each reacted against
prejudice in terms of escape to a land free of discrimination.
Both adopted a chauvinistic, even religious nationalism,
and both sought support from those groups most hostile
to their own minority group.[136] Both movements took on
elements of fanaticism in their belligerent determination
to secure a new life for their oppressed peoples. There is
nothing to suggest that Garvey was familiar with Herzl's
Judenstaat, published some twenty years before Garvey
launched his own program of black Zionism, though he
once described his followers as "Zionists" (Case A, 1699).
However similar the aims and origin of the two movements,
Zionism proved to be by far the stronger and more success-

ful, perhaps because it managed to secure heavy financial
and intellectual support from the Jews of the world. Garveyism, on the other hand, was greatly handicapped by the
fact that it always remained the personal crusade of a
single leader whose autocratic methods and slipshod financial practices alienated much of the support the movement
might otherwise have received. And regardless of the similarity between Jewish Zionism and Garveyism, the
U.N.I.A. leader entertained strong prejudices against Jews
in general.[137]

☆

Marcus Garvey's philosophy of race relations was inextricably bound up in his staunch belief that it was use-
less for the Negro to attempt to better his condition in a
country dominated by another, inherently hostile race.
Firmly convinced that the United States would always be
a white man's country, and concerned lest the Negro should
forget his racial and cultural background, Garvey willingly
relinquished Negro rights in America for the dubious right
to establish a black nation in Africa. His zeal in securing
this Negro state led him to co-operate with the most reac-
tionary and anti-Negro groups in the United States. It is
both a mistake and an injustice to assume, however, as
some careless writers have done, that Garvey was merely
an opportunistic demagogue anxious to build up a powerful
following for personal gain.[138] Demagogue he most certainly was, but his motives, mistaken as they often seemed
to many Negro Americans eager to win full status as citizens
of the only country they had ever known, were much more
complex than that. Garvey was determined to help his
suffering people and his devotion often led him to act in a
way that was incomprehensible to American-born Negroes.

In 1919, the year Garvey first began to be noticed in
the United States, Walter Lippmann concluded that Amer-

icans would have to work out a civilization where "no Negro need dream of a white heaven and of bleached angels." "Pride of race will come to the Negro when a dark skin is no longer associated with poverty, ignorance, misery, terror and insult," Lippmann declared. "When this pride arises every white man in America will be the happier for it. He will be able then, as he is not now, to enjoy the finest quality of civilized living—the fellowship of different men." [139] The creation of a powerful feeling of race pride is perhaps Garvey's greatest and most lasting contribution to the American race scene. Marcus Garvey is gone and with him many of the more spectacular yet ephemeral aspects of his colorful movement, but the awakened spirit of Negro pride that he so ardently championed remains an important legacy to the Negro people.

ECHOES

AND REVERBERATIONS

The heathen raged, the kingdoms were moved;
He uttered his voice, the earth melted.

—Psalm 46

Verily every man at his best state is altogether vanity;
Surely every man walketh in a vain show.

—Psalm 39

★ Even today it is probably easier to track down a yellowed stock certificate of the long-defunct Black Star Line than to give a balanced evaluation of Marcus Garvey and his amazing Negro movement. Strident demagogue or dedicated prophet, martyred visionary or fabulous con man?—these are a few of the difficult questions posed by this fascinating career. Unfortunately, the almost total lack of the usual biographical materials raises formidable mechanical barriers to an accurate reconstruction of Garvey's life and varicolored activities, while more than a decade after the pudgy little Jamaican's death the impact of his forceful personality still remains to override and obscure the effects and defects of his leadership. Certainly few would disagree with the U.N.I.A. member who once exclaimed, "Marcus Garvey opened windows in the minds of Negroes!" [1] Yet it is just as true, unhappily, as Ralph Bunche has said, that "when the curtain dropped on the Garvey theatricals, the black man of America was exactly where Garvey had found him, though a little bit sadder, perhaps a bit poorer—if not wiser." [2]

Marcus Garvey's success in capturing the imagination of the black masses cannot be ignored by the thoughtful student of Negro history. The enthusiastic response to Garvey's persuasive program of black nationalism shows beyond all question that the Negro masses can be reached through an emotional appeal based on race pride. As Gunnar Myrdal has pointed out, Negro intellectuals have been understandably reluctant to deal with this aspect of the Garvey movement, and its importance has generally escaped white observers in their concentration on the more flamboyant king-size schemes and dreams of the Jamaican prophet. [3] Yet it is precisely this aspect of Garveyism—its strong appeal for the unsophisticated and unlettered masses —that is most worthy of careful attention. Garvey's very success in selling an unrealistic escapist program of racial chauvinism to American Negroes throws into sharp relief the burning discontent and bitter disillusionment that he found in the Negro world. Marcus Garvey intuitively put his finger on the pulse of his race, and even today in many areas his prescription of Negro nationalism has wide appeal as the only tonic that will cure the world of discrimination, prejudice, intolerance, and injustice.

Garvey is now universally acclaimed as a master propagandist and gifted leader of men. "A West Indian charlatan came to this country, full of antiquated social ideas," recalled Claude McKay, himself a Jamaican, in 1937; "yet within a decade he aroused the social consciousness of the Negro masses more than any leader ever did." [4] "To hundreds of thousands of his own people he was and still is a magnificent leader, a Washington, a Lincoln, with a glorious program of emancipation," declared Mary White

Ovington after Garvey's banishment from the United States. "He was the first Negro in the United States to capture the imagination of the masses. Among the poor and the exploited, even among those whose money he misappropriated, he is defended with an ardor that abashes the critic. Charlatan or fanatic, profiteer or martyr, he has profoundly stirred the race consciousness of Negroes throughout the world." [5] Even Garvey's severe critic, Dr. W. E. B. DuBois, has admitted the sweeping popularity of the movement. "It was a grandiose and bombastic scheme, utterly impracticable as a whole," DuBois said in 1940, the year of Garvey's death, "but it was sincere and had some practical features; and Garvey proved not only an astonishing popular leader, but a master of propaganda. Within a few years, news of his movement, of his promises and plans, reached Europe and Asia, and penetrated every corner of Africa." [6]

While there is no question of Garvey's rapid rise to a position of potent leadership in the Negro world, it is next to impossible to give an accurate estimate of the size of his following at any time. Indeed, there is good reason to doubt whether even Garvey himself could have done so with any degree of reasonable exactitude. Unquestionably the actual dues-paying membership of the Universal Negro Improvement Association was far smaller than the number of Negroes who identified themselves with the exciting emotional atmosphere of the movement and gave its aims vigorous if informal support. There is no way of estimating this latter group, but it must have contained large numbers of Negroes who, though not actual members of the U.N.I.A., nevertheless accepted parts of Garvey's program and gloried vicariously in his promises of race advancement. It was this elusive element of Garvey's support that gave his movement its mass characteristics.

Garvey's heady arithmetic is quite unreliable. He once estimated that by the middle of 1919, three years after his arrival in the United States, the infant U.N.I.A. had enrolled more than two million members in thirty branches.[7] Broken down, these inflated figures would mean an average membership of better than 66,000 for each local U.N.I.A. division—often more than the total Negro population of the area! In 1920 Garvey began claiming a following of four million and by 1924 the figure had jumped to six million.[8] By 1928, at a time when all other evidence points to a decline in U.N.I.A. strength, Garvey's claims had spiraled to a membership of eleven million scattered throughout the world in some three thousand branches.[9]

Most observers have found it equally hard to fix the membership of the U.N.I.A. Inadequate financial accounts and the extremely informal system of records kept by the Garvey organization make it difficult to determine even the dues-paying membership. In January, 1923, W. E. B. Du-Bois used the available published records to estimate the U.N.I.A. membership at a figure somewhere between 9,703 and 17,784.[10] About the same time Warner A. Domingo, a former Garvey supporter turned critic, also concluded that the U.N.I.A. had fewer than 20,000 members in all countries.[11] Elsewhere DuBois admitted that there were perhaps 80,000 U.N.I.A. members, but suggested that these were mainly West Indian Negroes.[12] These figures do not take into account, of course, the far larger number of Negroes who followed the movement with keen interest and who acclaimed Garvey as a great race patriot.

Professor Kelly Miller, writing in 1927, concluded that the Garvey movement had attracted perhaps four million Negroes.[13] On the other hand, William Pickens charged in 1923 that Garvey's support was vastly overrated and that the U.N.I.A. had never enrolled as many as 30,000 members.[14] Time has mellowed Pickens' estimate of Garveyism, and he has recently suggested that Garvey built up the largest single organization of Negroes in the world, with a membership of several million in the United States, the West Indies, Central America, and Africa.[15] Other writers have put Garvey's following at between a million and two million Negroes throughout the world.[16]

At the Black Star trial in 1923 several of the defense witnesses, officials of local U.N.I.A. divisions, inadvertently gave some revealing figures on branch membership of the organization. After several years of attrition the New York City division of the association still had a respectable enrollment of about 30,000, by far the largest branch total. Other branches were much smaller but were still indicative of Garvey's widespread following: Chicago, 9,000; Philadelphia, 6,000; Cincinnati 5,000–6,000; Detroit, 4,000; Washington, 700; Jamaica, 5,000; Guatemala, 3,000. The president of the Boston division did not give total membership figures but testified that about 1,200 Boston members held Black Star stock.[17] It is worth recalling here that at the trial the government charged that Garvey and his Black Star associates had induced between 30,000 and 40,000 Negroes to invest in the bankrupt line. These figures would seem to explode Garvey's inflated boasts of a U.N.I.A. membership in the millions. Yet the figures also indicate that Garvey was able to maintain a sizable active following even in adversity, and they do not take into account the strong latent support Garvey was always able to draw from the Negro world. Garvey seems to have been well within his rights when he asserted in 1923 that the U.N.I.A. could muster twenty times the support given to all other Negro organizations put together and that at least three or four U.N.I.A. divisions had a local membership larger than the critics were willing to admit for the organization as a whole.[18]

"No one will ever know accurately the membership of the Universal Negro Improvement Association," Garvey once declared with perhaps more truth than he realized, "because every second Negro you meet, if not an actual member, is one in spirit." [19] It seems certain that by 1920 Garvey had attracted a large active following and that he had aroused the attention of most American Negroes and masses of blacks elsewhere in the world. Indicative of the world-wide interest in Garveyism is the report that the King of Swaziland in Africa later told a friend that he knew the names of only two men in the western world—Marcus Garvey and the prize fighter Jack Johnson.[20] "Garvey's movement received amazing support from the Negro masses of both North and South," concludes Ralph Bunche. "No other American Negro organization has ever been able to reach and stir the masses of Negroes to the same degree, or receive from them such generous financial support." [21] That this should have been accomplished in an alien land, by a young man of limited education, working with a people who had for centuries successfully resisted mass organization, was indeed a notable achievement.

☆

Marcus Garvey has been portrayed in a confusion of terms ranging from blackest denunciation to rosiest approbation. Few men have aroused greater fires of controversy in as brief a period of time. Garvey has been personally denounced as a "fabulous con-man," [22] "hardly more than a strident demagogue, with inflated ambitions and a swaggering attitude," [23] and his Negro redemption program has been condemned as "wild, imaginary," [24] and "hopelessly visionary." [25] Perhaps the unkindest cut of all

is the demonstrably untrue assertion that "there were probably not half a dozen educated Negroes in America who
were genuinely interested in Garvey's proposition." [26] Garvey's disciples employ even more powerful but equally
inaccurate phrases in his defense. One U.N.I.A. member,
swept away by the magnitude of his subject, observed with
eloquent pride: "This Negro genius combines in his person
the wisdom of a Solomon; the eloquence of a Demosthenes;
the courage of a Cromwell; the grit and determination of
a Robert Bruce; the iron will of a Bismar[c]k; the daunt-
lessness of a Toussaint L'O[u]verture and the cunning of
a Napoleon Bonaparte. This man has as much patience as
Carnegie has money." [27] A contemporary Negro writer
ranks Garvey as the greatest of all colored heroes: "He died
the death of a martyr, he ran his noble and gallant course
and yet lives as all great and illustrious immortals, for his
glorious, marvellous works and achievements continue
through time and eternity." [28]

Only a few of Garvey's enemies have ever impugned his
motives or charged him with personal dishonesty. William
Pickens in 1921 spoke with admiration of Garvey's "honesty
and his utter sincerity," [29] and other critics have concurred.
"He has been charged with dishonesty and graft," said
DuBois in summing up Garvey's other failings, "but he
seems to me essentially an honest and sincere man with
a tremendous vision, great dynamic force, stubborn determination and unselfish desire to serve." [30] There is no evidence that Garvey profited unduly from his missionary
activities. He seems never to have drawn more than a part
of the $10,000 salary voted him at the 1920 U.N.I.A. con-
vention, and his total salary over a three-year period as
president of the Black Star Line amounted to only
$6,343.84, certainly not an exorbitant return on the her-
culean services he rendered to the near million-dollar cor-

poration.[31] Garvey may have collected more money than
any other Negro leader, but he died a poor man and his
widow has had to rely in part on contributions from ex-
Garveyites to educate their two sons. There was more than
a little justification for the Universal Negro Improvement
Association's proud assertion that "Marcus Garvey has
worked for nothing to serve the Negro race." [32]

Even when Garvey's movement was under heavy fire,
critical observers were intrigued by some of the great projects the chunky Jamaican contemplated. The various
U.N.I.A. business enterprises in particular were viewed
with favor. "The creation of a steamship line, even in em-
bryo, is one of the greatest achievements of the twentieth
century Negro," exulted William Pickens before the Black
Star collapse. "A safe development of these business enterprises will mean more to the Negroes of the Western Hemis-
phere for some generations to come than will the hope of
the Republic of Africa." [33] "Shorn of its bombast and exag-
geration, the main lines of the Garvey plan are perfectly
feasible," DuBois admitted. "What he is trying to say and
do is this: American Negroes can, by accumulating and
ministering their own capital, organize industry, join the
black centers of the South Atlantic by commercial enterprise and in this way ultimately redeem Africa as a fit and
free home for black men. This is true. It is *feasible*. It is, in
a sense, practical." [34] Professor Abram L. Harris suggests
that Garvey's emphasis on Negro nationalism and an all-
black religion was but a device to arouse support for some
of the sounder but more prosaic features of his program—
co-operative housing and co-operative business ventures.[35]
Years after Garvey's banishment from the United States a
successful Negro merchant in Chicago recalled him as "one
of the few great leaders who taught the people to open
places of business." [36]

Few Negro leaders of his day agreed completely with either Garvey's program or his czarlike methods of implementing it. Yet Garvey's restless energy and driving force had an important effect on Negro leadership. His very success in welding large numbers of his people into a dedicated mass movement was itself an example not lost on Negro leaders who rejected the philosophy of the U.N.I.A. Moreover, his flaming words struck a spark that inspired others to take up the torch of leadership on behalf of the race.[37] A quarter century after directing the turbulent "Garvey Must Go" campaign in Harlem, A. Philip Randolph recognizes Garvey's indirect influence on American Negro leadership by way of stimulating an interest in organization as such.[38] Certainly the U.N.I.A. founder's organizational and promotional capacities were great when measured by any standard. "I think, with the possible exception of David Lloyd George," declared Dr. Lionel Francis, Garvey's successor as head of the American U.N.I.A., "Marcus Garvey is the greatest organizer the world has ever seen." [39] The Garvey magic success formula—bold, defiant words, colorful trappings, and a compelling and even audacious dream —remains a tempting legacy for present-day Negro leaders.

Today Garvey is remembered by the Negro masses chiefly for his fierce black nationalism. "All I know about Garvey is that he wanted to form the colored people into some kind of union and have us all go back to Africa and form a country of our own," says a Chicago domestic servant who was vague about other U.N.I.A. objectives. "That was a good idea. A union like that would make a strong nation. I'd like to try something like that." [40] A lower-class Harlem girl, interviewed in the year of Garvey's death, was also impressed with Garvey's vision of a Negro nation. "Rather drastic," she called it, but "a good idea." "But the question is," and here she touched a point that long had troubled American Negroes, "Would we be able to build a new civilization or would we revert to the primitive civilization of the Africans?" [41]

Although the vision of a powerful black nation in Africa thrilled many Negroes, Ralph Bunche has rightly concluded that "the plain truth was that very few Negroes were really interested in returning to Africa." [42] Garvey's lush descriptions of the past and future greatness of the race in its African motherland were chiefly an emotional escape for the U.N.I.A. audiences, actually the only sort of escape most American Negroes were really interested in. "The Negroes of America as a race are content to remain in America," asserted the Houston *Post* in an attempt to explain the failure of Garvey's African colonization scheme, and the Negro editors of *Opportunity* concurred.[43] "The main reason for Garvey's failure with thoughtful American Negroes was his African scheme," James Weldon Johnson said in 1930. "It was recognized at once by them to be impractical and fantastic." [44]

Garvey's chief claim to lasting fame lies in his vigorous efforts to stimulate Negro race consciousness. Garveyism was the forerunner of the native nationalism that is sweeping across Africa today. Garvey dedicated his life to the rehabilitation of Negro self-esteem and prestige, badly battered after centuries of slavery and mistreatment. His movement served as a focal point for a new appreciation by Negroes of their racial heritage and a growing sense of pride in their potentialities. Many Negroes consider this Garvey's greatest achievement. "He did more to teach the Negro race pride than any other man in our history," asserts one contemporary writer.[45] The Negro world is coming increasingly to accept the evaluation of the *Spokesman* magazine, which in 1925 admitted that the controversial little Jamaican had "performed a spiritual miracle in getting colored people together and inculcating race pride." [46]

☆

Garvey's reputation as the outstanding father of Negro nationalism has grown in the years since his death, a period that has witnessed nationalistic rumblings in many parts of the world, including his beloved Africa. Indeed, it is interesting to note the change of opinion toward Garvey that has come with the passage of time. If the once proud ranks of the U.N.I.A. are now depleted by several decades of discordant decline, at least new generations of Negroes are coming to look upon the association's founder with something approaching reverence. Typical of the swing-back in Garvey's favor, and in sharp contrast to the bitter debate of the twenties, is the Chicago *Defender*'s 1953 headline characterization of Garvey as the "Patron Saint of Restless Africa." [47] Indeed, at the time of Garvey's death the *Defender* had so far forgotten the heated battles of bygone days as to assert that "Garvey was easily the most colorful figure to have appeared in America since the historic times of Frederick Douglass and Booker T. Washington." [48]

Of particular interest has been the shift of opinion among Negro writers. At the time of Garvey's greatest triumphs in the United States, both he and his program were virtually ignored in the writings of Negro intellectuals. And if the U.N.I.A. leader was noticed, he was generally dismissed as just another opportunistic charlatan whose appeals to the masses tended to alienate any support his program might otherwise have received from the upper strata of the Negro world. Thus Professor Alain Locke, editing a book entitled *The New Negro* in 1925, gave but passing reference in his introduction to the Universal Negro Improvement Association and its "New Negro" activities, surely a significant omission from a book dealing with such a subject.[49] A surprising number of books dealing with contemporary Negro history written by Negroes during Garvey's lifetime either failed to make any mention of him or contained only a very brief, often unflattering reference to his work.

One of the first of the established Negro authors to attempt an evaluation of Garveyism, as well as to recognize the dramatic human interest quality of the subject, was James Weldon Johnson, who in 1930 chronicled a part of the Garvey story in his *Black Manhattan*. Other writers followed suit as the hard feelings of the 1920's gradually diminished and Garvey's critics began to realize that his banishment had eliminated the likelihood of a revival of his activities in the United States. Absence in this case may not have made hardened hearts grow fonder, but it did encourage more sober evaluation. In 1927 Benjamin G. Brawley, a professor of English at Howard University, first began discussing the Garvey movement in his high school history text, *A Short History of the American Negro*, and he expanded his generally sympathetic treatment in the 1931 and 1939 revisions of the work.[50] Brawley's study of Negro literary achievements, *The Negro Genius* (1937), contained a highly laudatory reference to Garvey's influence on the literature of the Negro Renaissance.[51] Merl R. Eppse's *The Negro, Too, in American History* (1938) also treated the Garvey movement sympathetically.[52] In 1940, coincidentally the year of Garvey's death, three Negro writers published books dealing wholly or in part with the zealous Jamaican prophet. In Jamaica Len S. Nembhard produced the first Garvey biography,[53] while in the United States the Jamaican poet Claude McKay devoted a chapter of his *Harlem* to an account of the rise and fall of Garvey's U.N.I.A.[54] Also published in that year was W. E. B. DuBois'

Dusk of Dawn, which took note of Garvey's astonishing popularity with the black masses.[55]

In the next decade there was by comparison a positive flood of Garvey material. Roi Ottley, a talented Negro journalist and writer, turned out two books dealing in part with Garvey's activities in the United States.[56] The indefatigable Negro historian Joel A. Rogers, who had promised a biography of Garvey since 1931,[57] devoted a chapter to the U.N.I.A. founder in his 1946 history of the lives of great Negroes.[58] Arna Bontemps and Jack Conroy included a section on Garvey in their popular study of Negro aspirations.[59] A comprehensive edition of important Negro writings and speeches included an impassioned address by Garvey on the subject of African redemption.[60] A dedicated Garvey disciple issued a new defense of the master.[61] There was even another in a long succession of attempts to evaluate Garveyism from the Marxian viewpoint.[62] The *Journal of Negro History* published its first article on Garvey,[63] and in France a literary magazine ran a somewhat fanciful account of the amazing *Moïse noir,* or black Moses.[64] The Harlem branch of the New York Public Library reports a steady reader demand for Garvey material. Clearly the interest in Marcus Garvey is by no means dead.

Some of these later comments on Garvey and his work are of interest because they illustrate the trend of Negro thought on the subject. The ideas of a new generation toward Garvey's race-redemption movement are being shaped by authors whose treatment of the U.N.I.A. leader is in marked contrast with the embarrassed silence or shrill condemnation of the 1920's. In general, the passing years have dealt kindly with Garvey, and his reputation as a great race leader with prophetic vision is growing. "Marcus Garvey was beyond question, the greatest organizer, and the most inspirational leader the race ever produced," asserted a California Negro in 1946. "Negro history does not record a single instance of any man to compare with him in this respect. The fidelity of his followers, and the extent and scope of his operations placed him on a throne that no other Negro has ever sat." [65] Even Garvey's racist ideas about religion, so shocking to Negro ministers in the twenties, now come in for a certain amount of praise from the clergy. Benjamin E. Mays, distinguished Negro minister and educator, writes that Garvey dramatized the idea of a black God "to arouse the Negro to a sense of deep appreciation for his race" and "to stimulate the Negro to work to improve his social and economic conditions." [66]

Benjamin Brawley's influential high school history text emphasizes Garvey's role in stimulating the new race consciousness. Garvey's ambitious U.N.I.A. program "served to give to the young American Negro a quickening that he might not otherwise have had and that even today continues to influence the group consciousness of the Negroes in this country." [67] The less comprehensive *Pocket Book of Negro Facts,* published in 1946 for the popular market, calls Garvey "a visionary and a prophet" who "consecrated his life to protest against oppression." [68] Others also link Garvey to the racial spirit of both pride and protest that pervades the Negro world. "The movement set in motion what was to become the most compelling force in Negro life—race and color consciousness," says Roi Ottley. "It has propelled many a political and social movement and stimulated racial internationalism. . . . It accounts for much constructive belligerency today." [69] Professor John Hope Franklin, in his excellent history of American Negroes, *From Slavery to Freedom,* stresses an even more important aspect of Garveyism: "Its significance lies in the fact that it was the first and only real mass movement among Negroes in the history of the United States and that it indicates the extent to which Negroes entertained doubts concerning the hope for first-class citizenship in the only fatherland of which they knew." [70]

American Negroes are not alone in their continuing interest in Marcus Garvey. In other parts of the world black men and women remember with pride his attempts to unify and redeem the race. In 1929 a Gold Coast author asserted that no other organization had done as much as Garvey's Universal Negro Improvement Association to focus world attention on African problems.[71] Twenty-four years later, in December, 1953, Garvey was lauded "for his early inspiration to the Negro race" at a West African nationalist conference presided over by the Negro prime minister of the Gold Coast, Dr. Kwame Nkrumah. Significantly, the delegates had gathered "to discuss ways and means of speeding up the liberation of Africa." [72] In Nigeria an obscure poet sang praises of the U.N.I.A. leader in a poem of African nationalism reminiscent of Garvey's own pan-African outpourings:

> Nigeria, oh my Nigeria,
> .   .   .   .
> For thy redemption brave Garvey fell,
> But yet in the gang of the immortals,
> Thy sons shall fight unseen by mortals,
> And ere long regain thy pride, oh Nigeria.
>
> Nigeria, oh my Nigeria,
> Preserve and arm thy nationalists,
> Infuse in them the immortals' genius,
> For thy sons to lead and thy shores to save
> From the traitor's bows and the oppressor's sceptre.[73]

After the dread Mau Mau terrorists began their murderous depredations in Kenya in 1951, Negroes in the United States and elsewhere were quick to tie the developments in Kenya to Garvey's African nationalist movement. "Is Mau Mau the Hand of Marcus Garvey?" asked the Chicago *Defender* in a banner headline over a feature article that concluded: "And wherever in Africa the natives seek to throw off white domination, the name of Marcus Garvey is revered." [74] The leading Jamaican newspaper, the Kingston *Daily Gleaner*, even credited Garvey with personally converting Jomo Kenyatta, the Mau Mau leader, to the philosophy of Africa for the Africans.[75]

As might be expected, in Jamaica the name Garvey is still magic. It was here that the first full-length book dealing with Garvey's life and philosophy was published, Nembhard's *Trials and Triumphs of Marcus Garvey*, a sympathetic work stressing Garvey's later years in Jamaica and England. A Jamaican minister today considers Garvey "unquestionably one of the architects of the new Jamaica," whose "international fame as a leader stands unequalled in the annals of twentieth century Negroes." "All leaders since have reaped where Garvey sowed," runs this contemporary account, "and his greatest failings are a trifle compared with the contribution he has made to the psychological and spiritual awakening of his people." [76] In its issue commemorating the mid-point of the twentieth century, the Kingston *Sunday Gleaner* paid tribute to Garvey as the "Father of Nationalism." "Indeed it would be true to say of Jamaica, and to a lesser extent of the other British West Indies," declared the *Gleaner*, "that national consciousness received its main impetus, if it was not actually born, from the racial movement associated with the still revered Marcus Garvey." " 'Garveyism' lies at the heart of the modern political movements through which West Indian nationalism is seeking to express itself." [77]

In keeping with the trend of island opinion, on July 8, 1952, the Jamaican House of Representatives passed a resolution recommending that Garvey's birthday be observed as a public holiday and urging the government to establish a scholarship in his memory. Representatives of various Jamaican parties joined in the general praise of Garvey's patriotic service. The U.N.I.A. founder was acclaimed as "the father of political parties in Jamaica," "a great man" who "did more in making the coloured people of Jamaica discover themselves than any other man before him." In supporting the Garvey memorial project, more than one member stressed the need to inspire an interest in Jamaican, as opposed to British, history. The Jamaican people must be given "a supreme pride in their origins and their significance and their racial strains," declared one legislator. "Marcus Garvey understood that and devoted his life to it. And if he succeeded in making people frightfully conscious of colour, that alone deserves perpetual recognition in Jamaica." [78] The leading island newspapers gave strong editorial support to the Garvey memorial proposal, one calling it "a turning point in our history." [79] When an English columnist writing in the *Gleaner* recalled Garvey's imprisonment in the United States and tactlessly questioned the propriety of honoring a convicted criminal, he was immediately denounced by an angry island correspondent for his "dastardly piece of impudent effrontery and malicious meddling." "England has its traditions," the British interloper was told brusquely. "Let us have ours. To us Garvey is a great figure of the past who lived before his time." [80]

In recent years American Negroes have also taken steps to give formal recognition to Garvey's services as a race patriot. In 1945, for example, Benjamin Gibbons, president of the Harlem Garvey Club, issued a call for an international conference to consider "various urgent problems confronting the African race." The proposed agenda was remarkably similar to those of Garvey's own international conventions of the 1920's. "Calling all UNIAists! Calling all Garveyites!" the promotional circulars proclaimed in bold type. "No red-blooded African can afford to miss this great historic event." [81] Significantly, the three-day conference opened on August 17, Garvey's birthday, and had the blessing of Mrs. Amy Jacques Garvey, who sent her greetings from Jamaica. The following year the energetic Gibbons presided over another African nationalist convention at which Mrs. Garvey and her two sons were the guests of honor. The 1946 convention mapped out an ambitious program of action along the old U.N.I.A. lines and canonized Garvey as the "Supreme Immortal Patriot." [82] Since 1949 Gibbons' United African Nationalist Movement has celebrated August 1 as Marcus Garvey Day, in honor of the opening of the first Garvey convention of the Negro Peoples of the World in 1920. An estimated two thousand Negroes attended the 1953 rally in Harlem. There were the customary eulogies of the dead U.N.I.A. founder and Garvey's program of racial nationalism was credited with sparking the nationalistic upheavals in Africa and Asia. On the lighter side, a silver loving cup was presented to a beauty-contest winner inscribed "To Miss Africa, 1953, on Marcus Garvey Day." [83] In Detroit William L. Sherrill, Garvey's one-time representative at the League of Nations, maintains his headquarters as the current president of Garvey's old Universal Negro Improvement Association. While the number of active Garveyites today is doubtless small, it would seem that Negroes the world over are tending to forget the unhappy results of some of Garvey's activities and are instead remembering only his fierce pride in things Negro and his dedicated zeal for effective race action.

☆

Amid the many conflicting interpretations of the meaning and importance of Garveyism, ranging from angry condemnation to uncritical praise, just what is Marcus Garvey's place in the pages of twentieth-century history? Certainly it may not be denied that here is one of the most interesting figures of our age. The sweeping range of his dreams, the startling audacity of his plans, the compelling authority of his inspired words, all acted to secure him a fanatically devoted following at a time when the despairing Negro people were awaiting a messiah. The extent of Garvey's following is itself significant, for it reflected the depth of the secret longings and bitter pessimism of the black masses. Marcus Garvey was an instrument through which the restless Negro world could express its discontent. His striking success in creating a powerful mass organization in a matter of months was possible only because he spoke the language of his people and told his followers what they wanted and needed to hear—that the black man was as good as any other.

And yet, despite Garvey's triumph as an unparalleled propagandist and organizer of the Negro masses, his success proved ephemeral, and his vaunted Universal Negro Improvement Association turned out to be only a transient, if extremely colorful, phenomenon. Personally honest, a sincere and dedicated visionary, Garvey might have hoped for more lasting success. Energy, imagination, daring, a commanding personality, superb oratorical skill—all these were his to use on behalf of the oppressed black people he yearned to serve. But his failings as a leader overbalanced the sounder aspects of his program. For all his impressive organizational activities, Marcus Garvey remains a tragic, even a pathetic figure, who is today remembered more for the size of his dreams than for the practical accomplishments of his once imposing race movement.

Garvey's reluctance to delegate responsibility, his difficulty in finding honest and capable subordinates, and his disinclination to listen to the advice and suggestions of men frequently better informed than he militated against any permanent gains from his work. By unconsciously seeking fawning courtiers rather than competent co-workers he opened wide the doors to blundering mismanagement and disloyal corruption. Garvey's egocentric, at times even arrogant, personality demanded that there be but one supreme U.N.I.A. leader and drove from his counsels those men who might have helped to avert the crippling misfortunes that ultimately overtook the movement. Those who remained were all too often dishonest and unscrupulous self-seekers who only accelerated the final collapse. The logical scapegoat for the Black Star fiasco, Garvey served a prison sentence for the financial chicanery of some of his two-faced associates and his own supremely confident but irresponsible and inexperienced leadership. A good lawyer could doubtless have won his acquittal, but Garvey's overweening conceit and irrational suspicions led him to reject his expert counsel and plead his own case—with disastrous results.

The inherent weaknesses of Garveyism itself also acted to limit its ultimate influence. Garvey sought to raise high the walls of racial nationalism at a time when most thoughtful men were seeking to tear down these barriers. His West Indian background led him rather ineptly to attempt to discredit much of the existing American Negro leadership by introducing a new and unfamiliar divisive symbolism based on the degree of color. The Back to Africa program provided an easy escape for Negroes hard pressed and weary of a life of oppression and frustration, but it was no real answer to the problems that beset the Negro world. Few American Negroes were seriously interested in a "return" to Africa, a mysterious land that none of them knew and few cared to see firsthand. In effect Garvey asked his followers to abdicate their hard-won, admittedly incomplete rights in the United States and to turn the country over to white supremacists of the Ku Klux Klan variety. Whatever their feelings for the other parts of the Garvey program, most Negro Americans were inclined to agree with the sober appraisal of a respected Garvey critic, N.A.A.C.P. secretary James Weldon Johnson: "As the world is at present, the United States, with all of its limitations, offers the millions of Negroes within its borders greater opportunities than any other land." [84]

Garvey's work was important largely because more than any other single leader he helped to give Negroes everywhere a reborn feeling of collective pride and a new awareness of individual worth. Young and unknown, this black Moses came out of the West Indies at a time when the shocking upturn in race riots and lynchings was graphically emphasizing to American Negroes the negation of their loyal contribution to the nation's victory in World War I. With the broken bodies of the victims of racial violence marking the broken hopes of the war years, the Negro world badly needed a message of hope and encouragement. This Marcus Garvey undertook to supply in terms bold and language uncompromising, with the result that in an astonishingly brief time he had captured the attention of his people to a degree no other Negro leader has ever attained. Because he made the Negro masses proud of their past and resolute to face the future, a surprising number of Garvey's devoted followers were willing to forget the erratic course steered by the Black Star Line and to forgive the vast sums that disappeared virtually without trace into the yawning emptiness of the U.N.I.A. treasury. Garvey appeared out of obscurity at a fortuitous moment in Negro history, at a time when American Negroes were ripe for a chauvinistic appeal to racial nationalism and ready for a black Zionism that could restore their shattered self-respect and promise a deliverance from present burdens.

Garvey demonstrated as no man before him had ever done the basic unrest within the Negro world. In capturing the imagination of millions of ordinary black men and women throughout the world, he showed the striking appeal that racial nationalism can, under certain circumstances, have for the Negro. Garvey helped to stir and set in motion much of the sweeping flood of race consciousness now inundating the colored world. His success in briefly harnessing the hopes and aspirations of large numbers of American Negroes to a wildly nationalistic program of African redemption, therefore, helps considerably to illumine an important chapter in the history of race relations in the United States. Garvey proved that the black masses could be organized through an emotional appeal based on racial chauvinism. But the steady decline in his following after 1925, in spite of Garvey's frantic efforts to revive and maintain the movement, suggests that the sort of appeal that worked so well in the years immediately after World War I was much less effective under later conditions. It is doubtful whether Garvey could find today, in the United States at least, the ready response that greeted his early proselytizing efforts.

In assessing Marcus Garvey's work as a Negro leader, one is hard put to discover any tangible gain resulting from the impressive movement he created. Garvey may have brought a much needed spiritual uplift to masses of discouraged and despairing blacks in the early twenties, but there remains today little of practical significance as a fitting monument to his labors. By undercutting most of the existing Negro leadership, even those elements worthy of support, and by rejecting all but the most extreme white backing—the dubious championship of the Klan and other racist groups—Garvey nullified much of the potential value of his movement in creating better conditions for his people in the United States. Garveyism failed largely because it was unable to come up with a suitable alternative to the unsatisfactory conditions of American life as they affect the Negro. Escape, either emotional or physical, was neither a realistic nor a lasting answer.

★REFERENCES AND NOTES

★INDEX

REFERENCES AND NOTES

PRIMARY SOURCES

Unfortunately, there is no collection of Garvey papers. Garvey's own files were scattered during the years of his imprisonment and exile from the United States and much of what remained of his personal records was destroyed in the London bombings of 1940–41. Apparently the institutional records of the Universal Negro Improvement Association also failed to survive the organization's decline. With respect to the Black Star Line, however, the picture is considerably brighter. There are original Black Star papers in the files of the United States District Court for the Southern District of New York, *United States of America* v. *Marcus Garvey,* dockets C31–37 and C33–688, and the record of Garvey's income tax troubles is contained in docket C38–771. The printed record of the federal trial of Garvey and his three Black Star associates, *Marcus Garvey* v. *United States of America,* United States Circuit Court of Appeals, Second Circuit, docket 8317, contains valuable testimony on Garvey's steamship fiasco as well as on larger aspects of the U.N.I.A. movement. The several hundred government and defense exhibits are perhaps the best single source of material on the Black Star Line. The record of Garvey's attempt to purchase ships from the government is to be found in the files of the United States Shipping Board in the National Archives of the United States. Similarly, the files of the Department of State in the National Archives also contain much interesting material on the voyage of Black Star ships, the extent of Garvey's influence and following abroad, the abortive U.N.I.A. colonization venture in Liberia, and, not least important, the apprehensive reaction of State Department officials to Garvey's activities.

Like the inadequate manuscript materials, the files of the various Garvey publications—the weekly *Negro World,* the daily *Negro Times,* and the monthly *Black Man*—are scattered and incomplete. The Moorland Collection of Howard University and the Schomburg

Collection of the New York Public Library have what can be described only as extremely broken files of these periodicals. The New York Public Library has several issues of the *Black Man*, published from London in the 1930's, but copies of this last Garvey propaganda organ are rare and, as far as I have been able to ascertain, are not filed in any London library. I have been most fortunate to secure copies of the *Black Man* from Mrs. Garvey and to use Mr. Hodge Kirnon's extensive private collection of the other Garvey publications.

Much Garvey material has appeared in printed form. Garvey's widow, Mrs. Amy Jacques Garvey, has edited two volumes of his early writings, *Philosophy and Opinions of Marcus Garvey* (N.Y.: Universal Publishing House, 1923) and *Philosophy and Opinions of Marcus Garvey or Africa for the Africans* (1926). Since, in spite of the lengthened title, the second of these books was published as Volume II, they are referred to in the notes as Volumes I and II of Garvey's *Philosophy and Opinions*. Mrs. Garvey also edited two volumes of her husband's poetry, *The Tragedy of White Injustice* and *Selections from the Poetic Meditations of Marcus Garvey* (N.Y.: Amy Jacques Garvey, 1927), and a pamphlet dealing with his trial and conviction, *United States of America vs. Marcus Garvey: Was Justice Defeated?* (N.Y.: Amy Jacques Garvey, 1925). Several of Garvey's organizational speeches have survived: *Speech of Marcus Garvey . . . Delivered at 71st Regiment Armory* (n.d.); *Speech at Madison Square Garden on the Return of a Delegation from Abroad* (N.Y., 1924); *Aims and Objectives of a Movement for the Solution of the Negro Outlined* (N.Y., 1924); *Speech Delivered by Marcus Garvey at Royal Albert Hall, London* (London: U.N.I.A., 1928); *Minutes of Proceedings of a Speech by Marcus Garvey at the Century Theatre, London, Sunday, September 2, 1928* (London: Vail, 1928). Both the 1922 and 1928 appeals to the League of Nations are included in *Renewal of Petition of the Universal Negro Improvement Association and African Communities' League to the League of Nations* (London: Vail, 1928). The *Constitution and Book of Laws of the Universal Negro Improvement Association and African Communities' League* (July, 1918, amended August, 1920) was issued in both English and Spanish. There is much autobiographical matter in Marcus Garvey, "The Negro's Greatest Enemy," *Current History Magazine,*

XVIII (September, 1923), 951–57; but more important for this study was Mrs. Amy Jacques Garvey's unpublished "Story of Part of the Life of Marcus Garvey," a biographical account of her husband's early years in Jamaica.

SECONDARY SOURCES

Although predominantly hostile to Garvey, the Negro press should be consulted for references to his movement. The Chicago *Defender* in the years 1920–27 was perhaps the most consistent Garvey critic. The New York *Age*, the New York *Amsterdam News*, the Washington *Bee*, the Pittsburgh *Courier*, and the Baltimore *Afro-American* also covered in generally critical fashion the more sensational and bizarre features of Garveyism. Other important Negro periodicals of the period include: *Messenger*, which spearheaded the "Garvey Must Go" campaign; *Liberator* and *Crusader*, which criticized Garveyism from the Marxist vantage point; *Challenge;* and *Spokesman. Crisis*, the organ of the National Association for the Advancement of Colored People, also was active in the opposition to Garvey, and its editor, Dr. W. E. B. DuBois, made several devastating analyses of the movement. Interesting attempts to revive Garveyism after its founder's death are to be found in the *New Negro World*, the *Voice of Freedom*, and the *African*. For a time the Garvey-sponsored African Orthodox Church published the *Negro Churchman*. The white press did not accord Garvey the attention that his activities deserved, but the *New York Times* and the New York *World* occasionally took notice of the more spectacular doings of the serious black prophet from Jamaica. The best source for Garvey's activities in Jamaica after his deportation from the United States in 1928 is the Kingston *Gleaner*.

Much has been written about Marcus Garvey and his interesting mass movement, and there is a wealth of material, of varying quality and usefulness, dealing with the aspects of the U.N.I.A. program for Negro redemption. As might well be expected with such a controversial subject, much of the published comment is hostile, and the careful reader will also want to consult the Garvey publications for a balanced interpretation. The following list of secondary works is by no means exhaustive and is presented merely as a guide to the more important books and articles dealing with the Garvey movement.

ARON, BURGIT. "The Garvey Movement." Unpublished Master of Arts thesis, Columbia University, 1947.

BAGNALL, ROBERT W. "The Madness of Marcus Garvey," *Messenger,* V (March, 1923), 638.

BARRETT, SAMUEL. *The Need of Unity and Cooperation among Colored Americans.* Oakland, Calif.: Voice Publishing Co., 1946.

"Black Magic Fails Again," *Independent,* CXX (June 23, 1928), 586–87.

"A Black Moses and His Dream of a Promised Land," *Current Opinion,* LXX (March, 1921), 328–31.

BLANTON, KELSEY. *Color-Blind and Skin-Deep Democracy.* Tampa, Fla.: Kelsey Blanton, 1924.

BONTEMPS, ARNA, and JACK CONROY. *They Seek a City.* Garden City, N.Y.: Doubleday, Doran, 1945.

BOONE, T. S. *Paramount Facts in Race Development.* Chicago: Hume, 1921.

BRAWLEY, BENJAMIN G. *The Negro Genius: A New Appraisal of the Achievement of the American Negro in Literature and the Fine Arts.* N.Y.: Dodd, Mead, 1937.

———. *A Short History of the American Negro.* N.Y.: Macmillan, 1927, 1931, and 1939.

BRIGGS, CYRIL. "The Decline of the Garvey Movement," *Communist,* X (June, 1931), 547–52.

BRISBANE, ROBERT HUGHES, JR. "Some New Light on the Garvey Movement," *Journal of Negro History,* XXXVI (January, 1951), 53–62.

BROWN, INA C. *The Story of the American Negro.* N.Y.: Friendship Press, 1936.

BROWN, STERLING A., ARTHUR P. DAVIS, and ULYSSES LEE. *The Negro Caravan.* N.Y.: Citadel Press, 1941.

BUELL, RAYMOND L. *The Native Problem in Africa.* 2 vols. N.Y.: Macmillan, 1928.

BUNCHE, RALPH J. "The Programs, Ideologies, Tactics, and Achievements of Negro Betterment and Interracial Organizations." Unpublished monograph prepared for the Carnegie-Myrdal study, 1940. Schomburg Collection, N.Y. Public Library.

CHARPIN, HENRI. "La Question noire," *Revue Indigène,* XVII (November-December, 1922), 275–85.

Chicago Commission on Race Relations. *The Negro in Chicago: A Study of Race Relations and a Race Riot.* Chicago: Univ. of Chicago Press, 1922.

Cincinnati Division, No. 146, Universal Negro Improvement Association. *Sixth Anniversary Drive, May 8th to 18th, 1927.* Pamphlet. Schomberg Collection, N.Y. Public Library.

CLARK, BRANSTAN S. *Is It the Color of Our Skin That is Responsible for Our Down-Trodden Condition all over the World? Also an Appeal for Racial Unity among Negroes.* Pittsburgh, Pa.: Branstan S. Clark, 1921.

COBB, IRVIN S. *J. Poindexter, Colored.* N.Y.: Doran, 1922.

COX, EARNEST SEVIER. *Let My People Go.* Richmond, Va.: White America Society, 1925.

———. *Lincoln's Negro Policy.* Richmond, Va.: William Byrd Press, 1938.

———. *The South's Part in Mongrelizing the Nation.* Richmond, Va.: White America Society, 1926.

Crisis, XXXVI (December, 1929), 419.

DAVIS, BEN, JR. "Marcus Garvey Dies as His Defeatist Program Is Replaced by a Fighting Negro Liberation Movement against Imperialism," New York *Daily Worker,* June 14, 1940.

DOWD, JEROME. *The Negro in American Life.* London: Jonathan Cape, 1927.

DRAKE, ST. CLAIR, and HORACE R. CAYTON. *Black Metropolis: A Study of Negro Life in a Northern City.* N.Y.: Harcourt, Brace, 1945.

DUBOIS, W. E. B. "Back to Africa," *Century,* CV (February, 1923), 539–48.

———. "The Black Star Line," *Crisis,* XXIV (September, 1922), 210–14.

———. *Dusk of Dawn.* N.Y.: Harcourt, Brace, 1940.

———. "Marcus Garvey," *Crisis,* XXI, 58–60 (December, 1920), and 112–15 (January, 1921).

————. "The U.N.I.A.," *Crisis*, XXV (January, 1923), 120–22.

ELMES, A. F. "Garvey and Garveyism: An Estimate," *Opportunity*, III (May, 1925), 139–41.

EPPSE, MERL R. *The Negro, Too, in American History*. Nashville, Tenn.: National Publication, 1938 and 1949.

Federal Writers' Project. "New York: Marcus Garvey." Unpublished studies in the Schomburg Collection of the New York Public Library.

FORD, ARNOLD J. *The Universal Ethiopian Hymnal*. N.Y.: Beth B'nai Abraham, n.d.

FRANKLIN, JOHN HOPE. *From Slavery to Freedom: A History of American Negroes*. N.Y.: Knopf, 1947.

FRAZIER, E. FRANKLIN. "Garvey: a Mass Leader," *Nation*, CXXIII (August 18, 1926), 147–48.

————. "The Garvey Movement," *Opportunity*, IV (November, 1926), 346–48.

————. *The Negro in the United States*. N.Y.: Macmillan, 1949.

"Garvey," *Opportunity*, II (September, 1924), 284–85.

"A German Appeal to Garvey," *Nation*, CXIII (December 28, 1921), 769.

GOSNELL, HAROLD F. *Negro Politicians*. Chicago: Univ. of Chicago Press, 1935.

GRANT, GEORGE S. "Garveyism and the Ku Klux Klan," *Messenger*, V (October, 1923), 835–36, 842.

GREEN, ZEBEDEE. *Why I Am Dissatisfied*. Pittsburgh, Pa.: Quick Printing, 1922.

"Gunning for the Negro Moses," *Literary Digest*, LXXIV (August 19, 1922), 40–45.

HARRIS, ABRAM L. "The Negro Problem as Viewed by Negro Leaders," *Current History*, XVIII (June, 1923), 410–18.

HARRIS, ABRAM L., and STERLING D. SPERO. "Negro Problem," *Encyclopaedia of the Social Sciences*, XI (1937).

HARTT, ROLLIN LYNDE. "The Negro Moses and His Campaign to Lead the Black Millions into Their Promised Land," *Independent*, CV (February 26, 1921), 205–6.

HAYFORD, CASELY. *The Disabilities of Black Folk and Their Treatment with an Appeal to the Labour Party*. Accra, Gold Coast: Palladium, 1929.

HAYWOOD, HARRY. *Negro Liberation.* N.Y.: International Publishers, 1948.

HENRY, EDWARD BARNES. *The Predictions of a Great Race Leader in Fulfillment.* N.Y.: Author, 1953.

JAMES, CYRIL L. R. *History of Negro Revolt.* London: Fact, 1938.

JOELSON, F. S. "The Farcical Black Republic," *Outlook,* LII (August 18, 1923), 130–32.

JOHNSON, CHARLES S. "After Garvey: What?" *Opportunity,* I (August, 1923), 231–33.

JOHNSON, JAMES WELDON. *Black Manhattan.* N.Y.: Knopf, 1930.

LOCKE, ALAIN. "Enter the New Negro," *Survey,* LIII (March, 1925), 631–34.

———— (ed.). *The New Negro: An Interpretation.* N.Y.: Boni, 1925.

LOGAN, RAYFORD W. *What the Negro Wants.* Chapel Hill: Univ. of North Carolina Press, 1944.

LOVETT, ROBERT MORSS. "An Emperor Jones of Finance," *New Republic,* XXXV (July 11, 1923), 178–79.

LUCAS-DUBRETON, J. "Le Moïse noir," *Les Oeuvres libres,* CCLXXXII (January, 1951), 81–116.

"A Lunatic or a Traitor," *Crisis,* XXVIII (May, 1924), 8–9.

McKAY, CLAUDE. "Garvey as a Negro Moses," *Liberator,* IV (April, 1922), 8–9.

————. *Harlem: Negro Metropolis.* N.Y.: Dutton, 1940.

————. *A Long Way from Home.* N.Y.: Lee Furman, 1937.

McKENZIE, F. A. "Is There a Black Peril?: The Story of Marcus Garvey, the Leader of the Negro Peoples," *Overseas,* VI (April, 1921), 43–45.

MANOEDI, M. MOKETE. *Garvey and Africa.* N.Y.: New York Age, n.d.

"Marcus Garvey," *Journal of Negro History,* XXV (October, 1940), 590–92.

"Marcus Garvey and the N.A.A.C.P.," *Crisis,* XXXV (February, 1928), 51.

MAYS, BENJAMIN E. *The Negro's God as Reflected in His Literature.* Boston: Chapman and Grimes, 1938.

MEIER, AUGUST. "The Emergence of Negro Nationalism: A Study in Ideologies; from the American Revolution to the First World War." Unpublished Master of Arts thesis, Columbia University, 1948.

MILLER, KELLY. "After Marcus Garvey: What of the Negro?" *Contemporary Review*, CXXXI (April, 1927), 492–500.

MINOR, ROBERT. "After Garvey: What?" *Workers Monthly*, V (June, 1926), 365.

———. "Death or a Program," *Workers Monthly*, V (April, 1926), 270.

———. "The Handkerchief on Garvey's Head," *Liberator*, VI (October, 1924), 17–25.

"Mr. Garvey's Black Republic," *World Tomorrow*, III (September, 1920), 265.

MUGDAL, HUCHESWAR G. *Marcus Garvey: Is He the True Redeemer of the Negro?* N.Y.: Author, 1932.

MYRDAL, GUNNAR. *An American Dilemma: The Negro Problem and Modern Democracy.* N.Y.: Harper, 1944.

"Negro Exodus Unnecessary," *Opportunity*, II (October, 1924), 312–13.

"Negro Leadership in America," *World's Work*, XLI (March, 1921), 435–36.

"A Negro Moses and His Plans for an African Exodus," *Literary Digest*, LXVIII (March 19, 1921), 48–51.

NEMBHARD, LEN S. *Trials and Triumphs of Marcus Garvey.* Kingston, Jamaica: Gleaner, 1940.

OTTLEY, ROI. *Black Odyssey: The Story of the Negro in America.* N.Y.: Scribners, 1948.

———. *"New World A-Coming": Inside Black America.* Boston: Houghton Mifflin, 1943.

OVINGTON, MARY WHITE. *Portraits in Color.* N.Y.: Viking, 1927.

PALMER, A. MITCHELL. "Radicalism and Sedition among the Negroes as Reflected in Their Publications," Exhibit 10 of *Investigation Activities of the Department of Justice* (Vol XII. of Senate Documents, no. 153, 66th Cong., 1st Sess., 1919, pp. 161–87).

PICKENS, WILLIAM. "Africa for the Africans: The Garvey Movement," *Nation*, CXIII (December 28, 1921), 750–51.

———. "The Emperor of Africa: The Psychology of Garveyism," *Forum*, LXX (August, 1923), 1790–99.

———. "Marcus Garvey," *New Republic*, LII (August 31, 1927), 46–47.

POWELL, ADAM CLAYTON, JR. *Marching Blacks*. N.Y.: Dial, 1945.

"The Press and 'Back to Africa,'" *Crisis*, XXIV (October, 1922), 273–74.

RECORD, WILSON. *The Negro and the Communist Party*. Chapel Hill: Univ. of North Carolina Press, 1951.

REDDING, J. SAUNDERS. *They Came in Chains: Americans from Africa*. Phila.: Lippincott, 1950.

REID, C. H. "Marcus Garvey: A Social Phenomenon." Unpublished Master of Arts thesis, Northwestern University, 1928.

Revolutionary Radicalism: A Report of the Joint Legislative Committee of New York Investigating Seditious Activities. Vol. II. Albany, N.Y.: J. B. Lyon, 1920.

ROGERS, JOEL A. *World's Great Men of Color*. Vol. II. N.Y.: J. A. Rogers, 1946.

ROSE, ARNOLD M. *The Negro's Morale: Group Identification and Protest*. Minneapolis: Univ. of Minnesota Press, 1949.

ROSE, ARNOLD M., and CAROLINE ROSE. *America Divided: Minority Group Relations in the United States*. N.Y.: Knopf, 1948.

ROSENTHAL, ERIC. *Stars and Stripes in Africa*. London: Routledge, 1938.

SHAW, A. P. *Christianizing Race Relations: As a Negro Sees It*. Los Angeles, Calif.: Author, 1928.

SHEPPARD, WHEELER. *Mistakes of Dr. W. E. B. DuBois: Being an Answer to Dr. W. E. B. DuBois' Attack upon the Honorable Marcus Garvey*. 2 vols. Pittsburgh, Pa.: Goldenrod Print, 1921.

SLOCUM, WILLIAM J. "Sucker Traps: Plain and Fancy," *Collier's*, CXXV (January 28, 1950), 49–50.

SPERO, STERLING D., and ABRAM L. HARRIS. *The Black Worker: The Negro and the Labor Movement*. N.Y.: Columbia Univ. Press, 1931.

STANDING, THEODORE G. "A Study of Negro Nationalism." Unpublished Master of Arts thesis, University of Iowa, 1929.

STOLBERG, BENJAMIN. "Black Chauvinism," *Nation*, CXL (May 15, 1935), 570–71.

STONEQUIST, EVERETT V. *The Marginal Man: A Study in Personality and Culture Conflict*. N.Y.: Scribners, 1937.

STREATOR, GEORGE. "Three Men: Napier, Moton, Garvey; Negro

Leaders Who Typified an Era for Their People," *Commonweal*, XXXII (August 9, 1940), 323–26.

TALLEY, TRUMAN HUGHES. "Garvey's Empire of Ethiopia," *World's Work*, XLI (January, 1921), 264–70.

————. "Marcus Garvey: the Negro Moses?" *World's Work*, XLI (December, 1920), 153–66.

TUTTLE, WORTH M. "Garveyism: Impressions from a Missionary School," *World Tomorrow*, IV (June, 1921), 183–84.

————. "A New Nation in Harlem," *World Tomorrow*, IV (September, 1921), 279–81.

VAN DEUSEN, JOHN G. *The Black Man in White America*. Washington, D.C.: Associated Publishers, 1944.

WALLACE, INEZ. "Marcus Garvey," Cleveland *Plain Dealer*, June 2, 1929.

WALROND, ERIC D. "Imperator Africanus—Marcus Garvey: Menace or Promise?" *Independent*, CXIV (January 3, 1925), 8–11.

WATKINS, SYLVESTRE C. *The Pocket Book of Negro Facts*. Chicago: Bookmark Press, 1946.

WEATHERFORD, W. D. *The Negro from Africa to America*. N.Y.: Doran, 1924.

WILLIAMS, ERIC. *The Negro in the Caribbean*. Manchester, England: Panaf Service, 1945.

ZICKEFOOSE, HAROLD E. "The Garvey Movement." Unpublished Master of Arts thesis, Iowa State University, 1931.

NOTES

Publication facts for items not included in the preceding lists of references are given in full at first citation. All other entries are in abbreviated form.

Chapter One

1   William F. Allen, Charles P. Ware, and Lucy M. Garrison (eds.), *Slave Songs of the United States* (N.Y.: A. Simpson, 1867), p. 76.

2   Garvey, *Philosophy and Opinions*, I, 37.

3 Myrdal, *An American Dilemma*, p. 749.
4 I am greatly indebted to Garvey's widow, Mrs. Amy Jacques Garvey, for much of the information upon which this chapter is based. In 1949 Mrs. Garvey prepared an unpublished manuscript, "Story of Part of the Life of Marcus Garvey," for this study of her husband's life and work. Except where otherwise noted, this chapter is based upon Mrs. Garvey's manuscript account, which is now in my possession.
5 Martha W. Beckwith, *Black Roadways: A Study of Jamaican Folk Life* (Chapel Hill: Univ. of North Carolina Press, 1929), pp. 183–97; Mary Gaunt, *Where the Twain Shall Meet* (London: John Murray, 1922), pp. 170–215; [Edward Long] *The History of Jamaica or, a General Survey of the Antient* [sic] *and Modern State of that Island* (London: T. Lowndes, 1774), II, 338–50.
6 Garvey, "The Negro's Greatest Enemy," *Current History Magazine*, XVIII, 951; Garvey, *Philosophy and Opinions*, II, 124.
7 McKay, *Harlem*, p. 144.
8 Garvey, *Philosophy and Opinions*, II, 124; New York *World*, August 5, 1923.
9 McKay, *Harlem*, p. 144.
10 New York *World*, June 29, 1923.
11 Douglas Dakin, London, to the author, November 23, 1953.
12 New York *World*, August 5, 1923; Garvey, *Philosophy and Opinions*, II, 124.
13 Garvey in *Current History Magazine*, XVIII, 952; Garvey, *Philosophy and Opinions*, II, 125.
14 W. P. Livingston, *Black Jamaica: A Study in Evolution* (London: Sampson Low, Marston, 1899), p. 237; *Jamaica in 1897: A Handbook of Information for Intending Settlers and Others* (Kingston, Jamaica: Institute of Jamaica, 1897), p. 1.
15 Stonequist, *Marginal Man*, p. 27; Livingston, *Black Jamaica*, p. 6. See also Fernando Henriques, *Family and Colour in Jamaica* (London: Eyre and Spottiswoode, 1953).
16 DuBois, "Back to Africa," *Century Magazine*, CV, 540.
17 McKay, *Harlem*, p. 145.
18 New York *World*, June 29, 1923.

19 See W. Ralph Hall Caine, *The Cruise of the Port Kingston* (London: Collier, 1908), pp. 214–31; C. L. Chenery, "The Jamaican Earthquake," *Barbados Advocate,* January 23–25, 1907.

20 McKay, *Harlem,* pp. 144–45; Aron, "Garvey Movement," p. 4.

21 New York *World,* June 29, 1923.

22 Aron, "Garvey Movement," pp. 4–5; McKay, *Harlem,* p. 145; DuBois, "Marcus Garvey," *Crisis,* XXI, 58; New York *World,* June 29, 1923.

23 See, for example, Duse Mohammed, *In the Land of the Pharaohs: A Short History of Egypt from the Fall of Ismail to the Assassination of Boutros Pasha* (London: Stanley Paul, 1911).

24 New York *World,* June 29, 1923; Garvey in *Current History Magazine,* XVIII, 951; Garvey, *Philosophy and Opinions,* II, 124.

25 Garvey, *Philosophy and Opinions,* II, 126.

26 *Ibid.*

27 U.N.I.A. Manifesto, Booker T. Washington MSS, Library of Congress.

28 Garvey, *Philosophy and Opinions,* II, 38.

29 *Ibid.,* pp. 37–38.

30 U.N.I.A. letterhead in Marcus Garvey, Kingston, to Booker T. Washington, Tuskegee, April 12, 1915, Washington MSS, Library of Congress.

31 Garvey in *Current History Magazine,* XVIII, 953–54; Garvey, *Philosophy and Opinions,* II, 127.

32 Marcus Garvey, Kingston, to Booker T. Washington, Tuskegee, April 12, 1915, Washington MSS, Library of Congress.

33 Booker T. Washington, Tuskegee, to Marcus Garvey, Kingston, April 27, 1915, *ibid.*

34 Garvey, *Philosophy and Opinions,* II, 128; Bunche, "Programs, Ideologies, Tactics, and Achievements," p. 394; Johnson, *Black Manhattan,* p. 252.

Chapter Two

1 Lawrence Gellert, "Negro Songs of Protest," *Negro Anthology, 1931–1933,* ed. Nancy Cunard (London: Nancy Cunard, 1934), p. 367.

2 Garvey, *Philosophy and Opinions,* I, 2.

3 See James B. Runnion, "The Negro Exodus," *Atlantic Monthly,* XLIV (August, 1879), 222–30; W. L. Fleming, "Pap Singleton, the Moses of the Colored Exodus," *American Journal of Sociology,* XV (July, 1909), 61–82.

4 Emmet J. Scott, *Negro Migration during the War* (New York: Oxford Univ. Press, 1920), p. 3.

5 Chicago Commission on Race Relations, *Negro in Chicago,* p. 602.

6 Samuel A. Stouffer and Lyonel C. Florant, "Negro Population and Negro Population Movements" (unpublished monograph prepared for the Carnegie-Myrdal study, 1940; Schomburg Collection, N.Y. Public Library), V, 3.

7 Chicago Commission, *Negro in Chicago,* p. 80.

8 Washington *Bee,* March 8, 1919; George E. Haynes, *Negro Migration and Its Implications North and South* (N.Y.: American Missionary Association), p. 5; Stouffer and Florant, "Negro Population," V, 18; Edward E. Lewis, *The Mobility of the Negro* (N.Y.: Columbia Univ. Press, 1931), p. 129.

9 Washington *Bee,* March 8, 1919; Scott, *Negro Migration,* p. 14.

10 Lewis, *Mobility of the Negro,* p. 116.

11 Carl Sandburg, *The American Songbag* (N.Y.: Harcourt, Brace, 1927), pp. 8–10.

12 Scott, *Negro Migration,* p. 14; Washington *Bee,* March 8, 1919.

13 Abraham Epstein, *The Negro Migrant in Pittsburgh* (Pittsburgh, Pa.: Univ. of Pittsburgh, 1918), pp. 23, 27.

14 Scott, *Negro Migration,* pp. 36–37.

15 Stouffer and Florant, "Negro Population," V, 14; Epstein, *Negro Migrant in Pittsburgh,* pp. 26–27, 35.

16 Quoted in Carl Sandburg, *The Chicago Race Riots* (N.Y.: Harcourt, Brace and Howe, 1919), pp. 10–11.

17   Scott, *Negro Migration,* p. 30.

18   See Emmett J. Scott, "Letters of Negro Migrants of 1916–1918," *Journal of Negro History,* IV (July, 1919), 290–340.

19   Quoted in Scott, *Negro Migration,* p. 31.

20   Washington *Bee,* March 8, 1919.

21   Emmett J. Scott, *Scott's Official History of the American Negro in the World War* (Chicago: Homewood Press, 1919), p. 32; Dowd, *Negro in American Life,* p. 189; Franklin, *From Slavery to Freedom,* p. 463.

22   Scott, *American Negro in the World War,* pp. 173 ff.; Franklin, *From Slavery to Freedom,* p. 457; Dowd, *Negro in American Life,* pp. 231–42.

23   See, for example, Robert L. Wolf, "Les Noires," *Messenger,* V (January, 1923), 578.

24   Scott, *American Negro in the World War,* pp. 40 ff.

25   Franklin, *From Slavery to Freedom,* p. 452.

26   [Finley P. Dunne] *Mr. Dooley's Philosophy* (N.Y.: R. H. Russell, 1900), p. 217.

27   Franklin, *From Slavery to Freedom,* p. 467.

28   *Ibid.*

29   Johnson, *Black Manhattan,* p. 246; DuBois, *Dusk of Dawn,* p. 264.

30   Franklin, *From Slavery to Freedom,* pp. 473–75.

31   Chicago Commission, *Negro in Chicago,* p. 1.

32   [Finley P. Dunne] *Mr. Dooley's Opinions* (N.Y.: R. H. Russell, 1901), p. 210.

33   Quoted in Chicago Commission, *Negro in Chicago,* p. 47.

34   Washington *Bee,* August 2, 1919.

35   Franklin, *From Slavery to Freedom,* p. 471.

36   *Ibid.*

37   Chicago *Defender,* May 5, 1923.

38   A. Mitchell Palmer, "Radicalism and Sedition among the Negroes as Reflected in Their Publications," Exhibit 10 of *Investigation Activities of the Department of Justice* (Vol. XII of Senate Doc., no. 153, 66th Cong., 1st Sess., 1919), pp. 161–87.

39   *Revolutionary Radicalism,* II, 1476–1520.

40 Quoted in Robert T. Kerlin, *The Voice of the Negro, 1919* (N.Y.: E. P. Dutton, 1920), p. 26.
41 See, for instance, Washington *Bee*, April 12, 1919.
42 A good example is Claude McKay's bitter sonnet, "If We Must Die," penned after the Washington race riot in 1919, in *The Book of American Negro Poetry*, ed. James Weldon Johnson (N.Y.: Harcourt, Brace, 1922), p. 134.

Chapter Three

1 Ford, *Universal Ethiopian Hymnal*, p. 11; Garvey Club Song Sheet, Schomburg Collection, N.Y. Public Library.
2 *Minutes of Proceedings of a Speech by Marcus Garvey at the Century Theatre, London, Sunday, September 2, 1928,* p. 22.
3 *Crisis*, XII (May, 1916), 9.
4 Garvey, *Philosophy and Opinions*, II, 128.
5 *Ibid.*, I, 10. See also pp. 29–30.
6 Johnson, *Black Manhattan*, p. 253.
7 See Kelly Miller, "The Harvest of Race Prejudice," *Survey*, LIII (March, 1925), 683; Case A, 68, 165.
8 McKay, *Harlem*, p. 147; Aron, "Garvey Movement," p. 22.
9 Garvey, *Philosophy and Opinions*, II, 128; McKay, *Harlem*, p. 147; Aron, "Garvey Movement," p. 23.
10 Amy Jacques Garvey, Kingston, Jamaica, to the author, February 19, 1949; interview with Amy Ashwood Garvey, London, January 22, 1951.
11 Wright, London, to Secretary of State, April 6, 1921, State Dept. files, 811.108G191/3, National Archives.
12 Garvey, *Philosophy and Opinions*, II, 128.
13 *Ibid.*, p. 129.
14 *Ibid.*
15 *New York Times*, October 15 and 17, 1919; New York *World*, October 15, 1919. See also Case A, 2208, 2331–32; Ottley, *"New World A-Coming,"* p. 69.
16 McKay, "Garvey as a Negro Moses," *Liberator*, V, 9. See also McKay, *Harlem*, pp. 147–48.

17   McKay in *Liberator*, V, 9; Aron, "Garvey Movement," p. 29; Bontemps and Conroy, *They Seek a City*, p. 168.

18   Amy Jacques Garvey, Kingston, Jamaica, to the author, February 14, 1951; Williams, *Negro in the Caribbean*, p. 57.

19   *Negro World*, August 2, 1919, quoted in Case A, 2443.

20   Clark, *Is It the Color of Our Skin?* p. 5.

21   *Negro World*, July 30, 1921.

22   *Nation*, XLI (September 17, 1885), 228.

23   See George S. Schuyler, "Shafts and Darts," *Messenger*, V (October, 1923), 842.

24   *Ibid.*, V (September, 1923), 819.

25   *Ibid.*, V (October, 1923), 842.

26   Aron, "Garvey Movement," p. 27.

27   *Negro World*, August 2, 1919, quoted in Case A, 2444–45.

28   *Case A*, 2474–75; DuBois, "Marcus Garvey," *Crisis*, XXI, 113.

29   *Negro World*, August 21, 1920; New York *World*, January 13, 1922.

30   *Negro World*, August 21, 1920.

31   Talley, "Garvey's Empire of Ethiopia," *World's Work*, XLI, 268; Amy Jacques Garvey, Kingston, Jamaica, to the author, February 19, 1949.

32   See photograph in Garvey, *Philosophy and Opinions*, II, 184.

33   B.S.L. Minutes, September 11, 1919, quoted in Case A, 1130. See also pp. 2127, 2212–15.

34   Ovington, *Portraits in Color*, p. 22; Tuttle, "Garveyism: Impressions from a Missionary School," *World Tomorrow*, IV, 184.

35   Columbia Records, No. 14024D, by Negro artists George and Roscoe. The reverse of the record was a piece entitled "My Jamaica."

36   Quoted by DuBois in *Crisis*, XXI, 113.

37   *Negro World*, February 14, 1920, quoted *ibid.*, p. 112.

38   Leon R. Swift, New York, to Mr. Johnson, New York, April 16, 1920, in Case B.

39   *Ibid.*

40   [————] to Louis LaMothe, Havana, August 23, 1920, *ibid.*

41   *Negro World*, August 21 and September 11, 1920.

42 *Ibid.*
43 *Ibid.*, September 11, 1920.
44 See, for example, Pickens, "Africa for the Africans: The Garvey Movement," *Nation*, CXIII, 751.
45 DuBois, "Back to Africa," *Century*, CV, 544; Aron, "Garvey Movement," p. 31; Chicago *Defender*, December 23, 1922, and February 3, 1923; Talley in *World's Work*, XLI, 269.
46 Garvey, *Philosophy and Opinions*, I, 10.
47 *Negro World*, August 21, 1920.
48 New York *World*, January 13, 1922.
49 Amy Jacques Garvey, Kingston, Jamaica, to the author, February 14, 1951.
50 Schomburg Collection, N.Y. Public Library.
51 Convention program, *ibid.*
52 *New York Times*, August 2 and 3, 1920; Aron, "Garvey Movement," p. 34.
53 *New York Times*, August 3, 1920.
54 *Ibid.*
55 *Ibid.*
56 *Ibid.*
57 New York *World*, August 5, 1920.
58 *Revolutionary Radicalism*, II, 1514.
59 *Negro World*, September 11, 1920.
60 New York *World*, August 4, 1920.
61 *Negro World*, September 11, 1920; Garvey, *Philosophy and Opinions*, II, 135–43.
62 Kansas City *Call*, May 10, 1929, cited in Standing, "A Study of Negro Nationalism," pp. 144–45.
63 *New York Times*, March 7, 1930.
64 Garvey, *Philosophy and Opinions*, II, 278–79.
65 *Negro World*, September 11, 1920; Garvey, *Philosophy and Opinions*, II, 140–41.
66 *Negro World*, January 28, 1922; McKay, *Harlem*, p. 148.
67 McKay, *Harlem*, p. 164. See also Joelson, "The Farcical Black Republic," *Outlook*, LII, 130, 132.
68 Chicago *Defender*, August 26, 1922.
69 William Pickens, Washington, to the author, May 27, 1949;

Pickens in *Nation,* CXIII, 750–51; *Negro World,* December 17, 1921.

70 Chicago *Defender,* July 29, 1922.
71 Quoted in McKay, *Harlem,* p. 154.
72 *Negro World,* August 21, 1920.
73 Quoted in B.S.L. circular exhibited in Case *A,* 2492.

Chapter Four

1 Quoted in Bontemps and Conroy, *They Seek a City,* p. 169.
2 Garvey, *Philosophy and Opinions,* II, 212.
3 *Negro World,* August 2, 1919, quoted in Case *A,* 2444–46. See also Garvey, *Philosophy and Opinions,* II, 129–30; *Crusader,* V (November, 1921), 24.
4 *Negro World,* August 21, 1920; New York *World,* August 11, 1920.
5 *Crusader,* V (November, 1921), 17, 24, and VI (January–February, 1922), 5; Chicago *Defender,* November 19, 1921.
6 Bontemps and Conroy, *They Seek a City,* pp. 171–72; Chicago *Defender,* August 6, 1921; DuBois, "The Black Star Line," *Crisis,* XXIV, 213.
7 Chicago *Defender,* May 21, 1921; Garvey, *Philosophy and Opinions,* II, 321–23.
8 *Negro World,* August 2, 1919, quoted in Case *A,* 2444–46.
9 Case *A,* 79, 87–88, 93–94, 97, and 172–73.
10 B.S.L. Circular, quoted in Case *A,* 2503.
11 B.S.L. Circular, quoted in Case *A,* 2500.
12 *Negro World,* October 16, 1920, quoted in Case *A,* 2511.
13 Case *A,* 148, 180. See also Garvey, *Philosophy and Opinions,* II, 188–90.
14 Joshua Cockbourne, Sagua La Grande, to Marcus Garvey, New York, December 2, 1919, in Case *B.*
15 Joshua Cockbourne, Sagua La Grande, to Marcus Garvey, December 5, 1919, *ibid.*
16 *New York Times,* August 22, 1922. See also George J. Nagy, New York, to Marcus Garvey, New York, January 19, 1923, in Case *B.*

17 Marcus Garvey, New York, to Captain J. Cockburn, New York, June 19, 1920, quoted in Case A, 2496–97. See also pp. 315–16 of this docket.

18 Case A, 2498; DuBois in *Crisis*, XXIV, 211.

19 B.S.L. Minutes, August 28, 1920, quoted in Case A, 1158.

20 Leon R. Swift, Norfolk, to Black Star Line, New York, August 14, 1920, in Case B.

21 Marcus Garvey, Kingston, Jamaica, to American Consul, Kingston, June 7, 1921, *ibid.*

22 Marcus Garvey, Kingston, to American Consul, Kingston, June 7, 1921, *ibid.*

23 [———] Kingston, to Secretary of State, April 12, 1921, State Dept. files, 811.108G191/5, National Archives.

24 Charles Evans Hughes, Secretary of State, to American Legation, San José, Costa Rica, April 26, 1921, *ibid.*, 811.108G-191/9.

25 Panama *Star and Herald*, April 28, 1921.

26 Walter C. Thurston, San José, Costa Rica, to Secretary of State, May 2, 1921, State Dept. files, 811.108G191/11, National Archives.

27 A. C. Frost, Guatemala City, Guatemala, to Secretary of State, March 9, 1922, *ibid.*, 811.108G191/27.

28 R. W. F., Office of the Solicitor, Memo to Doughton, June 21, 1921, *ibid.*, 811.108G191/31.

29 Hughes, Secretary of State, to American Consul, Kingston, May 10, 1921; Hughes to American Consul, Port Limon, Costa Rica, May 20, 1921, *ibid.*, 811.108G191/10 and /12.

30 Marcus Garvey, Kingston, to Chief Engineer, *Kanawha*, May 19 [1921], in Case B.

31 Cecil C. Beckford, Kingston, to Marcus Garvey, Kingston, May 21, 1921, *ibid.*

32 Marcus Garvey, Kingston, to Chief Engineer, *Kanawha*, May 18, 1921, *ibid.*

33 Marcus Garvey, Kingston, to American Consul, Kingston, June 1, 1921, *ibid.*

34 Marcus Garvey, Kingston, to American Consul, Kingston, June 7, 1921, *ibid.*

35   A. A. McInnez, Kingston, to Marcus Garvey, Kingston, June 7, 1921, *ibid.*

36   Charles L. Latham, Kingston, to Secretary of State, August 24, 1921, State Dept. files, 811.108G191/24, National Archives.

37   Marcus Garvey, New York, to Charles Evans Hughes, Washington, September 21, 1921, *ibid.*, 196.6/751.

38   G. T. Chareton and J. L. Crone, New York, to Marcus Garvey, New York, November 2, 1921, in Case *B.*

39   Marcus Garvey, New Orleans, to Charles Evans Hughes, Washington, July 13, 1921, State Dept. files, 811.108G191/32, National Archives.

40   C. L. Latham, Kingston, to Secretary of State, July 21, 1921, *ibid.*, 195.7/3424.

41   Black Star Line, New York, to Captain, *Kanawha,* Antilla, Cuba, August 26, 1921, in Case *B.*

42   [John S.] DeBourg, Antilla, to Black Star Line, New York, August 30, 1921, *ibid.*

43   Horace J. Dickenson, Antilla, to Secretary of State, December 12, 1922, State Dept. files, 195.91/2160, National Archives.

44   *Negro World,* November 8, 1919, quoted in Case *A,* 2483–85.

45   *Negro World,* November 6, 1920, quoted in Case *A,* 2515–17.

46   *Negro World,* October 16, 1920, quoted in Case *A,* 2510–11.

47   Orlando M. Thompson, New York, to Louis Lamothe, Havana, October 1, 1920, quoted in Case *A,* 2638–39.

48   Case *A,* 2639–47. See also pp. 1912–13, 2284–85 of this docket.

49   *Negro World,* March 5, 1921, quoted in Case *A,* 2376–77.

50   Case *A,* 2557. See also pp. 590–91 of this docket.

51   B.S.L. Minutes, May 28, 1921, quoted in Case *A,* 1168–69.

52   A. Rudolph Silverston, New York, to Alfred D. Lasker, Washington, June 29, 1921, U.S. Shipping Board, General Files, I, 605–1–653, National Archives.

53   A. Rudolph Silverston, New York, to Alfred D. Lasker, Washington, June 30, 1921, *ibid.*

54   A. D. Lasker, Washington, to A. Rudolph Silverston, New York, July 5, 1921, *ibid.*

55 Clifford W. Smith, Secretary, U.S. Shipping Board, Memo to Ship Sales Division, August 2, 1921, *ibid.*

56 J. Harry Philbin, Ship Sales Division, U.S. Shipping Board, Memo to Treasurer, August 3, 1921, *ibid.* See also Case A, 1985–87.

57 *California New Age,* September 23, 1921, quoted by DuBois in *Crisis,* XXIV, 212.

58 Chicago *Defender,* November 19, 1921; *Crusader,* V (November, 1921), 11, 19, and 23.

59 DuBois, "Marcus Garvey," *Crisis,* XXI, 58–60 and 112–15.

60 *Negro World,* March 12–December 10, 1921, quoted in Case A, 2573–2609.

61 See Wilford H. Smith, New York, to United States Shipping Board, Washington, December 13, 1921; J. Harry Philbin, Washington, to Black Star Line, New York, December 16, 1921, quoted in Case A, 2691 and 2693.

62 J. Harry Philbin, Ship Sales Division, U.S. Shipping Board, Memo to Treasurer, January 5, 1922, U.S. Shipping Board, General Files, I, 605–1–653, National Archives. See also Case A, 1878.

63 See Case A, 1926–39, 1942–47, 1969; *Negro World,* December 24, 1921, February 18, and July 8, 1922.

64 William J. Burns, Washington, to Frank Burke, Washington, August 31, 1921, U.S. Shipping Board, General Files, I, 605–1–653, National Archives.

65 Frank Burke, Washington, to A. J. Frey, Washington, September 1, 1921, *ibid.*

66 See *ibid., passim;* and Clyde Wenelken, Washington, to Chauncey G. Parker, Washington, March 31, 1924, U.S. Shipping Board, General Files, III, 1091–1250, National Archives.

67 *Congressional Record,* 70th Cong., 1st Sess., LXIX (April 17, 1928), 6627.

68 *Crusader,* V (November, 1921), 25.

69 George S. Schuyler, "Shafts and Darts," *Messenger,* V (December, 1923), 922.

70 Case A, 2–14, 21–33; *New York Times,* January 13, 1922; New York *World,* January 13, 1922.

71   *New York Times,* January 16, 1922.
72   Washington *Bee,* January 21, 1922.
73   *New York Times,* February 17 and 18, 1922; Chicago *Defender,* February 25, 1922.
74   *Crusader Bulletin,* February 18, 1922.
75   *Negro World,* April 1, 1922.
76   *Ibid.,* December 17, 1921.
77   *Ibid.,* May 13, 1922.
78   *Ibid.,* January 21, 1922.
79   *Ibid.,* December 24, 1921, and February 18, 1922.
80   *Ibid.,* July 8, 1922.

Chapter Five

1   George Alexander McGuire, "Preface," in Garvey, *Philosophy and Opinions,* II, vii.
2   Garvey, *Philosophy and Opinions,* I, 10.
3   Chicago *Defender,* May 20 and November 4, 1922; DuBois, "The Black Star Line," *Crisis,* XXIV, 214; Ovington, *Portraits in Color,* p. 28.
4   Case A, 387; *New York Times,* July 23, 1921.
5   *New York Times,* July 23, 1921.
6   *Ibid.,* September 12, 1922; Chicago *Defender,* September 9, 1922; Case A, 1449.
7   See, for instance, Chicago *Defender,* December 13, 1924; Kingston *Gleaner,* September 25, 1924.
8   Marcus Garvey to William Pickens, July 10, 1922, and Pickens to Garvey, July 24, 1922, quoted in Chicago *Defender,* July 29, 1922.
9   *New York Times,* August 7, 1922; Chicago *Defender,* August 12, 1922.
10   Chicago *Defender,* August 12, 1922. See also Manoedi, *Garvey and Africa.*
11   Bagnall in *Messenger,* V, 638.
12   *New York Times,* August 21, 1922.
13   Chicago *Defender,* August 26, 1922.
14   *New York Times,* August 28, 1922.

15 *Negro World,* August 5, 1922, quoted in Chicago *Defender,* August 12, 1922; Chandler Owen, "Should Marcus Garvey Be Deported?" *Messenger,* IV (September, 1922), 480.

16 Baltimore *Afro-American,* August 18, 1922; Garvey, *Philosophy and Opinions,* II, 297.

17' *New York Times,* September 6, 1922; A. Philip Randolph, "The Human Hand Threat," *Messenger,* IV (October, 1922), 499.

18 *New York Times,* September 7, 1922.

19 Randolph in *Messenger,* IV, 500.

20 Chicago *Defender,* August 26, 1922.

21 *New York Times,* September 11, 1922; Chicago *Defender,* October 7, 1922.

22 *New York Times,* January 13, 1923.

23 Chicago *Defender,* August 16, 1924.

24 *New York Times,* January 20, 1923.

25 *Ibid.,* January 21, 1923. See also *Garvey* v. *United States,* 292 F. 593 (2d Cir. 1923).

26 Quoted in Garvey, *Philosophy and Opinions,* II, 294–300. See also *Negro World* supplement, February 6, 1923; Pittsburgh *Courier,* August 20 and 27, 1927.

27 Garvey, *Philosophy and Opinions,* II, 294, 300–8.

28 See, for example, Case A, 939, 1283–86, 1525–26.

29 Chicago *Defender,* June 16, 1923.

30 Garvey, *Philosophy and Opinions,* II, 184–216.

31 Quoted in Chicago *Defender,* June 30, 1923; *Negro Times,* June 18, 1923.

32 Chicago *Defender,* September 15, 1923. For a court decision on Garvey's suit to obtain his release on bail see *Garvey* v. *United States,* 292 F. 591–93 (2d Cir. 1923).

33 Chicago *Defender,* June 30, 1923.

34 New York *Age,* June 30, 1923.

35 New York *Amsterdam News,* June 27, 1923.

36 Schuyler, "Shafts and Darts," *Messenger,* V (October, 1923), 841.

37 Garvey, *Philosophy and Opinions,* II, 180–83.

38 *Ibid.,* p. 218.

39 McKay, *Harlem*, p. 162.
40 Chicago *Defender*, March 17 and December 15, 1923, July 12, 1924, February 7, 1925; *United States* v. *Marcus Garvey*, no. C38–771, S.D.N.Y.
41 Garvey, *Philosophy and Opinions*, II, 231–35.
42 Marcus Garvey, New York, to Chairman, U.S. Shipping Board, Washington, June 3, 1924, U.S. Shipping Board, General Files, I, 605–1–653, National Archives.
43 J. Harry Philbin, Ship Sales Division, Memo to General Counsel, U.S. Shipping Board, June 11, 1924, *ibid.*
44 J. Harry Philbin, Ship Sales Division, to President, Fleet Corporation, June 16, 1924, *ibid.*
45 Garvey, *Philosophy and Opinions*, II, 264.
46 Chicago *Defender*, February 7, 1925.
47 Roscoe Simmons, *ibid.*, September 6, 1924.
48 *Ibid.*, August 23, 1924.
49 New York *Amsterdam News*, August 13, 1924.
50 Marcus Garvey and J. R. Hiorth, Agreement, January 28, 1925, State Dept. files, 811.108G191/39, National Archives.
51 José de Olivares, Kingston, to Secretary of State, March 13, 1925, *ibid.*
52 Jacob deRytter Hiorth, Kingston, to José de Olivares, Kingston, March 9, 1925, *ibid.*
53 Odin G. Loren, Colon, to Secretary of State, April 22, 1925, *ibid.*, 819.5032/– –.
54 Edwin Barclay to Elie Garcia, June 14, 1920, quoted in Garvey, *Philosophy and Opinions*, II, 365.
55 Quoted *ibid.*, pp. 399–405.
56 R. J. Sharp, New York, to R. C. Bannerman, Washington, October 2, 1920, State Dept. files, 812.00/673½, National Archives.
57 *Negro World*, November 6, 1920, quoted in Case A, 2517.
58 *Liberian Patriot*, May 21, 1921.
59 Marcus Garvey, New York, to Gabriel Johnson, Monrovia, February 1, 1921, State Dept. files, 882.00/705, National Archives; Garvey, *Philosophy and Opinions*, II, 366–67.
60 Memorandum of an Interview between Liberian Officials and

U.N.I.A. Delegates, March 22, 1921, State Dept. files, 882.00/705, National Archives.

61 Cyril A. Crichlow, Monrovia, to Marcus Garvey, New York, April 28, 1921, *ibid.*

62 Cyril Henry, Monrovia, to Orlando M. Thompson, New York, July 1, 1921, *ibid.*

63 Marcus Garvey to President C. D. B. King, December 5, 1923, quoted in Garvey, *Philosophy and Opinions*, II, 368.

64 *Ibid.*, pp. 371–78.

65 James J. Dossen, Monrovia, to U.N.I.A., New York, May 2, 1924, quoted *ibid.*, pp. 378–79.

66 Chicago *Defender*, May 14, 1921.

67 *Ibid.*, March 4, 1922.

68 Edwin Barclay, Monrovia, to Bishop C. S. Smith, Detroit, quoted *ibid.*, July 16, 1921. See also *World's Work*, XLI (March, 1921), 435–36.

69 Blaise Diagne to Marcus Garvey, July 3, 1922, quoted in Charpin, "La Question noire," *Revue Indigène*, XVII, 281, and in Buell, *Native Problem*, II, 81.

70 Chicago *Defender*, May 14, 1921.

71 *Ibid.*

72 Garvey, *Philosophy and Opinions*, II, 376–77.

73 T. V. O'Connor, U.S. Shipping Board, to Secretary of State, July 9, 1926, State Dept. files, 682.11253, National Archives. See also Garvey, *Philosophy and Opinions*, II, 379; Buell, *Native Problem*, II, 732.

74 Edwin Barclay, Monrovia, to A. H. Bull Line, Monrovia, June 30, 1924, State Dept. files, 811.108G191/38, National Archives.

75 Wall, Monrovia, to Secretary of State, July 31 and August 8, 1924, *ibid.*, 811.108G191/37 and /38.

76 Chicago *Defender*, July 19, 1924.

77 W. R. C[astle], Memorandum to Secretary of State, August 25–26, 1924, State Dept. files, 811.108G191/34, National Archives.

78 Quoted in Garvey, *Philosophy and Opinions*, II, 389–90; Buell, *Native Problem*, II, 732; McKay, *Harlem*, p. 166.

79   *Liberian News*, August, 1924, pp. 3–4, 9–11.

80   *Message of the President* (1924), p. 51, quoted in Buell, *Native Problem*, II, 732; "Liberia," *Spokesman*, I (March, 1925), 23.

81   Garvey, *Philosophy and Opinions*, II, 379.

82   "A Barefaced Coloured Leader," *Black Man*, I (July, 1935), 5–8.

83   See *ibid.*, III (November, 1938), 16; McKay, *Harlem*, p. 166.

84   Charles Evans Hughes, Washington, to the President, Washington, September 6, 1924, State Dept. files, 882.5511/10, National Archives.

85   Quoted in Buell, *Native Problem*, II, 733.

86   Garvey, *Philosophy and Opinions*, II, 385.

87   "About President King," *African World*, July 30, 1927, p. xx.

88   Garvey, *Philosophy and Opinions*, II, 384; "The Liberia-Firestone Rubber Scheme," *West Africa*, October 24, 1925, pp. 1384–85; "Liberian Development," *African World*, November 28, 1925, p. v; "The Firestone Concession," *African World*, December 31, 1925, p. v; interview with Amy Ashwood Garvey, London, January 22, 1951.

89   Garvey, *Philosophy and Opinions*, II, 385.

90   *Negro World*, June 7, and August 16, 1924.

91   "A Tragic Nuisance," *Messenger*, VI (December, 1924), 374. See also Chicago *Defender*, November 15, 1924.

92   Gosnell, *Negro Politicians*, p. 113.

93   *United States* v. *Garvey*, no. C38–771, S.D.N.Y.

94   *Ibid.*

95   *Garvey* v. *United States*, 4 F. 2d 974–76 (2d Cir. 1925); Garvey, *Philosophy and Opinions*, II, 173–77.

96   *Garvey* v. *United States*, 267 U.S. 604, 45 Sup. Ct. 464 (1924).

97   Quoted in "Opinion of the Negro Press," *Spokesman*, I (March, 1925), 29, 32.

98   *Ibid.*, p. 32.

99   George S. Schuyler and Theophilus Lewis, "Shafts and Darts," *Messenger*, VII (March, 1925), 129.

100   Quoted in *Spokesman*, I, 32; Garvey, *Philosophy and Opinions*, II, 149.

101 Buffalo *Evening Times,* February 24, 1925, quoted in Garvey, *Philosophy and Opinions,* II, 149–50.
102 New York *News,* February 7, 1925, quoted in *Spokesman,* I, 29.
103 "Watchman, What of the Night?" *Spokesman,* I, 4–5.
104 Garvey, *Philosophy and Opinions,* II, 237–39.

Chapter Six

1 Ford, *Universal Ethiopian Hymnal,* p. 11; Garvey Club Song Sheet, Schomburg Collection, N.Y. Public Library.
2 Garvey, *Philosophy and Opinions,* I, 14.
3 Cincinnati Division No. 146, U.N.I.A., *Sixth Anniversary Drive, May 8th to 18th, 1927,* p. 13; Aron, "Garvey Movement," pp. 36–37.
4 Nembhard, *Trials and Triumphs,* p. 90.
5 Ottley, *"New World A-Coming,"* p. 80; Bontemps and Conroy, *They Seek a City,* p. 172.
6 Cincinnati Division, *Sixth Anniversary Drive,* pp. 1–12.
7 *New Republic,* LII (August 31, 1927), 46–47.
8 Washington *Eagle,* September 9, 1927. Called to my attention by Mr. Hodge Kirnon of New York City.
9 The pardon application and its rejection are quoted in full in Garvey, *Philosophy and Opinions,* II, 241–71.
10 Quoted in Nembhard, *Trials and Triumphs,* p. 91.
11 New York *Amsterdam News,* undated clipping called to my attention by Mr. Hodge Kirnon of New York City.
12 *Ibid.,* January 11, 1928.
13 *Ibid.,* November 30, 1927.
14 Quoted in Nembhard, *Trials and Triumphs,* p. 96.
15 Quoted *ibid.,* pp. 98–99.
16 Quoted *ibid.,* p. 102.
17 "Marcus Garvey and the N.A.A.C.P.," *Crisis,* XXXV, 51.
18 Garvey, *Philosophy and Opinions,* I, 37.
19 Garvey, *Speech at Royal Albert Hall,* p. 5. See also McKay, *Harlem,* p. 171; "Black Magic Fails Again," *Independent,* CXX, 586–87.

20   Garvey, *Speech at Royal Albert Hall,* p. 3.

21   *Ibid.,* pp. 7, 10–11, 13–21, 24–25. See also Memorandum, July 6, 1928, State Dept. files, 811.108G191/49, National Archives.

22   McKay, *Harlem,* p. 171.

23   U.N.I.A., London, circular letter to editors, September 24, 1928 (in my possession).

24   *Renewal of Petition of the Universal Negro Improvement Association and African Communities League to the League of Nations* (London: Vail, 1928), pp. 21, 24, 28. See also Joseph C. Grew, Berne, to Secretary of State, September 25, 1922, State Dept. files, 800.4016/20, National Archives.

25   Garvey, *Minutes of a Speech at Century Theatre, London, 1928,* pp. 8–9, 22, 24, 26–27. See also Memorandum, June 16, 1928, State Dept. files, 811.108G191/51, National Archives.

26   Garvey, *Minutes of a Speech at Century Theatre, London, 1928,* pp. 30–31.

27   Wesley Frost, Montreal, to Secretary of State, November 8, 1928, State Dept. files, 811.108G191/50, National Archives.

28   Kingston *Gleaner,* August 2, 1929.

29   *Ibid.,* August 3, 1929.

30   *Ibid.,* August 16, 21, 23, and 29, 1929.

31   *Ibid.,* August 15, 1929; McKay, *Harlem,* p. 173.

32   Kingston *Gleaner,* August 16, 1929.

33   *Ibid.,* August 23, 1929.

34   *Ibid.,* August 6, 7, and 14, 1929; McKay, *Harlem,* p. 173.

35   Aron, "Garvey Movement," p. 57. See also Kingston *Gleaner,* August 29, 1929.

36   Kingston *Gleaner,* August 6, 8, 9, 22, 23, 24, and 29, 1929; Nembhard, *Trials and Triumphs,* pp. 150–66.

37   Nembhard, *Trials and Triumphs,* p. 167.

38   *Ibid.,* pp. 167–92.

39   Quoted in *Crisis,* XXXVI (December, 1929), 419–20; Kingston *Gleaner,* September 27, 1929.

40   Nembhard, *Trials and Triumphs,* pp. 198–225.

41   McKay, *Harlem,* p. 174.

42 Nembhard, *Trials and Triumphs,* pp. 228–30.
43 *Black Man,* I (December, 1933), 20, quoted in Bunche, "Programs, Ideologies, Tactics, and Achievements," p. 415.
44 Quoted *ibid.,* p. 414.
45 Quoted *ibid.* See also *Black Man,* I (July, 1935), 5–8, and III (March, 1938), 2.
46 Quoted in Bunche, "Programs, Ideologies, Tactics, and Achievements," p. 413.
47 *Black Man,* I (July, 1935), 13–16.
48 Bunche, "Programs, Ideologies, Tactics, and Achievements," p. 413.
49 *Black Man,* I (July, 1935), 20.
50 *Ibid.,* II (December, 1937), 6.
51 See *ibid.,* III (March, 1938), 11–13, and III (July, 1938), 19.
52 *Black Man,* I (September, 1935), 5, quoted in Bunche, "Programs, Ideologies, Tactics, and Achievements," p. 416. See also *Black Man,* I (November, 1934), 19–34, and I (July, 1935), 2–5.
53 U.N.I.A. circular letter, 1932, Schomburg Collection, N.Y. Public Library.
54 Baltimore *Afro-American,* June 1, 1935.
55 Amy Jacques Garvey, Kingston, to the author, February 14, 1951; A. L. Wilson, London, to the author, March 2, 1951.
56 *Black Man,* III (November, 1938), cover.
57 Bunche, "Programs, Ideologies, Tactics, and Achievements," p. 419. See also financial reports in *Black Man,* III (March, 1938), 12–13, and III (July, 1938), 19.
58 *Black Man,* I (July, 1935), 20.
59 *Ibid.,* II (July–August, 1936), 9.
60 *Ibid.,* p. 12.
61 Quoted in McKay, *Harlem,* p. 176.
62 *Black Man,* II (July–August, 1936), 4.
63 *Ibid.,* I (July, 1935), 11–13.
64 *Ibid.,* II (September–October, 1936), quoted in Bunche, "Programs, Ideologies, Tactics, and Achievements," p. 418.

65   *Black Man,* II (December, 1937), 4–5.

66   *Ibid.,* III (November, 1938), 8–9, cover.

67   Bunche, "Programs, Ideologies, Tactics, and Achievements,"
      p. 420.

68   See New York *Age,* November 18, 1939.

69   Bunche, "Programs, Ideologies, Tactics, and Achievements,"
      p. 423; Myrdal, *American Dilemma,* p. 813.

70   Bunche, "Programs, Ideologies, Tactics, and Achievements,"
      pp. 425–41; Myrdal, *American Dilemma,* pp. 812–15.

71   *Black Man,* III (November, 1938), 18–19; Bontemps and
      Conroy, *They Seek a City,* p. 184.

72   Harry Haywood, *Negro Liberation,* p. 203.

73   Bontemps and Conroy, *They Seek a City,* p. 186.

74   Garvey, *Philosophy and Opinions,* I, 9.

75   Daisy Whyte, "Private Secretary Reveals Details of the Illness
      and Death of Marcus Garvey," *Voice of Freedom,* I (August,
      1945), 1–2; Baltimore *Afro-American,* May 25, 1940; *New
      York Times,* May 25 and June 12, 1940; New York *Herald
      Tribune,* June 12, 1940.

76   Quoted in Bontemps and Conroy, *They Seek a City,* p. 186.

77   *New York Times,* June 13, 1940.

78   Ben Davis, Jr., "Marcus Garvey Dies as His Defeatist Program
      Is Replaced by a Fighting Negro Liberation Movement against
      Imperialism," New York *Daily Worker,* June 14, 1940.

79   Chicago *Defender,* June 22, 1940.

Chapter Seven

1   Garvey, *Tragedy of White Injustice,* p. 7.

2   Garvey, *Philosophy and Opinions,* I, 7.

3   Frazier, "The Garvey Movement," *Opportunity,* IV, 347.

4   Powell, *Marching Blacks,* p. 50.

5   Quoted in Hartt, "The Negro Moses and His Campaign to Lead
     the Black Millions into Their Promised Land," *Independent,*
     CV, 206.

6   Garvey, *Philosophy and Opinions,* I, 9.

7   New York *World,* August 7, 1920.

8   Garvey, *Philosophy and Opinions,* I, 9.
9   *Ibid.,* II, 15.
10 Quoted by Hartt in *Independent,* CV, 219.
11 Clark, *Is It the Color of Our Skin?* p. 20.
12 See, for example, Boone, *Paramount Facts in Race Development,* pp. 20–21.
13 Quoted by Hartt in *Independent,* CV, 218.
14 Garvey, *Philosophy and Opinions,* II, 12.
15 Garvey, *Selections from Poetic Meditations,* pp. 22–23; *Negro World,* October 13, 1928.
16 See James H. A. Brazelton, *Self-Determination: The Salvation of the Race* (Oklahoma City, Okla.: The Educator, 1918), p. 65; Weatherford, *The Negro from Africa to America,* pp. 427–28.
17 Hodge Kirnon, New York, to the author, March 28, 1949; Ottley, *"New World A-Coming,"* p. 75; advertisements in *Negro World,* August 21, 1920, and February 2, 1924, and New York *Amsterdam News,* December 21, 1927.
18 Cincinnati Division No. 146, U.N.I.A., *Sixth Anniversary Drive, May 8th to 18th, 1927,* pp. 9–10.
19 Garvey, *Philosophy and Opinions,* II, 19. See also p. 82.
20 *Ibid.,* I, 77.
21 Garvey, *Tragedy of White Injustice,* p. 3.
22 Garvey, *Philosophy and Opinions,* II, 82.
23 *Ibid.,* p. 415.
24 Garvey, *Tragedy of White Injustice,* p. 6.
25 Stonequist, *Marginal Man,* p. 21.
26 Joel A. Rogers, *Sex and Race: Negro-Caucasian Mixing in All Ages and All Lands* (N.Y.: J. A. Rogers, 1940), I, 254–71; James M. Webb, *A Black Man Will Be the Coming Universal King: Proven by Biblical History* (Chicago: Author [1918]), p. 12; Brazelton, *Self-Determination,* pp. 248–49.
27 Kelsey Blanton, *Color-Blind and Skin-Deep Democracy* ([Tampa, Fla.:] Kelsey Blanton, 1924), p. 60.
28 Amy Jacques Garvey, Kingston, Jamaica, to the author, July 5, 1949.
29 *Negro Churchman,* I (March, 1923), 1.

30   Quoted in McKay, *Harlem*, p. 166; Ottley, *"New World A-Coming,"* p. 73.

31   See, for instance, Garvey, *Tragedy of White Injustice*, pp. 4–5; Garvey, *Philosophy and Opinions*, I, 27; Marcus Garvey, "The White, Sinful Church," *Black Man*, I (July, 1935), 8.

32   Quoted in Talley, "Marcus Garvey: the Negro Moses?" *World's Work*, XLI, 165; "A Black Moses and His Dream of a Promised Land," *Current Opinion*, LXX, 330.

33   Quoted by Hartt in *Independent*, CV, 205.

34   *Negro Churchman*, I (March, 1923), 1.

35   "Garvey," *Opportunity*, II (September, 1924), 284–85; *Negro World*, August 16, 1924.

36   *New York Times*, August 6, 1924.

37   *Ibid.*

38   Garvey, *Tragedy of White Injustice*, p. 12.

39   *Black Man*, I (November, 1934), quoted in Bunche, "Programs, Ideologies, Tactics, and Achievements," p. 417.

40   Garvey, "A Black Man's Prayer," *Black Man*, I (July, 1935), 18.

41   Cover advertisements, *ibid.*, II (December, 1937), and III (March, July, and November, 1938).

42   Houston Stewart Chamberlain, *Foundations of the Nineteenth Century* (London: Lane, 1912), I, 211–12.

43   New York *News*, August 16, 1924. Called to my attention by Mr. Hodge Kirnon of New York City.

44   George S. Schuyler and Theophilus Lewis, "Shafts and Darts," *Messenger*, VII (March, 1925), 129.

45   New York *Amsterdam News*, February 16, 1927. Called to my attention by Mr. Hodge Kirnon of New York City.

46   Talley in *World's Work*, XLI, 165; "Black Moses and His Dream," *Current Opinion*, LXX, 330; Zickfoose, "The Garvey Movement," p. 62.

47   William Pickens, Washington, to the author, May 27, 1949.

48   A. Philip Randolph, New York, to the author, June 24, 1949.

49   Amy Jacques Garvey, Kingston, Jamaica, to the author, July 5, 1949.

50   See, for example, Mays, *The Negro's God as Reflected in His Literature*, pp. 184–85.

51 Frazier in *Opportunity,* IV, 347.

52 Garvey, *Philosophy and Opinions,* I, 10.

53 *Ibid.,* p. 6.

54 *Ibid.,* p. 5.

55 Quoted in Ovington, *Portraits in Color,* p. 18.

56 See Garvey, *Philosophy and Opinions,* I, 13; Garvey, *Speech at Madison Square Garden;* Garvey, *Speech at Royal Albert Hall,* pp. 26–27; "Black Moses and His Dream," *Current Opinion,* LXX, 331; Tuttle, "A New Nation in Harlem," *World Tomorrow,* IV, 279–81; Brawley, *Short History of the American Negro,* p. 266.

57 New York *World,* August 3, 1920. See also Garvey, *Philosophy and Opinions,* I, 40–41.

58 Quoted in Johnson, *Black Manhattan,* p. 254; *Revolutionary Radicalism,* II, 1513.

59 Garvey, *Philosophy and Opinions,* I, 39.

60 New York *World,* August 5, 1920.

61 Garvey, *Minutes of a Speech at Century Theatre, London, 1928,* p. 29.

62 Hartt in *Independent,* CV, 206.

63 Amy Jacques Garvey, Kingston, Jamaica, to the author, February 19, 1949, and February 14, 1951.

64 Garvey, *Speech at Madison Square Garden.*

65 Quoted by DuBois in "Marcus Garvey," *Crisis,* XXI, 114.

66 Quoted by Hartt in *Independent,* CV, 218.

67 Garvey, *Tragedy of White Injustice,* pp. 20–21.

68 Chicago *Defender,* September 13, 1924.

69 *Ibid.,* September 2, 1922.

70 *New York Times,* August 4, 1920.

71 See Victoria Earle Matthews, *Black Belt Diamonds: Gems from the Speeches, Addresses, and Talks to Students of Booker T. Washington* (N.Y.: Fortune and Scott, 1898), pp. 9, 19, 27, and 58–59.

72 Locke, "Enter the New Negro," *Survey,* LIII, 634; Locke (ed.), *The New Negro,* p. 15.

73 *Black Man,* III (November, 1938), 19. See also Chicago *Defender,* June 15, 1940.

74 Garvey, *Philosophy and Opinions,* II, 3, 40, 46, 49, and 97.
75 [Finley P. Dunne] *Dissertations by Mr. Dooley* (N.Y.: Harper, 1906), p. 190.
76 Quoted in Ovington, *Portraits in Color,* p. 30.
77 Quoted by Hartt in *Independent,* CV, 206.
78 *Ibid.,* p. 218.
79 Garvey, *Philosophy and Opinions,* II, 46.
80 *Ibid.,* p. 49.
81 *Ibid.,* pp. 97–98.
82 Cox, *Let My People Go,* p. 4. See also Cox, *The South's Part in Mongrelizing the Nation,* pp. 8–9, 93–94, 103, 108.
83 Garvey, *Philosophy and Opinions,* II, 338.
84 *Ibid.,* p. 347.
85 Blanton, *Color-Blind and Skin-Deep Democracy,* pp. 61–62.
86 Cox, *Lincoln's Negro Policy,* pp. 29–32; Cox, *South's Part in Mongrelizing,* pp. 93–94.
87 Quoted by Hartt in *Independent,* CV, 219.
88 Chicago *Defender,* August 16, 1924.
89 *New York Times,* July 10, 1922.
90 Chicago *Defender,* July 8, 1922; *New York Times,* February 8, 1923; DuBois, "Back to Africa," *Century,* CV, 547; Aron, "Garvey Movement," p. 117.
91 Amy Jacques Garvey, Kingston, Jamaica, to the author, February 19, 1949.
92 Quoted in Chicago *Defender,* July 22, 1922.
93 *Ibid.,* July 29, 1922.
94 "A Lunatic or a Traitor," *Crisis,* XXVIII, 8–9.
95 Garvey, *Philosophy and Opinions,* II, 71; Ottley, *"New World A-Coming,"* p. 74.
96 Hartt in *Independent,* CV, 219.
97 Garvey, *Philosophy and Opinions,* I, 6.
98 Quoted by Talley in *World's Work,* XLI, 163; "Black Moses and His Dream," *Current Opinion,* LXX, 330.
99 Garvey, *Philosophy and Opinions,* I, 29–30.
100 Ottley, *"New World A-Coming,"* p. 74; DuBois in *Century,* CV, 542; Johnson, *Black Manhattan,* p. 257.
101 New York *World,* June 29, 1923.

102 Garvey, *Speech at Madison Square Garden.*
103 *Münchener neueste Nachrichten,* November 25, 1921, in *Nation,* CXIII (December 28, 1921), 769.
104 Garvey, *Philosophy and Opinions,* II, 3.
105 *Ibid.,* p. 2.
106 See *ibid.,* pp. 39, 57, 86, and 324–25; Garvey, "A Barefaced Coloured Leader," *Black Man,* I (July, 1935), 5–8; New York *World,* August 4, 1920.
107 Frazier in *Opportunity,* IV, 346.
108 *Negro World,* August 26, 1922.
109 Chicago *Defender,* September 6, 1924.
110 Garvey, *Philosophy and Opinions,* I, 29–30; Myrdal, *American Dilemma,* p. 746.
111 Garvey, *Philosophy and Opinions,* II, 325–26; Franklin, *From Slavery to Freedom,* p. 482.
112 Garvey, *Philosophy and Opinions,* II, 62; Ottley, *"New World A-Coming,"* p. 73.
113 Garvey, *Philosophy and Opinions,* I, 37.
114 Quoted in Nembhard, *Trials and Triumphs,* p. 84.
115 Garvey, *Philosophy and Opinions,* II, 81.
116 Chicago *Defender,* March 29, 1924.
117 *Ibid.,* April 26, 1924.
118 *New York Times,* October 27, 1921.
119 Washington *Bee,* November 5, 1921.
120 *New York Times,* October 27, 1921.
121 Garvey, *Philosophy and Opinions,* II, 51.
122 *Ibid.,* p. 52.
123 Chicago *Defender,* March 31, 1923.
124 Harris and Spero, "Negro Problem," *Encyclopaedia of the Social Sciences,* XI, 350.
125 Bunche, "Programs, Ideologies, Tactics, and Achievements," p. 412; Haywood, *Negro Liberation,* p. 202.
126 Garvey, *Philosophy and Opinions,* II, 69–70.
127 *Ibid.;* Garvey, "The Future," *Black Man,* II (July–August, 1936), 8–9.
128 Garvey, *Philosophy and Opinions,* II, 70.
129 Record, *Negro and Communist Party,* pp. 40–41.

130   Minor, "Death or a Program," *Workers Monthly,* V, 270, quoted in *ibid.,* p. 41. Cf. I. Amter, *The World Liberative Movement of the Negroes* (Moscow: Soviet State Publishing House, 1925).

131   *Negro World,* February 2, 1924.

132   Garvey, *Philosophy and Opinions,* I, 18–19.

133   *New York Times,* January 21, 1923.

134   Quoted in Rogers, *World's Great Men of Color,* II, 602.

135   U.N.I.A. circular, January, 1920, quoted in Case A, 2667.

136   Rose, *The Negro's Morale,* pp. 43–44.

137   See, for example, Garvey, "The Jews in Palestine," *Black Man,* II (July–August, 1936), 3.

138   A good example of this sort of writing is to be found in Slocum, "Sucker Traps: Plain and Fancy," *Collier's,* CXXV, 49–50.

139   Walter Lippmann's Introduction in Carl Sandburg, *The Chicago Race Riots* (N.Y.: Harcourt, Brace, and Howe, 1919), p. iv.

Chapter Eight

1   Ottley, *"New World A-Coming,"* p. 81.

2   Bunche, "Programs, Ideologies, Tactics, and Achievements," p. 412; also quoted in Myrdal, *American Dilemma,* p. 748.

3   Myrdal, *American Dilemma,* p. 749.

4   McKay, *A Long Way from Home,* p. 354.

5   Ovington, *Portraits in Color,* p. 19.

6   DuBois, *Dusk of Dawn,* p. 277.

7   Garvey, *Philosophy and Opinions,* II, 129.

8   *Ibid.,* p. 131; DuBois, "The U.N.I.A.," *Crisis,* XXV, 121; James, *History of Negro Revolt,* p. 68; Franklin, *From Slavery to Freedom,* p. 482; Chicago Commission on Race Relations, *Negro in Chicago,* p. 493.

9   Garvey, *Speech Delivered at Royal Albert Hall,* pp. 7, 11, 14; Garvey, *Minutes of a Speech at Century Theatre, London, 1928,* p. 22.

10   DuBois in *Crisis,* XXV, 121.

11 See Garvey, *Philosophy and Opinions*, II, 299.
12 DuBois, "Back to Africa," *Century*, CV, 543.
13 Kelly Miller, "After Marcus Garvey—What of the Negro?" *Contemporary Review*, CXXXI, 495.
14 William Pickens, "The Emperor of Africa—the Psychology of Garveyism," *Forum*, LXX, 1795.
15 William Pickens, Washington, to the author, May 27, 1949.
16 Drake and Cayton, *Black Metropolis*, p. 751; Arnold and Caroline Rose, *America Divided*, p. 187; James, *History of Negro Revolt*, p. 68.
17 Case A, 1355, 1365, 1511, 1617–18, 1666, 1707, 1744, and 2289.
18 Garvey, *Philosophy and Opinions*, II, 305–6.
19 *Ibid.*, p. 306.
20 James, *History of Negro Revolt*, p. 68.
21 Bunche, "Programs, Ideologies, Tactics, and Achievements," p. 442.
22 Slocum, "Sucker Traps: Plain and Fancy," *Collier's*, CXXV, 36.
23 A. M. Chirgwin, "Negro Race Movements in America," *Contemporary Review*, CXXVII (February, 1925), 200.
24 Shaw, *Christianizing Race Relations*, p. 84.
25 Brown, *Story of the American Negro*, p. 114.
26 Van Deusen, *Black Man in White America*, p. 331.
27 Clark, *Is It the Color of Our Skin?* p. 10. See also Talley, "Marcus Garvey: the Negro Moses?" *World's Work*, XLI, 153.
28 Henry, *Predictions of a Great Race Leader in Fulfillment*, pp. 42, 48.
29 Pickens, "Africa for the Africans: the Garvey Movement," *Nation*, CXIII, 751.
30 DuBois, "Marcus Garvey," *Crisis*, XXI, 60.
31 Case A, 1053, 2197–98, 2219–20, and 2329.
32 *Things You Ought to Know*, undated pamphlet, Schomburg Collection, N.Y. Public Library.
33 Pickens in *Nation*, CXIII, 751.
34 DuBois in *Crisis*, XX, 114.
35 Abram L. Harris, Chicago, to the author, June 6, 1949.
36 Drake and Cayton, *Black Metropolis*, p. 752.

37 See, for example, Clark, *Is It the Color of Our Skin?* p. 5; Hayford, *The Disabilities of Black Folk;* Samuel Barrett, *The Need of Unity and Cooperation among Colored Americans* (Oakland, Calif.: Voice Publishing Company, 1946), p. 98; Ottley, *"New World A-Coming,"* p. 241.

38 A. Philip Randolph, New York, to the author, June 24, 1949.

39 Quoted in Bunche, "Programs, Ideologies, Tactics, and Achievements," p. 422.

40 Quoted in Drake and Cayton, *Black Metropolis,* p. 752.

41 Quoted in Margaret Brenman, "Some Aspects of Personality Development in a Group of Urban, Lower Class Negro Girls" (unpublished monograph prepared for the Carnegie-Myrdal study, 1940; Schomburg Collection, N.Y. Public Library), Appendix C, p. 18.

42 Bunche, "Programs, Ideologies, Tactics, and Achievements," p. 408.

43 "Negro Exodus Unnecessary," *Opportunity,* II, 312.

44 Johnson, *Black Manhattan,* p. 258.

45 Barrett, *The Need of Unity and Cooperation,* p. 36.

46 "The U.N.I.A. and Progress," *Spokesman,* I (June, 1925), 5–6.

47 Chicago *Defender,* June 6, 1953.

48 *Ibid.,* June 22, 1940.

49 Locke, *The New Negro,* pp. 14–15. See also Alain Locke, *A Decade of Negro Self-Expression* (Charlottesville, Va.: Slater Fund, 1928), p. 9.

50 Brawley, *A Short History of the American Negro* (N.Y.: Macmillan, 1927, 1931, and 1939).

51 Brawley, *The Negro Genius,* pp. 231–32.

52 Eppse, *The Negro, Too,* pp. 358–59.

53 Len S. Nembhard, *Trials and Triumphs of Marcus Garvey* (Kingston, Jamaica: Gleaner, 1940).

54 McKay, *Harlem,* pp. 143–80.

55 DuBois, *Dusk of Dawn,* pp. 277–78.

56 Ottley, *"New World A-Coming,"* pp. 67–81; Ottley, *Black Odyssey,* pp. 234–38.

57 J. A. Rogers, *World's Greatest Men of African Descent* (N.Y.: J. A. Rogers, 1931), p. 77.

58 Rogers, *World's Great Men of Color,* II, 599–610.
59 Bontemps and Conroy, *They Seek a City,* pp. 162–74.
60 Brown, Davis, and Lee (eds.), *Negro Caravan,* pp. 677–81.
61 Henry, *Predictions of a Great Race Leader.*
62 Harry Haywood, *Negro Liberation,* pp. 170, 197–98.
63 Brisbane, "Some New Light on the Garvey Movement," *Journal of Negro History,* XXXVI, 53–62.
64 Lucas-Dubreton, "Le Moïse noir," *Les Oeuvres libres,* CCLXXXII, 81–116.
65 Barrett, *The Need of Unity and Cooperation,* pp. 97–98.
66 Mays, *The Negro's God as Reflected in His Literature,* p. 185.
67 Brawley, *Short History of the American Negro* (4th edition, 1939), p. 197.
68 Watkins, *Pocket Book of Negro Facts,* p. 8.
69 Ottley, *"New World A-Coming,"* p. 81.
70 Franklin, *From Slavery to Freedom,* p. 483.
71 Hayford, *Disabilities of Black Folk.*
72 *West Indies Public Opinion,* December 24, 1953.
73 Osita Egbuniwe, "My Nigeria," *Nigeria Daily Comet,* November 23, 1948.
74 Chicago *Defender,* June 6, 1953.
75 Kingston *Gleaner,* October 23, 1952.
76 [R. A. L. Knight] "Outstanding Sons since Knibb," *William Knibb Memorial* (Kingston, Jamaica: Gleaner [1948?]).
77 E. H. J. King, "This Is Jamaica—at the Half Century Mark," Kingston *Sunday Gleaner,* December 31, 1950, p. 15.
78 Kingston *Gleaner,* July 9, 1952.
79 Kingston *Star,* July 19, 1952. See also Kingston *Gleaner,* July 9, 1952.
80 Vere Johns, "His Race Pride Entitles Him to Be Called—Great Garvey," Kingston *Star,* July 19, 1952.
81 Garvey Club Circulars, Schomburg Collection, N.Y. Public Library.
82 Aron, "Garvey Movement," pp. 26, 60–61; Convention Program, Schomburg Collection, N.Y. Public Library.
83 New York *Amsterdam News,* August 8, 1953.
84 Johnson, *Black Manhattan,* p. 259.

INDEX

Abbott, Robert S.: criticism of Garvey, 75–76; petition to attorney general, 111
Acosta, Julio, 88
Adams, Henry, 22
Advocate, 14
Africa: Garvey's emphasis on, 4, 15, 64–68 *passim,* 147, 148, 170–77, 183–88 *passim;* opposition to projects for, 76, 106–7, 127–32, 211; shipping connection with, 92–93; native opinion on Garvey, 106–7, 125–30, 216; colonization program for, 121, 124–32; religion in, 177
Africa Times and Orient Review, 15
African Blood Brotherhood, 198
African Communities League. *See* Universal Negro Improvement Association and African Communities League
African Legion, 63, 151, 153, 174
African Orthodox Church: established, 178–79; opposed by regular clergy, 182
African philosophy courses, 163–64
African Redemption: medals, 68; Fund, 126
African World, 49
Aldred, Eva, 18
Alexandria, Egypt, 176
American Negro Labor Congress, 152–53
Anarchism: Garvey accused of, 99, 110
Anglo-Saxon Clubs of America, 188, 190
Antilla, Cuba, 91–92
Antonio Maceo (ship). *See Kanawha*
Aron, Burgit, 5n

Ashwood, Amy. *See* Garvey, Amy Ashwood
Atlanta, Georgia: federal penitentiary at, 134, 136–37, 138, 141, 172; Garvey-Klan conference in, 189
Attucks, Crispus, 177

☆

Back to Africa movement: as part of Garvey philosophy, 4, 183–88; Negro opposition to, 106–7, 211; as colonization program, 124–32; evaluated, 221–22, 224
Bagnall, Robert W., 107, 111
Baker, Newton D., 30, 70
Barber, Rev. J. D., 180
Barclay, Edwin J., 125–26, 127
Basutoland, South Africa, 106–7
Battle, George Gordon, 134
Belgium, 184
Belize, British Honduras, 164
Berry and Ross Company, 175
Bethel African Methodist Episcopal Church, 41
Bilbo, Theodore G., 166, 186–87
Birkbeck College, 7, 15
Birmingham, Alabama, 194
Black Cross Navigation and Trading Company: history of, 121–24; as device for race consciousness, 174
Black Cross Nurses, 63, 151, 174
Black Hand Society, 106
Black Man: established, 157; described, 158–59; reports U.N.I.A. conventions, 160, 163; financial difficulties of, 161–62; attacks Haile Selassie, 162; and Bilbo Negro Repatriation Bill, 166, 186–87; mentioned, 49

266